THE BRUMBY WARS

Anthony Sharwood is a Walkley Award–winning journalist specialising in environment, sports, the outdoors, weather and climate. He started his career writing long-form magazine and newspaper features and has spent the last ten years as a writer and editor on leading Australian news websites. He has also presented television shows, radio programs and a podcast.

In 2020 he released the acclaimed *From Snow to Ash*, a love letter to the Australian High Country written while walking the Australian Alps Walking Track. *The Brumby Wars* is his third book.

Ant lives with his wife and two teenagers in a Sydney suburb nobody has ever heard of.

THE
BRUMBY
WARS

ANTHONY SHARWOOD

hachette
AUSTRALIA

hachette
AUSTRALIA

Published in Australia and New Zealand in 2021
by Hachette Australia
(an imprint of Hachette Australia Pty Limited)
Level 17, 207 Kent Street, Sydney NSW 2000
www.hachette.com.au

10 9 8 7 6 5 4 3 2 1

A catalogue record for this book is available from the National Library of Australia

ISBN: 978 0 7336 4720 8 (paperback)

Cover design by Luke Causby/Blue Cork
Front cover image courtesy Michelle Brown. 'In loving memory of Paleface, lost in the devastating summer bushfires of 2020 in the Mt Selwyn area of Kosciuszko National Park. Forever free, forever in the hearts of many, forever loved by all.' – Michelle Brown
Typeset in Bembo Std by Kirby Jones
Printed and bound in Australia by McPherson's Printing Group

CONTENTS

AUTHOR'S NOTE

I am not normally one for mottos or for plans, as I believe that writing, like life, is a journey of discovery.

But I did have one guiding principle informing every word of this book:

Everyone is heroic, even if they're not.

Anthony Sharwood
Sydney
July 2021

CHAPTER ONE

'FOR THE SAKE OF OUR COUNTRY'

For three years, they came at him. Three years of insults, harassment, smears, and intimidation. Despite it all, he sat down with them and listened. No neutral observer could ever accuse him of not looking them in the eye and genuinely attempting to find middle ground.

Every day of the working week, there are public consultation forums in local councils where nodding bureaucrats present a veneer of unbiased process when, in reality, a decision has already been made, a deal done, the bulldozers refuelled and ready to rumble. But as Kosciuszko National Park ranger and Wild Horse Project officer Rob Gibbs was helping to compile the Draft Wild Horse Management Plan for Kosciuszko National Park in 2016, he came in the spirit of compromise. His goal was to find a solution for the mobs of brumbies that were ravaging the park, trampling its delicate ecosystems, fouling its crystal streams and destroying the habitats of its native wildlife. At the same time, he knew that many people valued the brumbies for their links to High Country heritage and a dying way of life, for their wild-eyed freedom, for the fact that a mob of wild horses thundering across the snow grass tussocks is a hell of a thing to see.

Gibbs came bearing an olive branch, not a stick. He met the brumby advocates in their strongholds – the pubs and public halls of the mountains – and he calmly tried to explain the key strategy of the plan, which was to reduce the wild horse population in Kosciuszko National Park through trapping and, hopefully, rehoming rather than a cruel journey to the knackery. The 2014 estimate of 6000 horses in the park would be reduced to fewer than 3000 horses within five to ten years. A further reduction in the population to around 600 would take place within 20 years. Like many park rangers and scientists, Gibbs believed that in an ideal world, Kosciuszko would be horse-free. But the architects of the plan were willing to leave a pocket here, a pocket there – boutique mobs that horse lovers could visit. Mobs that would be out there, running wild and free in the mountains, as they had done for almost 200 years. A nod to postcolonial life in a landscape that had evolved over countless millennia without hard-hoofed animals.

It wasn't enough. It wasn't even halfway down the road to enough. To the brumby supporters, any plan to reduce numbers so dramatically was a declaration of war. And so they came at Gibbs. They came at him with venom and vitriol and pretty much everything except pitchforks. They came at him at public meetings, fuelled by beer and bravado. They called him a liar, a conspiracist, a greenie fuckwit and worse, their tone aggressive, their body language overbearing. They came at him on the modern battleground of social media. On pro-brumby Facebook groups, they called him a filthy brumby-murdering bastard and a thousand slurs just as ugly. They circulated memes, each more vulgar or menacing than the last. In one, Daniel Craig's James Bond walks alongside Queen Elizabeth II. 'And Gibbs, ma'am?' Bond asks. 'Make it look like an accident, 007,' the Queen replies. In another, Gibbs and another National Parks official stand semi-naked with their hands down each other's pants. The caption reads: 'Australia's greatest brumby murderer? I'll toss you for it.' One meme featured an image of a horse planting dynamite in a Parks office. Another post asked, 'If you could erase one person from history, who would it be?' Attached to it was a photo montage of some of history's worst dictators, including Pol Pot, Hitler, Stalin … then Gibbs.

Through it all, Gibbs never cracked, not because he was made of iron or steel but because, as he puts it, 'I was paid not to.' And when all that intimidation and online harassment still didn't stop him from showing up at meetings with a straight face and open mind, they made it personal. First, they called him homosexual. Then they tried to out his office relationship with a woman called Mel. When they eventually learned she was his wife, they told Gibbs they'd burn her in their house and have his kids beaten up at school. That's when the police stepped in.

Gibbs is far from the only person who has copped it. Across the High Country of New South Wales and Victoria, and in other brumby hotspots around the country, where the fight over wild horses pits science and the principles of sound land management against heritage and emotion, incidents of bad behaviour from brumby supporters are rife. In the Snowy Mountains of New South Wales, a pro-horse group made bumper stickers that said: 'Aerial Cull a Greenie: Save a Snowy Brumby'. Another group had coffee mugs made with the words: 'If you hurt my horse, I can make your death look like an accident'. To many in the mountains and beyond, 'my horse' means the brumbies.

Anyone in the mountains who does anything that might be perceived to threaten horses – even on a contract basis – has, at one point or another, become a target. In a major town in the Victorian High Country, when the helicopter is fired up for one of the regular deer culls, locals stand by, imitating the action of a rifle. Their message is clear: *Make sure you stick to deer.* Another helicopter pilot – much respected in the mountains for his good cheer and unmatched flying skills – was subject to a Facebook comment when contracted to do an aerial horse cull in Victoria which, for various reasons, has not yet happened. 'I see his advertising mentions Heli Fun,' a leading brumby campaigner posted. 'It doesn't mention Heli Kill. We might have to put that right.'

Those who work beyond the mountains are also not immune to the intimidation. Scientists who study the alpine environment have inboxes full of hateful, threatening emails. After presenting a Zoom webinar on horse damage, which brumby folks tried to disrupt online, the ecologist Don Driscoll got a message which called him a horse murderer, chillingly warning that what goes around comes around.

Sometimes the treatment is more subtle. Conservation campaigner Di Thompson, the daughter of a hard-bitten

West Australian drover, who has sat on more committees than anyone in the mountains in the name of preserving the ecology of her beloved High Country, has for years been sworn at and 'doored' at community meetings – her term for a large man standing over her in a doorway, intimidating her with a foul blend of aggressive language and armpit sweat.

Occasionally brumby supporters get creative, albeit no less nasty. Ahead of a pro-brumby rally in 2021, a poem was widely circulated on a popular pro-brumby Facebook group. One stanza read:

Lets all go up the mountains
And make the greenies run
With electric cattle prodders
To shove right up their bums.

Indigenous people have had it particularly bad. Elders led a narjong (water) healing ceremony in 2019 at the brumby-ravaged headwaters of the Murrumbidgee River in northern Kosciuszko National Park. It was attended by Indigenous people from along the Murrumbidgee and Murray, all the way to the Murray's mouth at the Coorong in South Australia. Members of a pro-brumby group stood nearby and booed like disgruntled football fans.

Richard Swain, an Indigenous man of the mountains, Snowy River guide and outspoken anti-brumby campaigner, has been stalked and photographed by brumby supporters, had his car tyres punctured repeatedly with the same brand of concrete nails, and endured every insult under the sun. One man on Facebook suggested that he deserved a dose of 1080, the poison used to kill foxes and other pest species. A woman suggested someone should take him for a walk in the forest and come back alone, a suggestion that drew laughing emojis from others. Another woman said, 'How about we hunt you and your family down to be shot', while another said, 'Let's cull Swain and be done with it'. Someone else said regarding the Invasive Species Council, whose Reclaim Kosci campaign Swain then worked for, she would 'like to use a double-barrelled shotgun on them, and then load these evil morons onto a truck and dump them. I am very wicked LOL!'

LOL indeed.

Journalists covering the issue have themselves become targets. Ricky French, who has written about the brumby debate extensively for *The Australian*, has been attacked by a brumby advocate and their social media followers, who trolled him with vile slurs.

Even some media outlets are in on the game. The narjong ceremony was an historic event which gained widespread national media coverage. In the notoriously pro-brumby local media of Cooma and surrounds, it rated not a word – effectively a more subtle form of booing. Meanwhile, one newspaper in the mountains accredited a photographer to cover a rally outside the Queanbeyan office of NSW Deputy Premier John Barilaro, where anti-brumby people were protesting Barilaro's *Kosciuszko Wild Horse Heritage Act 2018* (NSW), the first piece of legislation in Australian history that prioritised a non-native species in a national park. The photographer spent the entire afternoon snapping protesters – not for a news story in the paper, but to put faces to names who might later be intimidated by brumby supporters.

While Barilaro is regarded as a hero by many in the mountains, politicians who blow the other way have become targets. When NSW Energy and Environment Minister Matt Kean came out in support of emergency measures to remove brumbies that had moved into sensitive parts of Kosciuszko National Park after the Black Summer bushfires of January 2020, in a scene sourced straight from *The Godfather* a woman threatened to put a severed, bloody horse head on his front lawn.

Then there are the random outbursts of fury. In 2000, after 606 horses were culled in Guy Fawkes River National Park in northern New South Wales – an incident that still shapes the brumby debate in numerous ways – an irate local brumby supporter grabbed a brush turkey from nearby scrubland by the neck and flung it in disgust over the counter of the local National Parks office. He no doubt considered himself an animal lover.

While there's something almost darkly comic about the image of a brush turkey flying through a Parks office, scattering papers, hopping on the photocopier, gobble-gobbling its way down the corridors, there's an insidious side to the harassment and intimidation. Parks staff, land managers, scientists, activists, and anyone who speaks out in favour of substantially reducing brumby numbers genuinely fear for their safety.

Rob Gibbs is prone to snicker like Muttley (from the old Hanna-Barbera cartoon *Wacky Races*) at the sheer craziness of the whole debate. The occasional outbursts seem to help him let off steam. But his face turns ashen when he mentions Glen Turner, the NSW environment officer who in 2014 was shot with a hunting rifle by 79-year-old landowner Ian Turnbull in a dispute over land clearing at Croppa Creek in northern New South Wales. Turner, a 51-year-old father of two, was tracked down on public land, shot in the neck, chased and terrorised for more than 20 minutes then finally fatally shot in the back in front of his work ute.

'That really hit home to us,' Gibbs says over a generous barbecue dinner on the timber back deck of his Jindabyne home. 'Quite often, the comments you read on social media about Parks are saying things like, "They should be shot. If they're going to shoot horses, why aren't the parkies shot?" And at some of these horse meetings, we would raise the issue with the reps of the horse groups and go, "This isn't acceptable behaviour", and they'd laugh it off as, "Oh it's jokes", and you'd go, "Well, when does a joke become serious?" Because while they may be joking about it, we'd been dealing at the time of the draft plan with a community at the end of a long drought, with a lot of farmers and local people under high levels of stress, and you never know what could tip someone over to doing something stupid. Let's say there's a guy who lives down the end of the road who loves brumbies and hates Parks. And the next time I'm driving down that road in the Parks truck with the lyrebird logo on the side, what might be the thing that sends him over the edge?'

* * *

Why?

Why the abhorrent behaviour from regular people who run farms and businesses, who work in supermarkets and schools and offices and auto wreckers, who raise families, who love their children and teach them good manners? Where does the anger spring from? And why is all that fury funnelled through the issue of wild horses?

Because it's about horses but it ain't about horses, that's why.

As outspoken Victorian brumby advocate Phil Maguire put it: 'The brumbies have become emblematic of a cultural heritage that is besieged by leftists and fake environmentalists ... If the brumbies go ... Another huge slice of Australia's identity will be lost. We must win this war for the sake of our country.'

The first documented incident of serious intimidation against High Country land managers occurred in the 1940s, when an effigy of a prominent land manager hanging by a noose was left on the verandah of the old Jindabyne Hotel. The effigy was an angry message to rangers who'd been impounding stock which had been grazing illegally in the newly created Kosciuszko State Park. Before the declaration of the state park, pastoralists had never been told they were unwelcome anywhere in the High Country. Indeed, they had rarely been restricted from setting up shop anywhere in Australia. The story of Australia's postcolonial expansion and development was about the quest for good grazing land. Blaxland, Lawson and Wentworth crossed the Blue Mountains in 1813 seeking well-watered pasture to the west. Australia, as the saying goes, rode to prosperity on the sheep's back.

The first pastoralists arrived in the High Country in the 1830s. No doubt they could scarcely believe their luck. To use another well-worn piece of Australian vernacular, the proverbial 'wide brown land' had few places that were effectively immune to drought in summer. But up in the High Country lay green pastures that never failed, even right in the middle of summer, when they were most needed. So in the snow-free months, cattlemen would take their stock from the dry tablelands east of the mountains up into the High Country to feed on the evergreen pastures, from the broad snow grass plains at the mid-elevations, all the way up to the flanks of the rounded grassy summits of the Main Range around Mt Kosciuszko. In the early days it was pretty much a free-for-all. Grab it, graze on it. The High Country, after all, was a long way from any city or major town and virtually impossible to administer. By 1889, access to the highest peaks became regulated through a system of snow leases. Kosciuszko State Park was declared in 1944 and the much-prized leases began to be phased out in 1958.

William McKell, the NSW premier from 1941 to 1947 and a major force behind the creation of Kosciuszko State Park, spoke of it as providing a 'rich natural heritage for all'. As Graeme L Worboys and Deirdre Slattery note in their 2020 book *Kosciuszko: A Great National Park*, 'the idea that "heritage" could include fauna and flora, recreation and tourism, health and aesthetic appreciation was new'. All this environmentalism, or conservation as they called it back then, was indeed new-fangled stuff. For the first time, cattlemen were told that the land itself, untouched and ungrazed-upon, had a higher value than the profit that could be reaped from it. No one had ever told them anything remotely like that. It was incomprehensible. It was like being told that gold was more valuable in the ground than melted down into ingots. The cattlemen were blindsided. To them, conservation was a weapon as powerful and utterly unimaginable as firearms must have seemed to Australia's first people. And they were furious.

But the environmental evidence was in. Groundbreaking research by soil scientists in the 1940s showed that the ground on the Main Range around Mt Kosciuszko was indeed being broken. Erosion was rife and incredibly fragile plants found nowhere else in the world were being eaten out of existence. Before sheep and cattle, tiny mammals were the heaviest grazers in the highest alpine terrain above the tree line. A landscape that had evolved to cope with animals as light as plush toys was ill-equipped for beasts weighing half a tonne or more. Neither was it equipped to cope with the regular small fires the cattlemen set with wax matches to promote fresh pasture growth. That sort of practice might work on the lowlands – though there too it could be overused, to the landscape's detriment – but the highest parts of the High Country were different. The very highest parts had never burned, and their unique plants were suffering. A relatively small but incredibly beautiful and ecologically rich part of Australia, which looks like nowhere else on the continent, was dying.

But to the mountain cattlemen, it felt like their way of life was being killed off. The loss of High Country grazing rights was in very real terms a dispossession. Of course, that is a loaded term. Indigenous people were dispossessed of land across the country, and the Ngarigo and other Aboriginal tribes of the mountains were no exception. While the skills of local Indigenous people were valued by some – including by Polish explorer Paul Edmund Strzelecki, who came to appreciate the deep mountain knowledge of the Indigenous guides he employed on his ascent of Australia's highest peak in 1840, the first European to do so – the traditional way of life of the original mountain people was quickly extinguished. Many were moved on to missions. Others went to work for white High Country families. Many died from European diseases. Traditional ways soon died out, with local language and customs forbidden by many European settlers. It's a story that played out in most parts of Australia.

What's much harder to find in Australia are stories of the European landowning class being dispossessed, lawfully or otherwise. But that's what happened in Kosciuszko, and also in the Victorian High Country, where grazing was permitted in isolated areas as late as 2005, was briefly reintroduced as a trial in 2011 by the Liberal state government, and where the wounds are especially fresh. In both states, the shock and anger of being denied access to summer mountain pastures was real. Suddenly, properties below the mountains were no longer drought-proof. That changed everything and the economic pain was real. Many men and women of the land had to get jobs in town for the first time in their lives and their humiliation was real. The cattle families gazed up to the high mountains and saw massive hydro-electric schemes, ski resorts with mega-hotels, eight-seater chairlifts, multi-million-dollar snowmaking systems whose pipes chewed up the earth, the scars of vast car parks, ski runs cut through old-growth snow gum forests, mountain biking trails gouging ditches through the alpine heathland, and environmental degradation that they reckoned was far worse than anything a grazing animal ever inflicted. And their resentment was real. *Is* real.

All that pain, humiliation and resentment lives on today, and it is largely channelled through the fight to keep brumbies in the High Country, because brumbies are the last living vestige of their High Country way of life, and they'll be damned if those bastard greenies are going to take the brumbies too.

There are other reasons why they fight to keep the brumbies in the High Country. Brumby running – chasing and capturing wild horses for sport – is illegal in New South Wales, and on its last legal legs in Victoria, but many believe they've earned the right to keep doing it. Others believe that if the brumbies go, recreational horse riding privileges will be taken next as all horses are cleared out of the parks. There's an historical connection claimed – but not definitively established – between brumbies and the Walers; Australian-bred horses (originally exclusively from New South Wales) that served in the armed forces from the Boer War to World War II. There's the connection to poetry and stories. Others just love the idea of wild horses running free in the mountains.

But the struggle to retain the brumbies begins and ends with the idea of a way of life lost. The hoofprint on the landscape and everything it stands for. High Country photojournalist Lisa Hogben, herself the target of harassment, put it eloquently in an essay she wrote, 'The sacred cow has become a sacred horse'.

Horses first set hoof in Australia after disembarking with the First Fleet in 1788. There were seven in total, and after eight and a half months at sea they arrived better fed and in better all-round condition than most of the human passengers. As Europeans eventually spread out across the vast, unfenced country, some horses inevitably strayed into the bush and became wild. Some claim the word 'brumby' derives from a Sergeant James Brumby, whose horses ran loose when he was transferred from New South Wales to Tasmania in the 1830s. Others say it has Indigenous linguistic origins. Whatever the source, the word brumby has a pleasing quality. It's one of those wonderful Australian B-words that is incredibly satisfying to enunciate, like bludger, bogan, brekky or billabong. It's *our* word for *our* wild horses. This is no small matter. Banjo Paterson mythologised the brumbies in the late 19th century in poems like 'Brumby's Run' and 'The Man from Snowy River', and the mythology grew, solidifying in the minds of countless young Australians in the mid-20th century with Elyne Mitchell's *Silver Brumby* books. This, too, is no small matter.

Today, Australia has the largest wild horse population in the world, with numbers estimated in the range of half a million. In the outback, they are regularly shot from helicopters – along with feral camels, goats, donkeys and pretty much anything with four legs and hooves that's not a future beef burger – and nobody bats an eyelid. But authorities are reticent to shoot the High Country brumbies, the numbers of which were estimated to have reached an historical high of 25,000 in 2019. Brumby advocates dispute that figure. Some say it was as low as 3000. Whatever the actual number, anyone who's walked or worked in the High Country for more than a couple of decades can see that their numbers have skyrocketed in recent years. But if you so much as mention managing or reducing the mobs – especially with guns – watch out.

In certain communities, and particularly in High Country communities where typically you'll see a yellow-and-green sticker that says 'Mountain Cattlemen Care for the High Country', you'll have individuals who are pillars of a community, who come across as being logical and reasoning. They'll give their time to volunteer for the community, and they will be respected and have friends. But the red button for some of these people is trying to get their head around the idea that you might need to cull some of those feral horses in sensitive alpine environments ... no matter how logically you describe what that management is and why it's justified and needed, they won't get any of that because the ideology has started from their first learnt language and their parents, from their community. To talk about the idea of culling is a direct threat to their history, to their entitled bush heritage, to what their parents gave them and what their grandparents gave their parents. And what drives them is similar to what drove the mob to turn on the Capitol Building in Washington. That same mentality pervades a bigger part of those High Country communities than you might think.

These words come from a uniformed High Country land manager who cannot afford to be identified lest he lose his

15

standing in the community, his livelihood, and perhaps more. He continues:

> It could even be the well-respected bush nurse or the doctor, the people who are used to grappling with science and reason and logic. But this folklore of the brumby in the High Country is so deeply ingrained and embedded into their DNA that suddenly, the person that they present 364 days a year disappears and this primal feral persona suddenly just comes out. And what happens is that person, plus others with similar standing in the community, feed into each other. They create their own little feedback loop and this validates the fringey people. So it all becomes this self-fulfilling righteousness, and once that occurs, no logic or reason gets through. And many of them have grown up riding and have close relationships with their domestic horse, so they humanise horses, or see them as having something akin to a soul. And this all feeds into this position that will never shift for a lot of these people. And no matter how good you are at prosecuting the arguments, you could be David Attenborough and you won't cut through.

Rob Gibbs knows only too well how effective the feral persona is in the fight to control what many call feral horses. 'They're happy,' he says. 'They've achieved their goal through bullying and intimidation.'

High Country brumby supporters haven't achieved their position of ascendancy alone. They have co-opted hundreds of thousands of supporters on social media, including big-name celebrities like Russell Crowe, who played the role of the man trying to capture the horse in the movie version of *The Silver Brumby*. Tom Burlinson, who played the title role in the 1982 film *The Man from Snowy River*, is another high-profile brumby lover. There are more pro-brumby Facebook groups than you could list on a horse blanket, the biggest with upwards of 50,000 followers. The cause is an easy one to recruit support for. Who doesn't love horses? Who doesn't love wild horses even more? What's that? Those terrible park rangers want to kill the brumbies? What the hell is THAT all about? ANGRY EMOJI! #brumbylivesmatter. (Yes, they really use a hashtag borrowed from the Black Lives Matter movement.) When pro-brumby groups go to court to prevent trapping or planned culls, money for legal representation is easy to raise. Little girls from pony clubs gladly donate the $20 they got from their grandpa for Christmas. One leading brumby advocate proudly displays an email from a pensioner who gave all she could afford: two dollars. It's the sentiment that counts.

Meanwhile, the scientists toil on in relative silence and often in despair. Professor David Watson of Charles Sturt University, who quit his post on the NSW Threatened Species Scientific Committee when John Barilaro's brumby legislation was passed, wrote in a February 2021 essay:

> How can environmental scientists find and sustain hope in the modern world? How can we continue to inspire when our lamp begins to flicker and wane? With all that we know about threats, about the fallibility of governance structures

and the creaking instability of planetary processes that make breathable air and drinkable water; how can we keep on keeping on?

Study after study shows the degradation to the High Country caused by brumbies. There are numerous environmental issues. The broad-toothed rat is a cheeky alpine rodent which makes tunnels in the thatch of snow grass tussocks to shield itself from predators. Guess what happens when the grass is eaten till the ground is bare? Of particular concern are the degraded sphagnum bogs. Sphagnum is nature's miracle moss. A semi-fluorescent greeny-yellow, it grows in big pillowy pads along High Country streams, storing the snowmelt and rainfall and releasing it slowly, slowly, like water from a sponge. Because of sphagnum, many High Country streams run clear and true even through the worst drought. Without sphagnum, the reservoirs of the great hydro-electric schemes of the mountains would be starved of a constant inflow of water as streams intermittently dried up. Those streams would also run muddy instead of clear. Sphagnum bogs support communities of rare plants and animals, like the spectacular corroboree frog, a tiny black-and-yellow amphibian which would fit comfortably inside a matchbox with a couple of its friends. There is nothing remotely like sphagnum anywhere else on mainland Australia, and while the horses rarely eat it, they eat the carex grass that grows out of it and trample it in their daily search for water.

But who on Facebook cares about moss? Moss is boring. Who cares about swamps? Donald Trump said he'd make

America great again by draining one. Who gives a rat's about rats? And what chance does a frog have against a horse? There's a reason people swoon over pop songs about wild horses while *The Muppet Show*'s Kermit the Frog sang, 'It's Not Easy Being Green'. Up against horses, moss and bogs and rats and frogs are a public relations basket case. The brumby wars are a classic case of head versus heart, and in the contest of emotion versus science, emotion wins every time.

'So, we may ask ourselves, how did we get here?' Charles Darwin University ecologist Dr Dick Williams said in his keynote speech at the Kosciuszko Science Conference on Feral Horse Impacts, convened in November 2018 as a response to the Barilaro legislation, which had been passed in June of that year:

> We can perhaps explore that question by looking at the way the issue of feral horses in the Alps has been differentially framed ... Science has told its story on the basis of evidence, rationality, history and authority: livestock and the Alps do not mix. The pro-brumby lobby have told a different story – one of the companions to the heroic settler, the free-range iconic animal.

When emotion rules, science is not just disregarded but denied. A recent post on a pro-brumby site illustrated the irrationality perfectly: 'Nature will do its own thing. The moss will grow back. The moss is what your going on about? Your kidding me. I guess the brumbies killed the Great Barrier Reef too.'

But the sphagnum moss will not grow back, or not within decades anyway, because everything grows slower in the cold alpine and subalpine environments, and the High Country is in many ways Australia's inland Great Barrier Reef – an incredibly fragile ecosystem with a million threats to existence. And brumbies are not an abstract threat, like coal is to the reef. The chain from mining to burning to warming to bleaching may be clearly scientifically established, but it's circuitous. In the High Country, you can walk in any of a number of areas and see the hoof marks, the huge piles of poo, the silty water, the trampled sphagnum firsthand. Even then, the loudest voices in the mountains and beyond will tell you that the damage is overstated, or that it just doesn't matter, or even that horse poo is good for the alpine environment. And those are the voices that reach beyond the mountains to people who are disengaged in the debate, or who only come across it when the issue of wild horse management pops up in the news from time to time. In one survey, 78 per cent of Victorians didn't know that brumbies are listed by Parks Victoria as a pest animal. In the popular imagination, brumbies are synonymous with the High Country. In the popular imagination, they belong there. Mythology has become reality.

'People have been sold the nonsense that brumbies are part of our heritage,' says Dr Alec Costin AM, the venerable 95-year-old ecologist whose pioneering soil conservation work was instrumental in ending the grazing era in Kosciuszko. 'They are part of our imagination now and people don't give a damn about the beautiful environment which is still recovering from the grazing era. You only need a couple of films like *The Man from Snowy River* and *The Silver Brumby* and people are sold. They don't understand all the other implications.'

When you drive to the Snowy Mountains from Sydney, the iconography is all about wild horses and the cattlemen's days. Just over the ACT border is the Snowy Monaro Regional Council welcome sign alongside a sculpture of four running brumbies, manes and tails flying in the breeze. In early 2021, someone covered each horse in an Australian flag, just to ramp up the you-beaut true-blue flavour. On the Visit Cooma tourism website, one of the header images shows eight brumbies glowing in late afternoon sunlight. The first motel you pass in Cooma has a restaurant called The Stockmen's, while a local removalist is called The Van from Snowy River. In Jindabyne, the first hotel you pass is the Banjo Paterson Inn. It doesn't have much parking on site and the car park across a laneway out the back is called The Overflow, a dry bush humour nod to one of the poet's best-loved works. Up the road in Perisher, you've got The Man from Snowy River Hotel. Or if you turn left out of Jindabyne, you'll pass the Wild Brumby Distillery on the road to Thredbo, where the enormous Silver Brumby ski lodge surveys the village from the highest point. Past Thredbo and over on the Victorian side of the mountains, Corryong has The Man from Snowy River Museum, the grave of Jack Riley, and holds The Man from Snowy River Bush Festival each autumn, with rodeos, bushcraft skill demonstrations and more, including a re-enactment of The Man's daring ride. The town has made the poem and legend its own. Virtually every town, ski resort and settlement in and around the mountains has folded the iconography of Banjo and brumbies into its identity. Even Canberra's rugby team is called the Brumbies. Corroboree

21

frogs, on the other hand, make lousy emblems. They just don't cut it in the folklore stakes.

So revered are the brumbies, so sanctified, so woven into the fabric of High Country mythology, that it hardly matters to their supporters that they were considered a pest back in the day of Banjo Paterson. Consider the storyline of 'The Man from Snowy River', in which the colt from Old Regret escapes to join the 'wild bush horses'. A party of riders is immediately dispatched to retrieve the valuable thoroughbred which those pesky wild bush horses lured away. Paterson employed a generous dollop of poetic licence in all of his characterisation and storytelling, but in real life he knew the score. He is on record as saying that 'the wild horses got to be as big a plague as the wallabies and rabbits', and that, while trapping and shooting horses on a wholesale basis was a 'terrible thing', 'it had to be done for, if they didn't get rid of the horses, the horses would get rid of them'. By which he meant, the brumbies would devour the precious mountain pastures, and were therefore a threat to the cattlemen's way of life.

The Silver Brumby author Elyne Mitchell also understood that brumbies needed to be culled when the number of mobs grew too high, according to her youngest daughter and biographer, Honor Auchinleck. 'Elyne would have ensured she was well briefed about the research,' Auchinleck says. Mitchell wrote *The Silver Brumby* in the postwar period. 'This was a time when there was a quest for finding a beauty in the world because the world had been through such a rotten experience, and I think that the horses symbolised that,' Auchinleck adds.

But she says their numbers are 'out of control' partially because pastoral families are no longer culling or removing them due to the establishment of national parks, and believes her mother would see it the same way.

That's right: according to her daughter, Elyne Mitchell, the author of *The Silver Brumby*, would think there are too many brumbies today. Not that Mitchell would want them all gone. Not by a long stretch. 'If you bring the brumbies' right to life into question, you bring all creatures' right to life into question, and you bring our right to live here in Australia into question. Yet we're here and we have a right to be somewhere, and we can't have that right diminished and I think it is being diminished in many respects,' Auchinleck says.

This view might be categorised as that unfashionable thing – almost forgotten in our increasingly polarised world – known as the sensible middle ground. Yes, the unique High Country plants and animals need protection. And yes, families who have worked the High Country for generations deserve to keep their emblems, their memories. The trick is to find the balance. Rob Gibbs tried and he's still scarred from the experience. It shouldn't have to be that way.

'I think Elyne would find the debate quite frightening … I think she'd find it very toxic,' Auchinleck says.

She'd be right. This is one of the most toxic debates in Australia today. It's the culture wars through the prism of horses, encompassing all the elements of the polarised Australia Day/Change the Date debate. Do we prioritise the culture of postcolonial Australia or the culture and ecology of pre-colonial Australia? In essence, that's what people are asking.

But it's more complicated than that because we're talking about horses. Any other introduced species and the debate would be over before lunchtime.

The brumby wars, as they are currently playing out, have two sides firmly ensconced in their respective trenches. But when you travel through the mountains and beyond, on foot and by road, and you meet people on both sides of the debate, you start to think there might just be a way through.

CHAPTER TWO

THE REAL MAN FROM SNOWY RIVER

You've never seen a man cook sausages like Richard Swain.

There's an old saying in advertising: you sell the sizzle, not the sausage, and when most of us throw a few snags on the barbie they sizzle, the grease hissing and popping like wet sticks in a fire. Richard Swain's sausages make no such racket. They are not seared, scalded, torched and tortured until pustules of sausage pus bubble out of the skin. Swain's sausages cook slowly, coaxed out of rawness in a pan resting on the very edge of the coals, their skin never breaking, their complexion darkening as gradually as a London suntan. If you're hungry, so be it. If you absolutely can't wait to wrap one of those bangers in white bread and drown it in sauce, or bung it on a camp plate with peas and gravy and mashed potato, well … you're going to have to be patient.

There's a chance you'll give up. You might find yourself waiting so long for those fatty little flesh fingers that you decide to crawl into your tent, falling asleep to the sound of your stomach grumbling and the river gurgling and the night creatures chittering and scampering. But that would be a mistake, because this whole trip is about the slow burn. About listening, savouring, understanding. 'I take people into this place and allow country to sing to them,' Swain says in the promotional video for his Snowy River paddling adventures. And if you keep your trap shut long enough, you might just hear the country's song.

But on this misty spring evening on an elevated riverbank beside the Snowy, the calm, industrious babble of the river and the gentle crackle of the fire are drowned out by the small talk of campers trying to keep their minds off their hunger. There is song, but it's an actual tune, not the song of country. If you didn't know better, you'd swear that Swain was humming the chorus of 'White Noise' by Australian band The Living End. Could he really be humming that? Is this proud Indigenous man making a point? Maybe your mind is playing tricks on you. Out here in the Byadbo Wilderness – a large boot-toe of rough, dry, gorge country that was tacked onto the south-eastern corner of Kosciuszko National Park in 1970 – you quickly find yourself second-guessing your thoughts.

If you're smart, you don't fight it. You let your mind flow like the river rather than trying to sort thoughts into a Dewey decimal system of order. You use words sparingly and avoid superfluous questions. You don't ask whether the day's paddling will bring large rapids because it either will or it won't, and what's the difference if you know beforehand? You don't inquire about the dinner menu because what's for dinner is what's for dinner, and it'll be ready when it's ready.

When Swain requests fire sticks the size of your arm, you don't ask whether he means Arnold Schwarzenegger's biceps or the forearms of your elderly piano tutor. You just fetch the driest sticks you can find that don't have creatures dwelling underneath them. And when you lay those timber limbs on the fire, you don't cross them the way they taught you in the Scouts or Girl Guides, because the flames will burn too hot, too high, too rapidly. Instead, you gently place them parallel, just one or two at a time, so their heat spreads evenly, the fuel consumption minimised, the finite resources of the forest floor respected. The song of country that Swain wants you to hear? It's that this country yearns to be treated gently.

But for the best part of two centuries, the silent song has gone unheard. Byadbo has been brutalised. The cattlemen came first, stripping the topsoil to dust through overgrazing, and burning the land too frequently in a quest to promote fresh grass shoots. The topsoil washed away and Byadbo's natural open woodland was transformed into much denser regrowth forest beneath widely spaced old trees. In the denser forest, the native grasses, mosses and lichens that held Byadbo's steep slopes together struggled to survive ongoing chewing and trampling, exacerbating soil loss. Around the turn of the 20th century, a rabbit plague arrived and further undermined the soil. Larger, hungrier ferals followed. Goats, deer and pigs chewed what was left of the landscape bare, all the way to the riverbank. And then came the horses.

Brumbies are the most recent visitors to this area. They spilled over from higher, snowier parts of Kosciuszko in the early parts of the 21st century and quickly became one of the worst pests. Former National Parks and Wildlife Service ecologist Ian Pulsford commenced research on the density of herbivores in Byadbo in 1984. He measured the amount of herbivore dung at six different sites. Back then, he found virtually no horse dung. Most was from rabbits, with a small amount from wallabies or kangaroos. In 2017, ANU researcher Jessica Ward-Jones replicated Pulsford's study. She revealed a fourfold increase in all types of dung per square metre. A whopping 84 per cent of that was from horses. 'This area is currently trying to recover from 150 years of grazing, changes in fire regimes and rabbit plagues,' she said in a February 2020 video for pro-conservation group Reclaim Kosci. 'Since it was included in Kosciuszko National Park, it should have had a chance to recover, but since horses and deer are here, we've found that it just hasn't had an opportunity to.'

Brumbies, and to a lesser extent deer, have been chewing and pooing Byadbo to death. And while there are deer carcasses all over the landscape from a recent cull, no one dares to touch the brumbies, whose numbers reached an estimated 8500 in southern Kosciuszko in mid-2019, almost double the 2014 estimate. But that would be the peak. As drought took hold, the brumbies began to starve. Byadbo couldn't cope and neither could the horses themselves. They ate anything and everything – even the seed heads of the phragmites reeds that were once a character of the Snowy's banks and its small feeder creeks. But there just wasn't enough feed. Carcasses of emaciated wild horses soon dotted the denuded banks of the Snowy, grotesque graffiti on an already tarnished landscape. It was a silent equine famine that went largely unrecorded and unreported. Byadbo's like that. What happens in Byadbo stays in Byadbo.

* * *

When most people visit the Snowy Mountains of New South Wales, they're too mesmerised by the snow-clad mountains visible to the west through the car windscreen on the approach to Jindabyne to wonder about the low-lying, snow-free country up and over the hills to the south. Most don't even know Byadbo is there, let alone appreciate its value. There's only one road through it. It's called the Barry Way on the NSW side of the border and the Snowy River Road on the Victorian side, and was completed in 1961, with the optimistic goal of encouraging tourism between East Gippsland and the Snowy Mountains. But the unsealed road never became a popular tourist route. It was always too rough, too remote. To this day, few people pass through Byadbo. Fewer still see its wildest parts, which are accessible only via treacherous, poorly signposted four-wheel drive tracks that plunge towards the Snowy River. If you turn south along the Barry Way at Jindabyne, drive past Moonbah and Grosses Plain, then veer onto one of those tracks, you'd better hope like hell you've got a driver as calm, cheerful and competent as Richard Swain's 20-year-old daughter, Hayley.

The managers of open-cut mines in outback Australia are said to prefer female drivers because they're less likely to make mistakes in the enormous pit trucks. Hayley Swain inspires exactly that sort of confidence. She drives heavy vehicles for a living on worksites near Bega on the NSW south coast, and occasionally pilots the family off-roader on resupply trips for her father's river tours. Swain says he finds it hard to sleep the night before Hayley drives down to the river. Shotgunning alongside her on the Paupong Trail, you can see why – not because of her driving skills, but because of the track itself. The Paupong was built for convenience, not comfort, lurching terrifyingly down a ridge towards the river. On old maps, they call such ridges 'ladders'. In truth, they're more like slippery slides, especially in wet conditions. After overnight rain it's triply cheek-tightening. Hayley handles it like she's driving to the shops.

She's happy to chat while she drives, which is both unnerving and reassuring. She talks about her upbringing and her mum, Leanne – Richard's first wife – whom she describes as 'a typical Aussie horse lady'. She says she grew up around horses and was familiar with them from a young age, but she has no love for the wild brumbies roaming the mountains, nor the people who champion them. No doubt influenced by her father, a prominent anti-brumby voice in the mountains, she says she understands the damage brumbies do and that it pisses her off. She says the whole horse debate pisses her off. But it would be wrong to categorise her views as entirely her father's. Hayley Swain is nothing if not her own person. She's an interesting one. Blonde hair, thongs with the insignia of Winfield Blue cigarettes, a Southern Cross tattoo just above her ankle. In the brumby debate, people who display symbols of Australiana on their person or property are usually on the side of the horses. Not this feisty filly. 'Fuck the brumbies. I love Australia,' she declares with a big, cheeky smile.

Hayley says her dad's fighting for the bush, while her cousins (on her mum's side) and her former schoolmates are fighting for a made-up thing. Many of those ex-schoolmates hang out in the brumby groups on Facebook, a platform that Hayley reckons 'gives stupid people an audience'. She says most brumby lovers on social media are 'fat-arsed old bitches that are divorced and stuck at home pondering how great the brumbies are'. She calls them 'Karens'. And before you know it, you've made it down the Paupong Trail without skidding into a ditch and you're on a sandbank of the Snowy at the resupply point.

You bid farewell to Hayley, greet her father when he arrives shortly thereafter, and thank him for squeezing you in to another group's trip. The other paddlers are members of a bushwalking club, all aged in their 60s or early 70s, and you can't help admiring them for roughing it out here. You bundle your gear in dry bags, watching carefully as Swain shows you how to secure the bags to the boats, and take to the water, making the paddling mistakes everyone makes in their first hours on the river, but somehow staying upright through the first few rapids. In gentler reaches between the white water, you take in the country.

'Surely the Creator of the Universe must have raked together all the spare, rough mountain ranges, gorges and boulders into one vast heap, meaning to level them out when he had nothing more important on hand,' adventurer Arthur Hunt wrote of Byadbo in the Canoe Club of NSW newsletter of 1938. Hunt and his companion Stanley Hanson audaciously navigated the largely uncharted Snowy from Jindabyne to its mouth at Marlo in Victoria in 1937, travelling in a pine canoe less than four metres in length. It was the sort of mad adventure that deserves to be as well known as the Burke and Wills epic, not least because Hunt was an entertaining diarist. And the man was right about Byadbo. God had a good laugh when he made this place. There's nowhere like it anywhere in the entire Australian Alps.

Even at the quickest glance, three key factors make the geography of Byadbo different. First, it's dry. Most of the Australian Alps bioregion is exceedingly wet by Australian standards. Indeed, the area around Mt Kosciuszko is the wettest place in non-tropical mainland Australia. That's because the mountains act like a barrier against the prevailing westerly weather systems, trapping clouds and squeezing them dry. East of the mountains, different story. The tablelands near Jindabyne and the Monaro plains near Cooma are in a rain shadow. Any moisture is as scant as Oliver Twist's second helping, even on days when it snows heavily in the mountains. To the south-east in Byadbo, the low country is drier still. Viewed on Google Earth, Byadbo's furrows and ridges are greyish-brown, a stark contrast to the bottle-green forests of nearby higher areas. Though barely 50 kilometres south-east of Thredbo ski resort as the mountain raven flies, Byadbo is another world. It's much warmer too, which is why its pastures, though meagre, were favoured by 19th century cattlemen in winter.

The second thing that makes Byadbo different is its trees. Descending the Paupong Trail, gnarled snow gums give way to sturdier box gums. About halfway down to the river, cypress pines kick in. They're a sparse sort of tree, their branches set apart from each other like the arms of a turnstile. They're not majestic like the snow gums or soaring alpine ash, but they suit this place. Cypress pines grow in dry and semi-arid regions of inland Australia like the vast Pilliga forest in north-central New South Wales. Because of the rain shadow effect, Byadbo is the only place in the whole of Australia where cypress pines grow east of the Great Dividing Range.

The third unique feature of Byadbo is its crazy topography. Australia's highest mountains are among the oldest in the world, sculpted to roundness by a million blizzards, their highest parts ground smooth by glaciation. Byadbo is rugged. Viewed from the channel of the Snowy River, its slopes rise so steeply that they seem to have no business not being cliffs. This low country is in many ways more mountainous than the high mountains. For that, the river is the culprit. Fuelled by the snowmelt of the high Alps, it scythed its way through here. 'The mountains and the rivers share a deep connection,' Swain says. He's right. But that connection has been broken.

The Snowy might have cut Byadbo's gorges and jagged slopes, but these days it would struggle to slice through white bread. All along the river are signs that this was once a much broader, swifter stream. It's October, prime spring snowmelt season after a reasonably snowy winter, yet huge sandbanks sit high and dry. On every large rock, you can see signs of the waterline which once lay metres above the current river level. For all the damage wrought to the land and soil of Byadbo by man, beast and fire, the Snowy River itself has endured the harshest treatment. 'By 1991, the river was little more than a greasy trickle in a huge channel choked with willows, weeds, sand and slime,' Deirdre Slattery and Graeme L Worboys wrote in *Kosciuszko: A Great National Park*.

How did it come to that? How was the mighty Snowy, the river of Banjo Paterson's dreaming, reduced to a greasy trickle? And how has the Snowy's story not been shared as widely as the stockman's daring ride? One of the key factors behind the Australian Labor Party's 1983 federal election win was its promise not to dam Tasmania's Franklin River, which would have ruined a pristine wilderness. While that relatively obscure Tasmanian river changed the course of Australian history, the course of the Snowy was drying up. Why are we oblivious to the sad fate of this waterway which is so prominent in the national imagination?

It doesn't help that most Australians don't even know where the Snowy flows. We can't name its principal tributaries or pinpoint where it rises or enters the sea. We know that our longest river, the Murray, rises ... oh, somewhere in the High Country before emptying out into Lake Alexandrina at the Coorong in South Australia. We know that its principal tributary, the Darling, rises in outback New South Wales and flows the colour of caramel – when it's not a series of intermittent pools – before meeting the Murray somewhere out west. We know about the Hawkesbury, the Murrumbidgee, the Yarra, the Brisbane, the Derwent, the Torrens, and the Swan because these rivers flow through or near our cities. But most of us couldn't point out the Snowy on a map. The river is a place in a poem, a feeling, an idea. It is something exotic – as snow always is in the Australian consciousness – but far from a real concern. But the Snowy is a real river with a sad story to tell.

When you hike the unchallenging 13-kilometre round trip from the top station of Thredbo's Kosciuszko Express Chairlift to Mt Kosciuszko – as tens of thousands of people do each year – you walk upon a steel mesh walkway, specially designed to protect the delicate alpine plants from being trampled. About three kilometres into the trek, just after the Mt Kosciuszko lookout, the walkway crosses a small, unmarked stream flowing north-east, fed by a large snow patch which usually clings to life until January. That's the infant Snowy. Like a wild animal, it matures quickly. Within a few kilometres, the Snowy is a gushing torrent strewn with huge, rounded granite boulders before it's dammed for the first time at Guthega, not 15 kilometres into its course. Again, it's dammed just a few kilometres downstream at the former Snowy Mountains Hydro-Electric Scheme settlement of Island Bend. In these interrupted higher reaches, the Snowy collects swift mountain rivers – the Guthega, the Munyang, the Gungarlin. For a few fleeting kilometres after Island Bend, it roars like the river of old. Then at Lake Jindabyne, a flooded valley where once its rushing waters merged with the Eucumbene and the Thredbo, the Snowy is silenced.

Lake Jindabyne both dams and damns the Snowy. Before the lake filled in 1969, the Snowy's precious water flowed more or less straight from the mountains to the Victorian coast without anyone taking more than a few drops. After Jindabyne, the Snowy wound its way through the tablelands, dropping to the low Byadbo country then dashing almost due south to its outlet in the Southern Ocean, through country too steep and remote for any kind of irrigation or cropping. To the nation-builders of the time, that was a shocking waste of water. Their solution was as dastardly and brilliant as any James Bond villain's plot: dam the Snowy and pipe its water through the mountains into the westward-flowing Murray, thus irrigating the food bowl of Australia. Special bonus: generate hydro-electric power as the water tumbles down the western face of the mountains.

When the first sod was turned in 1949 at the launch of the watery blood transfusion known as the Snowy Mountains Hydro-Electric Scheme, Australia's Governor-General William McKell – the former NSW premier who had presided over the creation of Kosciuszko State Park – was as gushing as the river itself:

> I was born not far from this spot. I was brought up within hearing of the song of the Snowy, which has always been more than a river to me. I stood on its banks at the delightful Arcadian spot, Jindabyne, watched the clear waters singing their way to the sea at a rate of two million acre feet per year. I have heard it say, 'I can work for Australia'. Today the prayer of snow is answered. The river is to be put to work for its people, and what great work it will do.

Even a High Country conservationist like McKell was blind to the need to conserve the Snowy. When he spoke of 'the clear waters singing their way to the sea', he was hearing a very different tune to Richard Swain's song of country. Swain calls the Snowy 'The River of Life'.

To old Bill McKell, the Snowy River's lifeblood – its water – was a resource to be channelled to nation-building. So it came to pass that Lake Jindabyne filled and the Snowy's flow was reduced by 99 per cent, with barely a garden hose worth of water allowed to pass below Jindabyne Dam. Meanwhile, the old town of Jindabyne was submerged and relocated up the hill, becoming considerably less delightful and Arcadian and significantly more windswept.

But they weren't done killing the river quite yet. Just below the Lake Jindabyne dam wall, a montane river enters the Snowy. Officially called the Mowamba, locals call it the Moonbah because it flows through a valley of that name. The Mowamba rises in the high peaks behind Thredbo and is the last Snowy tributary that reliably carries heavy snowmelt each spring. Its cold, nutrient-rich water would have done wonders for what was left of the Snowy's ecology, but they built an aqueduct to divert the Mowamba back up into Lake Jindabyne. Thus did the Snowy become the choked-up, greasy trickle. And because so few people travel the Barry Way, the river's fate – like Byadbo itself – was out of sight, out of mind.

It wasn't until the 1990s that environmental concerns over the Snowy bubbled over into action. The Snowy Water Inquiry was commissioned in 1998. Its final report, published later that year, recommended that releases below Jindabyne Dam should increase from 1 per cent to 22 per cent of natural flows. The targets changed over the years but one constant was that the river never got as much water as promised. By 2009, it was supposed to be receiving 15 per cent of natural flows. It got 4 per cent. By 2012, it was supposed to be getting 28 per cent. Never happened. There are statistics on Lake Jindabyne water releases on the Snowy Hydro website that you need a PhD in pure mathematics to understand. How much water is actually coming out of that dam? In lieu of easily digestible information, there's no better person to ask than Richard Swain.

Though his people are Wiradjuri from central New South Wales, Swain was born and bred in the mountains and now lives on a property near Cooma. In his early 50s with salt sprinkles in his pepper hair, Swain began guiding along the Snowy in the 1990s, running trips down towards the Victorian border, where the river is bolstered by tributaries like the Jacob and the Pinch. The first environmental releases from Lake Jindabyne in the early 2000s, meagre though they were, provided enough water to make areas further upstream navigable. So Swain ramped up his business, conducting semi-regular spring river tours through Byadbo. This river is his workplace, but it's much more than that. The Snowy is his dreaming. A place of stories, of ancient songlines, of pathways travelled by Australia's first people for tens of thousands of years. Swain had stories of the river passed on to him by local elders Uncle Snappy and Uncle Max. And when the mood strikes him in spare moments between river guiding duties, he passes those stories on. Like the one about a massacre somewhere far away when they hid the kids in the giant phragmites reeds like the ones that used to be found in Reedy Creek. Today, the reeds on Reedy Creek are gone, every last one destroyed by horses.

River guiding is tough, relentless work. The hours are long and the demands many. There are meals to cook and dishes to clean. There's the packing up of the campsite each morning, all gear stowed in dry bags and tied securely into the boats. There are hapless paddlers to steer through the rapids and scoop up when they capsize. There are a hundred micro-requests to deal with throughout the day. Someone needs to stop and pee. Someone needs their camera from a bag tied up threefold at the very bottom of a boat. Someone forgot to smear on sunscreen and needs their bottle. Then there's the setting up again in the evening, the erection of tarps to ward off the Byadbo drizzle which barely wets the ground but will soak you through within minutes. There's the checking of campers' tents, ensuring they haven't erected them clumsily, which happens far more frequently than it should. Then there's the stress of the unknown. The fear of a river or campsite accident. The worry over Hayley negotiating the Paupong on resupply day. 'It's been a tough year,' Swain says in a rare, almost apologetic moment of openness around the fire. That's putting it mildly.

In the Black Summer bushfires, Swain was out with a neighbour who runs a wildlife sanctuary when a C-130 Hercules water-bombing aircraft came down on a neighbouring property, killing three American firefighters. Swain spent the ensuing months building emergency wildlife enclosures and providing accommodation for wildlife volunteers. It was a deeply traumatic time for everyone in the mountains and surrounding districts. Though replenished by heavy autumn rains, the river on his property still runs black with ash and he reckons it will for years. Then, in April, there was a sudden death in his immediate family.

'The river loves a smile,' Swain says in his promotional video, and the video cuts to a good-looking woman paddling her inflatable kayak in slow motion and smiling an Instagram-wellness smile. But Swain himself isn't smiling much. Whether it's preoccupation with work, disgust at the state of country, or despair at the sheer cruelty and indifference of the universe is anyone's guess. 'There aren't many parallels you can't draw with your own life and what happens on the river,' he says in his promo video. He's right. Life is messy – and the river is a mess.

What really gets Swain animated is the notion that there's something quintessentially Australian about the brumbies which have done so much damage to this country – just at a time when it was recovering, when it had been incorporated into the national park, when it stood half a chance. 'Costume play,' he hisses when talking about the brumby advocates and their reverence for the symbols of pastoral life. 'They're all just having a big costume party. Vegemite and horses and thongs. Is that really Australia? What's Aussie about a thong? There are 20 million Vietnamese people with thongs. You can buy a jar of Vegemite in New York. They have horses in America.' Someone around the fire mentions the claim, often made by farmers, that they are the best custodians of the land. 'You show me the square millimetre where they looked after it,' Swain replies. 'If you're looking for an honest appraisal of our history, this land is your answer.'

At last, dinner is ready. And the salty sausage fat squirts inside your mouth in a delicious explosion, like the aspic-turned-to-liquid inside a Chinese soup dumpling. Cook your sausages slowly and they will burst forth in abundance. Treat the land well and it'll do likewise. The song of country in a Woolworths banger.

In the morning, cereal and English muffins are on the menu and you'd better believe Swain cooks his muffins slowly, gently, till they're toasty and golden all over like the outback from the air. This camper cooks a *No Entry* sign – uncooked edges and a burnt black stripe down the middle. You hope Swain doesn't notice, but he doesn't miss much. He found the dirt you accidentally put in his hollow tent poles within three minutes. Then, sitting down to eat the underdone yet burnt muffin, you plonk your backside too firmly on a camp chair, ripping its fabric. Apologising profusely, and standing now, you change the subject to something, anything. You tell Swain you saw rock wallabies on the edge of a rocky outcrop beside the river on an early morning walk. He tells you that local rock wallabies died out years ago – yet another victim of grazing – and that the wallabies on the rocks were plain old wallabies, not rock wallabies. It's not often in suburban, middle-class life that you feel your whiteness as a burden on someone else. But you feel it out here and it's a clumsiness, a wrongness, a smear. Between the muffin and the broken chair and the dirty tent poles and the misidentified macropods, you feel like a poster of everything Swain is struggling against. You've come here to understand country, but ended up showing how little you know, and how incapable you are of caring for it. Half of you wants to explain how useless you feel. The other half just wants to go home. There's no way to do either.

After breakfast, Swain takes the campers on a walking tour around the vicinity of the campsite. He walks sure-footedly and silently through the bush in camo boardshorts and bare feet. He doesn't use the phrase 'sacred site' but this elevated patch of open woodland above all but the highest flood mark was clearly a place much visited by Australia's first people. Scattered on the ground are artefacts like grinding stones and hand-chipped blades. Some trees bear scars where canoes were cut from them. Others have holes that were fashioned to smoke out possums. Swain demonstrates how the bark from kurrajong trees was used to make a strong twine. The kurrajongs are rare in Byadbo now, juvenile specimens almost non-existent. He finds a small clump of yam daisies – a plant prized for their nutrient-rich tuber. They too once flourished throughout Byadbo, before the horses got to them.

When you're back on the river threading your way through valleys the shape of a capital V, you remind yourself how special it is here. Perhaps Swain thinks similar thoughts. He does seem to be happier afloat. The river loves a smile. And the river, like him, has moods and modes. In one section where the country momentarily opens up into a broader valley, the river becomes shallow, braided, with giant round pebbles and small grassy islands through which little cascades run. It has the feel of a giant Japanese garden. In another section the river runs sullen and slow, with giant casuarinas overhanging dark pools where black swans paddle and platypus plop and dive. Then there are the rapids. The trick is to lean towards the rocks, not away from them. Most adventure sports have similar moments of cognitive dissonance to overcome. In skiing, when your skis are pointing directly downhill and your survival instincts scream 'lean back!' you have to lean forward. So too with these boulders in the rapids. 'There aren't many parallels you can't draw with your own life and what happens on the river.' Swain's video monologue rings true again. Face up to something hard. Be rewarded.

Paddling a river, you travel at the pace of country. It's something we don't often do in a fast-paced world. On a quiet reach of dark water, Swain points out a hill with a craggy, near-vertical rocky summit. Though it's not marked as such on any map, Swain says the hill is called Where Dick Got Frightened. The unusual name derives from a stockman called Dick, surname unknown, who Swain says was half Irish, half Aboriginal, like many 19th century stockmen of this area. One day, a mob of cattle took off from the tableland and scarpered down towards the cliffs. To go after them would have been suicide. So Dick sensibly decided to cut his losses. The cattle were gone. Canoe adventurer Arthur Hunt wrote up a version of the story in the journal of his 1937 trip:

> It appears that many years ago the flat country towards Ingebyra was taken up by one of the earliest settlers and used as a cattle run. This man had in his employ a native stockman called Dick. Dick had the reputation of being absolutely fearless and was a splendid horseman. One day some cattle broke away from him and ran out on a spur. Dick rode hard trying to wheel them. He was galloping when he saw that the timber ended abruptly, and he pulled his horse into a slithering stop at the very edge of a precipice. It was the only time Dick ever admitted to being frightened, and to this day the spur bears his name and is reference to the incident.

Valuable escaped animals, a perilously steep mountain, and the Snowy River. It irresistibly evokes thoughts of 'The Man from Snowy River'. Could this be the tale on which Banjo's legend was founded? Did The Banjo, with his poet's magic wand, turn cows into horses? Did he throw a valuable colt into the mix to increase the dramatic tension tenfold? Did he turn a reluctant non-chase into a heroic descent? When AB Paterson published his iconic poem in 1890, he was a lawyer, harbour rower, tennis player and Sydney Grammar old boy. Did this relatively unknown writer paint his stockman white to appease the literary tastes of the times?

It has become accepted over the years that the character of The Man is a fictional amalgam of High Country stockmen, crafted from a mixture of campfire tales and Banjo's vivid imagination. The Man from Snowy River Museum in Corryong, on the Victorian side of the mountains, maintains the one-size-fits-all official position that the poem was a work of fiction drawing from tales told by Jack Riley and other stockmen whom Paterson met in his High Country travels. Riley's grave in the Corryong cemetery tells a less ambiguous tale. Its inscription reads:

In Memory of
THE MAN FROM SNOWY RIVER
JACK RILEY
BURIED HERE
16th July 1914

Irish immigrant Riley lived in a remote hut near Tom Groggin Station, on the upper Murray River about halfway between

Corryong and present-day Thredbo. His existence was humble, but he had friends in high places. One of them was Walter Mitchell, a grazier who ran local station Towong Hill. Mitchell introduced Riley to Banjo, and the two journeyed through the mountains, where Riley regaled the poet with tales of mountain riders and their horseback derring-do. The Mitchell family would become the nearest thing to Australian High Country royalty. Walter Mitchell's son Tom became attorney-general of Victoria and husband to Elyne Mitchell, author of the iconic *Silver Brumby* books. Tom Mitchell met Banjo and, according to the 2012 book *Searching for the Man from Snowy River* by WF Refshauge, he wrote a 1983 letter to the Royal Australian Historical Society stating that Banjo told him 'point blank' that The Man was Riley himself.

But was he?

Riley lived on the Murray, not the Snowy. Of course, it's possible that Paterson used the evocative phrase 'Snowy River' to mean the High Country generally, the way 'Kosciuszko' means a wider area than just the mountain or the national park. But there are strong hints that the poem was inspired by Byadbo to the east of the mountains rather than Riley's stamping ground to the west. A major clue lies in the first two lines of the final stanza:

And down by Kosciuszko, where the pine-clad ridges raise
Their torn and rugged battlements on high.

Nowhere else in the mountains or their adjacent flanks is there anything even remotely resembling pine-clad ridges. The only native conifer in the true High Country is a knee-high shrub called the mountain plum pine, which nestles among the boulders in the high alpine zone and is all but unidentifiable as a pine. When Banjo wrote of pine-clad ridges, he had to be thinking of the ridges of Byadbo. Where else could it be? There's simply nowhere else within a very loud cooee of the mountains that comes close to fitting that description.

As for the torn and rugged battlements, that too must be Byadbo. As mentioned, the mountains around Kosciuszko have rounded summits. There are clumps of smooth, granite boulders here and there, but nothing like a torn and rugged battlement, even with a large dose of poetic licence. And though the mountains drop off steeply to the western side towards Corryong, the ground cover is generally soft and wet. It changes from grassy alpine herb field to heathland, then to dense, mossy, ferny forests of alpine ash and mountain ash. Nowhere on the damp, western flank of the mountains is there ground that would make 'a horse's hoofs strike firelight', as described early in the fifth stanza. But look how dry Byadbo is. Look at the flint stones Richard Swain unearthed this very morning.

He hails from Snowy River, up by Kosciuszko's side,
Where the hills are twice as steep and twice as rough,
Where a horse's hoofs strike firelight from the flint stones every
  stride,
The man that holds his own is good enough.

There are of course other claimants to the identity of The Man apart from Riley. Just about every valley in the mountains has residents who reckon it was a local stockman who rode down a hill out the back of their neck of the woods. *Searching for the Man from Snowy River* author WF Refshauge believes The Man may well have been Charles Lachlan McKeahnie of Adaminaby, who famously chased a runaway stallion in 1895 in the north of the mountains. McKeahnie was just 17 at the time, which well and truly qualifies him as a 'stripling', the evocative word for young man used in Banjo's third stanza.

But another highly respected author points to Byadbo. In *On Track: Searching out the Bundian Way*, outdoorsman and naturalist John Blay chronicles his trek along an ancient pathway that passes through Byadbo on the way from the NSW far south coast to Kosciuszko. Blay makes the excellent point that while history remembers and celebrates the landowners, the 'main players' were more often their employees and contractors. That, of course, is the genius of Banjo's signature poem: he lionises the unsung Aussie battler. His hero, The Man, is the man who would have been written out of history and forever remained in lower case if the poet hadn't come along.

But maybe Banjo himself wrote The Man out of history. Maybe he turned an Indigenous battler white. Maybe 'The Man from Snowy River' is literary *terra nullius* – the black man erased from history. John Blay is unaware of the story of Dick or the hill Where Dick Got Frightened, but he mentions other riders of the Byadbo region by name in *On Track*. One was an Aboriginal stockman called Harry Bradshaw, another was a character with the extravagantly formal name of George James Howitt Patterson Johnson, who always went by the nickname The Joker. As Blay wrote:

Maybe Joker was The Man. Maybe he was just a typical character. Maybe The Man stands for individual human spirit triumphing over a hostile environment. But then again, maybe we should rename him the man from Nurudj Djurung [Snowy River]. Aboriginal friends tell me, 'That "Man From Snowy River" feller, he was a Koori. Who else coulda done what he did? Who else woulda known the country that well?' (p. 68)

The possibility of The Man from Snowy River being an Indigenous man, or at least being based on an Indigenous man, has bubbled up occasionally before, most notably in 1988 when Victoria's official historian, Dr Bernard Barrett, argued the case. Barrett cited a story published in 1887 – three years before 'The Man' was published – by High Country cattleman CW Neville-Rolfe which told of an 'exciting chase in which the horseman hero was a slightly built Aboriginal lad named Toby', who was renowned for being a skilled rider.

David Dixon, a descendant of the Ngarigo people of the mountains and the Djiringanj people of the NSW south coast, wrote more recently that the best mountain stockmen were Indigenous people. 'But Banjo Paterson would not have been able to make a hero out of our people in his day,' he argued in the *Bega District News* in 2018. Dixon says it doesn't much matter what he says or writes because white people will only listen to what white people say or write because they still see history through the colonial lens and mindset. He might have a point. Barrett's claim kicked up quite the stir in 1988. Dixon's, 30 years later at the height of the culture wars, didn't.

But it's worth saying again, even if this author is white. On balance, there's overwhelming evidence that 'The Man from Snowy River' was based on the exploits of an Indigenous man. There is just too much Byadbo in the poem. The pine-clad ridges and rugged battlements on high are like signposts saying, 'It happened here!' And if the poem was sourced from stories of the Byadbo area, then the stockman had to be Aboriginal because all the best riders in the area had Indigenous blood.

'Banjo knew he was making a myth, and he knew that parts of the ballad didn't ring true, but it didn't matter. This was a piece of impressionism,' the journalist and author Grantlee Kieza wrote in his 2018 biography of Paterson, simply titled *Banjo*.

Impressionism and mythmaking are of course the artist's prerogative, perhaps even their duty. But the thing about myths is that they have a habit of morphing into truth. Today, the accepted truth is that The Man was a white man. Another 'truth' to emerge from the poem is the natural place of brumbies in the mountains. The mere fact that 'wild bush horses' are mentioned in the poem has elevated them to iconic status. Forget that Paterson knew they were pests and advocated for them to be shot to protect the pasture for cattle. None of that matters now. The brumbies are characters in the poem and that makes them sacred, eternal, untouchable, as quintessentially Australian as Vegemite and thongs. That old saying that 'a lie can fly around the whole world while the truth is lacing up its boots'? The same could be said for reality and myths. The myth of The Man. The myth of the noble brumby.

Irrespective of the true identity of Banjo's Man from Snowy River, this much is indisputable: the modern day Man from Snowy River is Richard Swain. Some people in the mountains would reel at that suggestion because of his Wiradjuri bloodlines, but Swain has earned the title. 'He was brought up with huge respect for the environment and country and he has the respect of traditional owners of that area,' the naturalist Ian Pulsford says. But he doesn't have everyone's respect. And as you bump and wind up the Barry Way towards Jindabyne after three days on the river and pop out at Grosses Plain, Swain points out the property of Leisa Caldwell, one of the leading brumby advocates in the mountains. 'Costume play,' he says under his breath, and leaves it there.

When you meet Leisa Caldwell to hear her side of the brumby story, she shows you something interesting. It's an old brochure for Swain's river trips. At number five on the 11-point list under the subheading 'Highlights', it says: 'The iconic Snowy River brumby is often seen along the riverbanks.'

Yes, Swain once included the brumbies in his marketing. It's a 'gotcha' moment. But it's also yesterday's news. Who's to begrudge a tourist operator doing whatever was necessary to attract custom in the fledgling days of a business? Swain was told that people wanted to see brumbies and, back then, he was prepared to take the advice. The point is, he's moved on. He's stopped showing people what they think they want to see and started showing them what they need to see.

As for Leisa Caldwell, she's spent years making something that she reckons people need to see too.

CHAPTER THREE

'THE LAST LITTLE BIT WE'VE GOT'

When the organisers of the Sydney 2000 Olympics planned the opening ceremony, they knew it would be a once-in-a-generation moment for Australia. A moment when a global audience of hundreds of millions would be watching us, trying to understand what makes us tick. The minute the ceremony started, the world would know that these were not the Games of Asia, North America or Europe, where every previous winter and summer Olympic Games (except Melbourne 1956) had been held. These were Australia's Games, and they would look, feel and sound like Australia.

So when they decided to kick off proceedings with an iconic Australian animal, did they opt for a kangaroo? A cuddly koala? An emu? A platypus? Two amorous quokkas cavorting in the moonlight? And when they chose an unmistakably Australian sound as the aural backdrop to their opening scene, did the 110,000 hushed, expectant people at Stadium Australia hear the simple, haunting rhythm of clap sticks and didgeridoo?

Men at Work's 'Land Down Under'? The relentless chime of cicadas on a scorching day in the bush? The raucous cackle of kookaburra song? The drawn-out whistle and crack of whipbirds?

Well, there was indeed the sound of a whip. Except it came not from a pair of slim, olive-green forest birds, but from a horseback rider dressed in traditional bush attire. Steve Jefferys galloped alone into the stadium on his seven-year-old stock horse, Ammo. The horse reared twice, then Jefferys cracked his whip and galloped swiftly across the arena. Other riders followed, carrying white flags with the five Olympic rings, atop a surface the colour of the bush in drought. And as they galloped, Australian composer Bruce Rowland's *The Man from Snowy River* movie theme filled the stadium. It was the moment Banjo Paterson and Australian bush culture went global. It was the moment when we announced: this is what matters to us, what defines us. This is the little nugget of Aussie culture that beats loudest in our hearts. All those giant jellyfish and flying children still to come? A nod to our lighter side. But this – *this* – is how we see ourselves. And then, in another salute to The Banjo, *The Man from Snowy River* theme morphed into 'Waltzing Matilda'. And across a nation, throats choked with lumps the size of Pacific oysters.

Sitting on her black leather couch covered in cowhide, Snowy Mountains horsewoman Leisa Caldwell couldn't help herself. She let those warm, salty teardrops flow like the Snowy used to run in the old days. Twenty-odd years later, when she sits down and watches those first few minutes, the same thing still happens every time.

'Where does the feeling come from?' Caldwell asks. She answers the question herself. 'I don't know, but it's a bit like: how do you define love?' There's no answer to that question, so she asks another. 'Have you read the poem "Green and Gold Malaria"? It's exactly the same as when you read that.'

'Green and Gold Malaria' is a 44-line single stanza poem by Brisbane lawyer-turned-poet Rupert McCall. The plot is simple enough. A bloke goes to the doctor and says he's got some sort of rash. Tells the doc he gets it on Anzac Day and at assorted big sporting events where Australians are performing. Doc diagnoses him with green and gold malaria, which is so named by the medical profession from 'the Great Australian Bight to the Gulf of Carpentaria'. And if McCall's job the day he wrote that line was to rhyme a disease with a geographic location, here's hoping he knocked off early, job well done. Caldwell's point is that the poem celebrates unabashed patriotism. And that's exactly what she felt as her favourite symbols of Australiana were trotted out, literally and figuratively, one after the other, in front of the whole world.

Not that she was 100 per cent happy. The riders were not Snowy Mountains folk but horsemen and women from up Scone way, north-west of Newcastle, a region famed for being Australia's thoroughbred breeding centre. That aside, those first moments of the Sydney 2000 opening ceremony hit the sweetest of sweet spots for Caldwell. What a sight! Anything that happened on the track or in the pool in the ensuing two weeks would be cheese and crackers after roast beef and pavlova. And if you ask her whether kangaroos or koalas might've done the trick in those opening moments, well, you'd be missing the point. Because it's pretty clear that Caldwell believes an animal doesn't earn its full allocation of iconic Australian points by merely being endemic to this continent. Its status is elevated through its relationship with people.

'We haven't partnered with kangaroos or koalas physically,' she says. 'Horses helped humanity evolve and have done so for thousands of years. There's no other species of animal on the planet that has had such a profound partnership or relationship with humanity like horses have.'

Some brumby advocates are all bluster and no muster. Give Caldwell her due. No one has done more groundwork for the cause, and she's respected across the mountains for her work on the Kosciuszko National Park Wild Horse Community Advisory Panel and much more. Caldwell works as the heritage officer for Snowy Monaro Regional Council, so you could excuse her from writing heritage documents in her spare time at home. But in 2016, as Rob Gibbs was helping compile the Draft Wild Horse Management Plan for Kosciuszko National Park, Caldwell put together a detailed, highly articulate, intensively researched 71-page submission. On the first page, she asked a poignant question: 'How is it that brumbies have been living in the now Kosciuszko National Park for approximately 180 years in often immense numbers but it is only recently in the past two decades that they are deemed inappropriate?'

In a sense it's a slightly misleading question, because for the best part of 180 years brumbies were often considered pests that interfered with the prized pastures of mountain cattle, as Banjo himself made clear. Historically, brumbies were chased, rounded up and killed, sometimes en masse. The killings were often brutal. A favoured method was to slit their necks as they were driven out of corrals, so that they'd run into the bush and die in discreet locations rather than in one bloody heap that would have to be dealt with. And no one batted an eyelid, let alone shed a tear. Brumbies were also prized for the sport of catching them on brumby running trips, for the price their hides would fetch in town, and as working horses if they made it out of the mountains in good-enough condition after brumby runs, which could be rough-and-tumble affairs. On balance, it was a love/hate relationship that the mountain cattlemen had with wild horses. They were both a weed and a crop.

So when Caldwell asks why brumbies are only now considered inappropriate, it's pretty clear that she's querying why government land managers, scientists and people who live *outside* the mountains consider them inappropriate. The answer is that the science of environmentalism has only relatively recently brought the threat of so-called invasive species in Australia to mainstream consciousness. Viewed through the prism of preserving what's left of Australia's pre-colonial ecology, any invasive species must go.

That singular focus, to the exclusion of all other considerations, doesn't wash with Caldwell. Unsmilingly, she shifts her gaze towards the mountains and says, 'There's nothing else left in the mountains to demonstrate that we ever existed, or that our heritage ever existed. Our children and grandchildren are prohibited from following in their families' footsteps.'

* * *

Jindabyne is a town where everyone wears a uniform, even if it's not a uniform. Snowboarders wear baggy pants. Skiers wear puffy jackets, or whatever this year's fashion happens to be. Winter tourists visiting the snow for the first time comically wear too many clothes, as though Nugget's Crossing shopping centre is the top station of the chairlift at Perisher or Thredbo. Mountain bikers wear shorts and T-shirts with gear motifs, bushwalkers wear earth-coloured long-sleeved shirts, and people of the land wear blue jeans with striped or plaid shirts and a hat. Always the hat.

Leisa Caldwell, woman of the land, walks into the Parc Cafe in Jindabyne wearing no hat. She's just knocked off work at her desk job, so fair enough. But she's wearing a red-and-white striped shirt with jeans, so two out of three ain't bad. Caldwell's choice of venue is an odd one. The café is in the National Parks building, one of the few places in town where the uniform is actually uniform, as in the earth tones of National Parks and Wildlife Service gear with the lyrebird insignia. Brumby advocates are generally no fans of Parks. But the staff are friendly, the coffee is good – she has chai tea – and the vibe is relaxed. In her late 50s or thereabouts, Caldwell presents a serious, almost stern face. If she were a school headmistress, you'd be scared of her. In truth, she's probably just nervous. It's not easy to talk about her passion for brumbies with someone she believes to be from the other side of the fence. She risks being trivialised, even mocked. She risks her words being twisted, weaponised against her. But when you assure Caldwell you'll put your personal views to the side and allow her to tell her story, she slowly loosens up. First rule of interviewing: everyone loves to talk about themselves. So who is this woman, one of the strongest, most impassioned and most proactive voices in the mountains on the brumby issue?

Caldwell was born in Sydney but has lived in the mountains for 44 years. She says that with a hint of apology, because anyone whose family has been up there less than a few generations is generally considered a blow-in. She married into a High Country family: her husband Garry's great-great-great-grandmother was born in a hut in an area called Biddi in what is now the Byadbo Wilderness. Leisa just happened to meet Garry down that same way on a family camping trip; Leisa was 14, Garry was 15. They wrote letters to each other at school after that. Garry Caldwell's people have been in the mountains since the mid-1800s. His great-great-grandfather was James Spencer, a noted mountain stockman who escorted many early visitors and scientists up to the highest peaks, including the esteemed meteorologist Clement Wragge, who set up an ill-fated observatory on the summit of Mt Kosciuszko in the late 1890s.

Spencer lived at Waste Point, which was on the Snowy back then but is today a strip of land fronting an upper arm of Lake Jindabyne, just past the point where the wild river is tamed. He had a horse called Paddy which had a mind of its own and used to disappear from Waste Point all the time. Old Paddy would inevitably turn up at a spot down by the nearby Thredbo River, which soon became known as Paddy's Corner and is still called that today. Paddy's Corner is right near the trout hatchery where Garry Caldwell has worked for the last 25 years. And get this: he's got a horse called Paddy which he often takes out riding in the exact same area where the original Paddy used to roam. Here's the really spooky part: Garry's Paddy is not named after the old wayward Paddy, it was purchased from an Irishman, hence its name. Indeed, the Caldwells only learned the story of the original Paddy years after Garry had bought Paddy II and regularly ridden him in the stomping ground of Paddy I.

'*Doo-do-doo-do, doo-do-doo-do, doo-do-doo-do.*' That's the sound of Caldwell mimicking the theme from *The Twilight Zone*, to illustrate the strange case of two horses called Paddy who favoured the same patch of turf in the lee of the mountains several human generations apart. And sure, you could throw that story in a basket named coincidence. But there's another way you could read it. You could acknowledge that when you have deep connection to a place forged over time, strange little ghosts work their way into family stories. When your people have inhabited the country for multiple generations, your bond becomes stronger than mere continuity of tenure. It becomes a little mystical. It becomes – dare you say it? – something akin to the connection felt by Indigenous people.

'In today's climate, we are taught to recognise the Indigenous connection to the land and value it and understand it,' Caldwell says. 'So why aren't we allowed a connection? Because we're so young? Does that mean we're not valid because we come from convict stock or we've only been here 200 years? I can't help it, but our connection to the mountains to me feels just as strong.'

This view would doubtless invite ridicule in certain circles, especially if expressed as a throwaway line that essentially says, 'We're white. We have dreaming too' without its full context. So Caldwell, with great thoroughness, has encapsulated her views on heritage in a way that people will take seriously. Building on the foundation of her submission to the 2016 Draft Plan, she has written a fresh report called 'Kosciuszko National Park Wild Horse Heritage – Identified Values'. Flicking through, it's clear that this is an even more comprehensive piece of work, professionally laid out and with referencing. The report documents the history of wild horses in the mountains on several levels, with the aid of old news clippings, photos and quotes from heritage experts and professionals as well as old-timers.

It talks about the aesthetic significance of the horses, how 'catching just a glimpse of elusive brumbies running through the bush and hearing the galloping stampede of hooves or a whinnying call from one horse to another can be breathtakingly exhilarating and thrilling for many', noting how a wild horse can add 'its noble majesty to the frame which instantly changes and heightens the senses'. It cites art, photography and literature which have found 'significant meaning and value in the brumbies'. The report also speaks of the social significance of the horses, stating that 'brumbies are recognised and esteemed by associated communities as a part of their story and their identity'. Caldwell writes about the symbolism of the wild horse, stating that, 'the wild horses continue to represent a dichotomy between civilisation and wildness'. She even covers the wellness angle, claiming that 'there is plenty of evidence that horses both wild and domesticated can be utilised in mental health therapy programs around the world'.

That point invites a line of questioning: are not the mountains therapeutic without the horses? What's more therapeutic than sitting by a pristine babbling mountain stream, or taking in the sweeping views from Australia's highest summits? Is there anything more soul-enriching or sublime for a lover of the Australian Alps than making wide, arced ski turns between the snow gums on spring corn snow – the base frozen, the surface the consistency of a melting 7-Eleven Slurpee, a perfect harmony of firmness and silkiness giving both stability and fluidity to your turns? How is a wild horse going to improve that experience?

'You find the bush and nature therapeutic on its own without horses,' she says. 'But you've never done it with horses as well to know if it gives you another level of therapy.

'As I've said in here, with the mental therapy kind of stuff, people are using horses these days for therapy not only up close as domestic animals, but to sit and watch them in the bush or on the plains. We are learning more about our connections with horses every day. The bond between horses and humans is profound and emotional.'

Caldwell concludes her report by saying that the brumbies have 'significant cultural heritage value to many people at all levels, not just in mountain communities, but throughout Australia'. She says they must be protected and managed 'for the preservation of the Australian culture and identity'. She says brumbies are 'intrinsic to communities' sense of wellbeing and if removed from the landscape would result in a strong sense of loss'.

Sitting with Caldwell as she drinks her black chai tea, you can't help noticing a significant similarity between her and Richard Swain. This statement would surprise both and please neither, but the likeness is in their manner. Both say more with their faces than their mouths, and what their faces show is loss. Swain had his moody silence as he contemplated the degraded landscape while campers small-talked by the campfire. Caldwell carries a strained, almost pained expression, as if she knows nothing she says will make a non-believer understand, which is why she's gone to the trouble of writing it all down. Some might call Caldwell embittered, but exasperated would be more accurate. Resentful of those who would dismiss the gravity of her own sense of loss.

'It's the blatant unfairness and inequity that is the kick in the guts,' she says. 'Many sacrifices have been made by the local people over several generations but we are forever seeing more concessions made for tourists and developers. The brumbies may not be native, but they are important to many people ... It's about time some concessions were made for those local people that have given up so much already.'

At least Gloria Gaynor is listening. She belts out 'I Will Survive' through the café's speakers while the waitress, Ash, shuts down the coffee machine and prepares for closing. We move out into an unexpected burst of late afternoon sunshine on the deck at the front of the building. Do you think Leisa Caldwell will crumble? Do you think she'll lie down or die? Oh no, not her. She will survive, and she'll be damned if the brumbies don't survive too. How much have they taken over the years? How much more do they want? First they came for old Jindabyne, inundated it with water. Then more recently they flooded it with Sydney money so that even the new Jindabyne doesn't feel like itself anymore.

'They want the heritage of our brumbies destroyed, and yet here we are in what used to be a country town and we're seeing our town destroyed, our mountains destroyed by their tourism. That's okay?'

'Their' tourism. Interesting word choice there. Pretty good chocolate brownies and coffee here in this town destroyed by 'their' tourism. Are there not some positives to change?

'But it's not a High Country town anymore. Jindabyne 30 years ago used to be a country town in summer. We all knew each other and now we don't. You see someone and you wonder, "Are you a resident?" And the thing is, it's changed so much, so fast. It was dribs and drabs in the '80s, dribs and drabs in the '90s, it sped up in the 2000s, and in the last ten years, it's just gone boom! And people are cashed-up in Sydney and moving here and they're changing it because they're city people coming here expecting their city services. I see that in council and you see it in attitudes around town. And it hurts us. My mother-in-law, who was born in the old town under that lake, she has just moved to Berridale because she felt like a stranger in her own town. This was her heritage.'

And the brumbies in the mountains are all that's left of your heritage?

'It's the last little bit we've got.'

* * *

There's a sense in this debate that you're watching a dysfunctional game of checkers play out, where half the players are playing on the white squares, the other half on the black squares. And the game can never be won or lost or even really played at all, and the naysayers will never see eye to eye with the neigh-sayers, and everyone is just yelling at clouds.

The views of Richard Swain are typical of many Indigenous people. Ngarigo woman Aunty Rhonda Casey, who grew up on country in the Snowy Mountains, is another strong, consistent voice in opposition to the horses. 'The explosion of horse populations up on country is absolutely horrific,' she once said. 'Do we really want to bear the shame of inaction in the future? What are we going to tell our kids, that the feral animals were regarded as more important than Indigenous culture and the natural environment?'

But there are Indigenous people with a different perspective on the issue. One such person is David Dixon and his views straddle the divide between black and white in all senses. Dixon, 50, is a descendant of the Ngarigo people, who lived in the Kosciuszko region, and the Djiringanj of the NSW south coast. Based in Bega, where he works in social services, the issue of the brumbies came to his attention when he was a young fella, through stories handed down by his Ngarigo mother, Margaret Rose Dixon.

Margaret told young David that his great-great-grandfather on her side and his great-great-uncles on the other side of the family were stockmen in the 1800s who had good relationships with High Country landholders. They drove brumbies from Kosciuszko all the way down to the small coastal town of Tathra, a journey of around 200 kilometres through terrain that was extremely rugged, especially near the coastal escarpment. At Tathra wharf, the brumbies would be loaded onto steamer ships and taken to Sydney, where they were sold as stock horses. It wasn't gold or whales, but it was a lucrative enough trade.

The Indigenous stockmen used old ancestral pathways to drive the brumbies out of the mountains, upon which the European colonists soon constructed rough tracks and roads to drive stock, realising the old routes were the best way from the mountains to the sea. Capturing the brumbies in the first place was work which was well suited to Indigenous stockmen because of their knowledge of country. The brumbies would then be broken in, or 'tamed', as Dixon prefers to put it, at Blackfellows Lake near Tathra, a place of great significance for the Djiringanj.

Dixon says his mother always took great pride in this history and today, he shares her pride. 'It's part of my family story and part of the Alps' story,' he says.

To Dixon, the equation of history is not as simple as times before white people's arrival equals good, times after white people's arrival equals bad. He takes a broad, pragmatic view towards the fate of Indigenous people in the face of global forces beyond their control. 'We are part of a wider story of the Australian wave of the industrial revolution, and that was going to happen whether we liked it or not,' he says. 'Our people are very adaptable. We all have to adapt all the time to change, whether it's national or global. I'm proud that we were able to take up some sort of industrious activity that gave us value within the economic system'.

The brumbies were the key to that. They were the entity that enabled Dixon's people to use their bush skills and ancestral knowledge in places like Wollondibby, a valley that was a wild horse stronghold about halfway between present-day Jindabyne and Thredbo. 'Tracking and trapping wild horses in the vast territory of the Alps would not have been an easy task. There's a lot of country in the Snowy Mountains,' Dixon says. Dixon has always been interested in family and local history and has studied a few units of history at university in his limited spare time – he'd like to undertake a full degree one day but his work doesn't leave him much time. 'You've got to eat,' he says. Dixon quotes the mid-20th century black American writer and activist James Baldwin, who said, 'People are trapped in history and history is trapped within them'. People and horses alike.

'We need to be accepting of history,' Dixon adds. 'We have to learn from it. If we push it away and don't acknowledge it, it brings bitterness and misunderstanding. The brumby was a conduit between two cultures and two peoples. Some people want to wipe that out and say, "They're bloody feral animals and they need to be wiped out." I'm not saying that the mountains shouldn't be protected – I want that as a traditional owner – but I don't think we should wipe out a history that happened. We should confront and respect that.'

Dixon's appreciation for the brumbies goes a step beyond the lifeline it gave his people in the unfamiliar economic and social system which was imposed – often brutally – upon them. He actually appreciates the beauty of the horses. 'Our old people were animal lovers. They would have had great respect for these powerful horse spirits, and the beauty of them. They are part of nature and there would have been respect for that.' He also believes his ancestors would have respected the resourcefulness of the wild horses who forged an existence in the High Country, where life could be tough, especially in winter. 'Like our ancestors, the brumbies built their own knowledge and connection with the land for their survival,' he says. Dixon also takes pride in the fact that thinning out the wild herds, as his people did, was a service to the mountains. 'The work they did was a form of environmentalism,' he adds.

Dixon would be a louder voice on this issue but he's smart enough to steer well clear of politics. 'The old people told me how both sides can use you as a political football. And if you don't go along with their narrative, then you become invisible to them. They pick the Aboriginals out who can be a mouthpiece to repeat political lines.'

There's a good-natured defiance about Dixon. He detests the knee-jerk assumption that traditional owners want the land left the way it always was. He reckons the world these days is far too polarised. The last thing it needs is another right-winger or left-winger, and buggered if anyone will slot him easily into one of those categories. The world is complicated and nuanced, the brumby issue is complicated and nuanced, and a man's views should be complicated and nuanced. The culture wars aren't all black and white. This is the David Dixon take on the brumby wars, and it appears to be his world view too.

Dixon actually travelled up to the mountain a few years back for a meeting of a community wild horse management panel. He listened as traditional owners expressed the view that there needed to be controls on the number of brumbies in Kosciuszko National Park, but that brumbies should remain in some areas if they don't do too much damage. 'We were willing to go along with whatever the science was on it,' he recalls.

But his concern for the environmental damage inflicted by brumbies is balanced, as mentioned, by cultural considerations. It's also mitigated by the damage done by people, and especially people with money. 'There's another environmental predator up there that doesn't seem to get the same attention,' he says. 'The brumbies are being looked at like noxious weeds, but what about all the development up there? The Snowies are a playground for people with money. I call it the whitefellas' playground. They all believe they're in Europe or something. I looked at the master plan for the area. They were predicting $3 billion a year, a lot of visitors in there. It's one of the wealthiest national parks in Australia. And the traditional owners? None of that money comes to us.'

* * *

Leisa Caldwell and David Dixon are united in their resentment of tourism in the mountains, but their main common ground is the belief that the heritage work with horses is worth celebrating and worth protecting, by keeping brumbies running wild and free in the mountains. That protection was enshrined in John Barilaro's *Kosciuszko Wild Horse Heritage Act*, the stated objective of which is 'to recognise the heritage value of sustainable wild horse populations within parts of Kosciuszko National Park and to protect that heritage'. Surely that was a victory for Caldwell?

Well, here's the thing. When the legislation passed, the 2016 draft plan prepared by Rob Gibbs and others effectively became confetti. Three years later and a new draft wild horse heritage management plan is yet to be made public, though its release is said to be imminent. Kosciuszko National Park is still operating under the 2008 plan, which is hopelessly outdated for numerous reasons, not least the fact that horse numbers have exploded. In accordance with the *NSW National Parks and Wildlife Act 1974*, the new 2021 plan will identify the heritage value of sustainable wild horse populations within certain parts of Kosciuszko, set out how that heritage value will be protected, and ensure that the environmental values of the park are maintained. In short, it means some horses will continue to be removed, probably by trapping. But how many? Virtually no horses have been removed since 2017, give or take a few hundred that had strayed into previously horse-free areas after the 2020 fires. So the fight, in Caldwell's eyes, is far from won, especially with NSW Environment Minister Matt Kean, who is no friend of the brumbies or of John Barilaro.

In her heritage report, Caldwell concludes the section on the social significance of brumbies with the following quote:

Here in the Snowy, the Brumbies are an integral part of our High Country heritage and its folklore. They reflect the history of our ancestors, a history that in this part of the world gives us our own identity which we are rapidly losing. The Snowy Mountains stockmen now almost extinct, rightly or wrongly had their cattle taken from the mountains, then their homes and history flooded for hydro-electricity, and more recently their way of life of riding their horses in the mountains was prohibited too. The horsemanship, bush craft and bush lore that was once passed down and celebrated by Australians is all but gone. What is there left now if not for the brumbies to even demonstrate that our history ever existed?

The origin of that quote is significant. It's Caldwell quoting herself, from a paper called 'Why the Emotion?' which she penned back in 2002 for the Kosciuszko National Park Wild Horse Steering Committee on the Guy Fawkes cull. The Guy Fawkes 'massacre', as she and many brumby supporters call it, was the single biggest event that shapes today's brumby debate.

CHAPTER FOUR

FAWKES NEWS

Just after 6.30 pm on a Sunday evening in October 2000, barely a month after Australia's bush horse heritage had been celebrated at the Sydney Olympics opening ceremony, NSW Environment Minister Bob Debus took a phone call from his press secretary at home. 'We knew the moment the story broke that this was very bad trouble,' Debus recalls of the immediate aftermath of the report that had just run on Channel 9.

Debus today is 77, a tall, dignified man who pronounces the word 'issue' so that it sounds like 'issyoo'. And oh boy, did he have himself an issue to deal with.

NBN, Channel 9's affiliate in the large NSW mid-north coast town of Coffs Harbour, had broken the story of a cull of 606 brumbies in Guy Fawkes River National Park, a rugged area of deep gorge country that cuts into the high tableland west of Coffs. The Guy Fawkes River was named by a certain Major Edward Parke, who camped there on Guy Fawkes Day in 1845, the 240th anniversary of the treasonous plot to blow up the British parliament's House of Lords. The Guy Fawkes

River National Park wild horse cull of 2000 was a saga scarcely less volatile.

The Guy Fawkes brumbies had been there since at least the late 1800s, some say a little longer. Unlike Kosciuszko and the Victorian Alps, they had no link to 'The Man from Snowy River'–type mythology, nor was there then a mass movement championing their right to live in the area. The vocal, sometimes aggressive pro-brumby movement was still in its infancy and was barely visible outside of the High Country. But the story wasn't about heritage destroyed; it was about the cull itself. Graphic scenes of dead horses ran across the Nine Network, blowing up into a story of alleged animal cruelty which enraged a nation.

Paradoxically, the cull had been conducted to prevent animal cruelty. After years of drought, the Guy Fawkes area was parched. Feed for both native and introduced herbivores was already scarce. Then the fires came. As the spring leading up to the Black Summer of 2019–20 showed, fires often strike early in that part of the world. Winter is usually the driest time of year, and with the first hint of warmth in late August fire authorities are always on high alert. In the year 2000, they would need to be.

'At that time, Guy Fawkes River National Park was 90,000 hectares and fire had burnt around 60,000 hectares. That's two-thirds of the park, including the majority of the areas that provided habitat for horses,' recalls Alan Jeffery, who at the time was the National Parks north coast regional manager, based in Coffs Harbour. Jeffery had fire management crews and others working in the park at the time, including staff who had worked with horses in the area for over 20 years. All had noticed emaciated horses congregating on the river flats. 'There was very limited feed and the horses were in poor condition and getting poorer,' he says. 'Some were down on the ground and had lost the strength to move. At least a couple were already dead. So while we had fire operations going on, we had serious concerns about the horses and discussions had started about the issue.'

Jeffery's concerns were shared by others. One professional shooter had been culling feral pigs by helicopter in the top half of Guy Fawkes. Flying over the area, it had become clear that there were a lot more horses than most people believed. The shooter rang Jeffery's pest management officer, Brad Nesbitt, and told him that the horses of Guy Fawkes were 'looking pretty bony'. He reckoned the kindest thing would be to cull them. Nesbitt took the shooter's perspective on board and passed it up the chain to Jeffery.

'When we realised there were large numbers of horses in such poor condition, we really started to firm up the planning to cull them humanely,' Jeffery recalls. 'It was not a simple decision. We needed to pull together resources, to ensure we had ammunition and accredited shooters, to ensure the park was clear. We undertook a risk assessment and worked through all the protocols. I put forward a proposal on behalf of our team to say this is what we should do. There was no objection and the decision was taken.'

NPWS staff had engaged locals in the trapping and removal of small numbers of horses in the 1990s with limited success. On occasion there had been ugly mishaps with horses injuring themselves in trap yards. But Parks were on generally good terms with locals, many of whom saw brumbies as pests that damaged fences and caused other problems. And while some valued them as horses that could be captured and put to work on farms, or sold for a reasonable sum at the Grafton sale yards, Jeffery had no cause to fear a wholesale backlash for what he considered a sensible, humane act of land management. Nor did he consider it necessary to consult with the RSPCA or media beforehand. Culling feral animals was a routine park operations issue, one of many unpleasant but necessary tasks that parkies performed as part of their job. 'Given the situation with the fires we didn't think a public consultation program was warranted,' Jeffery says of the consensus among his team at the time.

On the morning of Sunday 22 October 2000, Parks staff, helicopter pilots and accredited shooters met for a briefing around 8.30 am. There were two helicopters and three shooters – one shooter per helicopter with a third on rotation. The extra shooter was on hand to give each marksman an emotional break as much as anything. As the professional aerial shooter explains, shooting horses is heartbreaking work.

'No one really likes shooting horses. Some people get a little bit … a little bit emotional, you know? I guess mentally, you need a bit of time out to sort through what's happened, particularly if you've got to shoot a few foals and stuff, because you can't leave foals and mares. You've got to shoot young animals and old animals and people need time to process that emotionally.'

The professional shooter says people should always have empathy when shooting any animals, and particularly horses, because of the significant bond between horses and humans. 'One of the other shooters had his own horses,' he says. 'But you've got to put all that to one side to a certain extent. It was far better to shoot these horses than have them die from starvation or exposure to fire. It was the best of two bad situations.'

The shooter grew up in the bush and from a young age had experience using firearms in a responsible way. He was a teenager when he first held a gun, and soon became adept at shooting foxes, rabbits, you name it. Today, he is one of the most respected shooters in the country. Based on his extensive experience, he firmly believes aerial shooting of wild horses is more humane than trapping and transporting them to an abattoir. 'Trapping is a totally foreign experience for the horses,' he says. 'They're confined, transported, pushed up races … and they know fear, they know something's not right. It's completely different to when they're running in the wild.'

The view that wild horses are better culled on the spot than taken to the knackery is today held by the RSPCA. 'The RSPCA accepts in some circumstances shooting may be justified but causes less stress to wild horses than the process of trapping, transporting, breaking and rehoming wild animals, as demanded by brumby groups,' RSPCA CEO Steve Coleman told the *Sydney Morning Herald* in October 2020, in a story marking the 20th anniversary of the Guy Fawkes cull. 'That is the practical, brutal reality. It's not nice, it's not palatable, but it is the truth.' That's quite the turnaround, because after the 2000 Guy Fawkes River National Park cull the RSPCA took the National Parks and Wildlife Service to court over multiple counts of alleged animal cruelty.

And so the shooting began.

The professional shooter, as ever, was careful to wait till the helicopter was in the right position to take a shot. Sometimes they would wait for a minute or more. He was also mindful of the need not to run the horses too hard. 'Most of the Guy Fawkes horses were pretty run out,' he says. 'These weren't big, fat shiny horses. They basically had all the feed burnt out under them, so they weren't galloping at high speed. They were just sort of trotting along. You just had to pick the right time.'

Timing was crucial, aim doubly so. 'You're always going for a heart or lung shot, which is a pretty big target on a horse. It's all about the first shot that hits.' Experts from further afield who specialise in feral animal culling will tell you that when an animal is struck by a projectile, it's a significant impact and they don't know what's going on. It's likely that they don't feel pain initially for a good few seconds. So the clock starts from those first few seconds before the realisation sinks in. If you hit a major artery, then the blood pressure starts disappearing off the scale. If you get it right, they just go down straight away.

The cull took three days, but most of the work was done on the first two. They shot 326 horses on day one, 221 the next day and 59 on day three. In the end 606 horses were shot, which was more than expected. In the interests of transparency after the event, Alan Jeffery had the foresight to suggest that the media be informed. In 2000, with the enthusiastic support of Minister Debus, regional managers of the National Parks and Wildlife Service had far more autonomy than they have now. Today, all communications go through Sydney, which means that simple requests can be mired in procedural red tape. Back then, a sign-off from a director one or two steps up the chain was all that was required for an operation like the Guy Fawkes cull. Unfortunately for Jeffery and his colleagues, the streamlined, practical bureaucratic process within Parks turned out to be a weakness. 'Senior management within NPWS were aware of the operation and I had advocated that we should get on the front foot and take the story to the media, but that wasn't supported,' he recalls. 'For whatever reason, the decision was taken that effectively said, "No, let's not create a story we don't need."'

So the cull proceeded. One or two local landholders had half an inkling something might be up, but apparently not Minister Debus. That turned out to be a huge public relations blooper. 'It left a large section of the public with the belief that, somehow or other, the NPWS was secretly murdering horses,' Debus now admits.

In the immediate aftermath of the cull, as the helicopters returned to base, Parks believed the cull had been a success. They felt that an animal welfare catastrophe had been averted. Within days, most of Australia would believe that an animal welfare catastrophe had been created.

* * *

Greg Everingham is a lean, lanky sort of fella with a no-bullshit manner and a bushman's way with words. Which is to say, he doesn't mince them. Now 67, he has lived in the Guy Fawkes River area most of his life and owns a parcel of country up near the national park. He had ridden in the park for years, both before and after it was gazetted, and knows 'the gullies and creeks and hidey holes that most people wouldn't even know about'. In 2000, he also knew and loved its mobs of wild horses. At the time of the cull, Everingham was managing a large local cattle property. The property was out of earshot of the park, but a day or two after the shooting had stopped Everingham got a call from a neighbour who lived a little closer to the park and who'd said in the days prior he'd heard distant gunfire. At dawn the next day the two men drove to the edge of the park to investigate, in a truck towing horses in a float.

'We rode a fair way into the park and never saw anything,' Everingham recalls. 'It was unusual that we weren't seeing horses, so we knew there was some form of trouble because normally you'd see tracks or a group of horses somewhere along the way. But there was nothing till we got to a place called Paddy's Basin, a big, flat area in open country with some mud holes where horses love rolling to keep biting insects off. That's where we saw the first two dead horses. One was shot through the wither and one through the head.'

That first pair of horses was killed cleanly enough. But when the two men rode into rougher country, where aerial shooting was a much more difficult proposition, the picture became very different. 'The whole thing was bullshit up in that rough country,' Everingham says. 'Never seen a mess anything like it. The cold, callous butchery was unbelievable. I'd never seen anything as cruel or barbaric in my life.' Everingham reckons the best marksmen in the world had no chance of shooting accurately in country where frightened horses were bolting along ground hemmed in by cliffs and spurs that helicopter pilots had to swerve around. And he backs up that claim with graphic descriptions of the seven dead horses he and his mate saw before they set up camp for the night.

'There was one horse … someone tried to finish it off by shooting it in the head, but they missed and blew half its jaw off. A bay horse had its whole foot shot off. Another horse had half his back foot missing. We couldn't go to sleep because of the smell. The next morning, the heli came overhead – I guess it was doing mopping-up – and I flagged 'em down to land but they wouldn't land. Probably a good thing 'cos I would've pulled them out of the heli and flogged the piss out of them because of how this job was done.'

Worse sights were in store the next day as the two men continued through the park. 'I must have seen seven or eight holes, these dig-outs where the horses fell and scratched holes with their front legs, trying to get up. Other horses had more than ten shots in them. They shot them from the arse to the head – where did they start, the head or the arse? One young mare had blood all over her, which meant she'd travelled some distance before they finished her off. A lot of older mares were lying dead next to little tiny foals, some of them only a week old. I asked Brad Nesbitt once which ones they shot first – the foal or the mother?' Needless to say, Everingham never got an answer.

Perhaps the most distressing sight to Everingham was a white mare that lay dead with two legs of an unborn foal coming out of her. 'Why would you find it necessary to shoot a pregnant mare?' he says. 'It wasn't right, it just definitely wasn't right. I was in a bit of a bad state for a couple of weeks afterwards. Even talking about it now is hard.'

When Everingham got home, he knew what he had to do. He knew a bloke whose brother was a reporter at NBN in Coffs Harbour. The media had to be informed. The public had to know. He also contacted a friend, Graeme Baldwin, who went to take a look for himself. Baldwin's partner, Erica Jessup, is an expert horsewoman who was working on a thoroughbred horse stud up in Toowoomba, about five hours north over the Queensland border, and who today is the founding member, treasurer, and stud book registrar of the Guy Fawkes Heritage Horse Association, which she formed in 2004. Baldwin had contacted Jessup in Toowoomba to tell her he was going to take a look, and she knew he might be in the park for a few days. But she was surprised when she didn't hear from him for nearly a week afterwards. 'I rang a few times and the phone just rang out,' she said. It wasn't too unusual for the landline to ring unanswered, as Baldwin was often outside doing farm work. But Jessup became worried when day after day, there was no answer. Eventually, Baldwin picked up the phone.

'Have you been down the river all this time?' Jessup asked. Baldwin said no, he hadn't. He'd been physically sick for three days after what he'd seen. He had known it was Erica calling, but he just couldn't bring himself to talk about it. 'Graeme knew those horses and he was just so upset about what happened to them,' Jessup recalls. 'He said, "You've got no idea what those bastards have done." He said there was this buckskin colt laying there dead with his front legs shot off and a hole three feet deep where it was digging with its hind legs, trying to get up. Another horse was paralysed in the back and trying to get up with its front feet. He said there were just heaps and heaps and heaps of them.'

A week after the cull, Alan Jeffery was at a function organised by NPWS in Dorrigo National Park, at the top of the coastal escarpment about halfway between Coffs Harbour and Guy Fawkes. The local Parks regional manager was enjoying some brief time out on a rare clear evening in a town that is often drizzly and wet, even when the nearby country is drought-stricken. Mobile phone reception was still a little sketchy in those days, but when Jeffery walked out along the Skywalk – a local tourist attraction in the national park at the edge of the escarpment overlooking the green Bellinger Valley – his phone rang. It was a tip-off that a local TV crew had hired a helicopter and was flying into the park to film a story on the cull with Greg Everingham.

In *Star Wars*, Luke Skywalker was the hero. This Skywalker, in the eyes of Greg Everingham, was a villain. Awkwardly for both Everingham and Jeffery, the two men were about to share a day together in the helicopter.

Jeffery was adamant that Everingham and the news crew should be accompanied by a senior Parks person. So on the day of the flight, he met the news crew at the heli base at Coffs Harbour. 'They said something like, "We're going to present this as it is – nothing too outrageous and no terrible images,"' Jeffery recalls. They took off and the first stop was at Everingham's property.

'Greg Everingham is incredibly passionate about horses but he can be a pretty aggressive character,' Jeffery recalls. When discussing options for the removal of horses over the years, he had told NPWS staff, '"If you ever try to shoot horses in Guy Fawkes River National Park again, it'll be over my dead body."' The awkwardness of the confrontation was magnified by the cramped scenes inside the chopper. 'It was only a little helicopter, I don't know how we all managed to fit in there. Anyway, we flew in there and the cameraman got lots of footage of dead horses. While the program is necessary, it's a bloody business. The aim is to ensure the animals are dead, that can require multiple shots, and there are no pretty images of shot horses. I knew a lot of that imagery would come out. And at the end of that day, I thought, "Shit, this is going to be a big, difficult issue to deal with."'

When the news story broke, every major print and broadcast media outlet in the country covered it. With few exceptions, the reporting contained emotive, often brutal language that played directly into the hands of those who already carried resentment against National Parks. It was full of terms and phrases associated with war, like 'cut down', 'gunned down', 'killing fields', 'carnage' and 'slaughterhouse'. The helicopters were often referred to as 'gunships'.

'This unfounded rhetoric around slaughter gave many people the view that this was a botched operation, when in fact it was well planned and skilfully undertaken,' Alan Jeffery says.

But the rhetoric worked, by design or otherwise. Australians were outraged. In an age before social media, they vented their fury in the form of street protests, in angry calls to even angrier talkback radio hosts like John Laws and Alan Jones, and in letters to the editorial pages of newspapers. Meanwhile, the original rationale behind the cull took not so much a back seat to the anger as an untethered ride in the tray of a ute.

'The killing of hundreds of brumbies in the area around Coffs Harbour by the National Parks and Wildlife Service is a tragedy of huge dimensions,' one reader wrote in *The Daily Telegraph.*

'I am outraged at the actions of the National Parks and Wildlife Service when more than 600 beautiful creatures were shot dead for the feeble reason that they were "wrecking the environment",' thundered another. 'It makes me angry and sick to the stomach that someone could commit such a brutal act. That bush was home to those horses long before the NPWS was established. It had no right to do what it did.'

The vitriol travelled all the way to the NSW Environment Minister's office. 'There was just mayhem. Every day, wall-to-wall complaints,' Bob Debus recalls. 'I was accused of cruelty and heartlessness. A year later, I still got occasional messages, including one from France calling me a horse murderer. It went worldwide. People felt it was utterly unacceptable and utterly beyond forgiveness, and many of these people had nothing to do with the bush, nothing to do with farmers. But I guess that's the majority.'

Meanwhile, a not-so-silent and very powerful minority harnessed the moment as a soapbox for their views. Peter

Cochran, a cattle farmer from a valley adjacent to Kosciuszko National Park, had been the National Party member for the NSW seat of Monaro from 1988 to 1998 and was a long-time agitator against Parks. He continues this crusade today and was a major force behind John Barilaro and his 2018 brumby bill. 'There's certainly no excuse for what they did,' Cochran told a national TV audience at the time. 'It was wholesale slaughter and it destroyed for all time the reputation of the National Parks and Wildlife Service.'

Even the Australian Veterinary Association (AVA) spoke out against the cull. 'The very rugged forest terrain in the Guy Fawkes River National Park is not suitable for this [type of operation] because of the obvious difficulty in conducting the operation in the most humane manner possible,' said vice-president Dr Garth McGilvray, a Coffs Harbour local. The AVA also issued a press release, denying claims that the cull had been conducted with its blessing.

Both Parks and the state government were copping blow after blow. Everingham was in high demand as a spokesperson. His straight-talking, deadpan speech delivered from a stable with a row of saddles behind him came across extremely powerfully. 'It was a damn mess. It was a disgrace to call yourself an Australian,' he told one network's cameras.

One exception to the relentlessly negative, often bloodthirsty media coverage was News Corp's Simon Benson. Not known for being the least controversial reporter in the Murdoch stable, he was on this matter a rare source of perspective. As he wrote in a piece headlined, 'Led astray by Banjo's dream':

More than 50,000 kangaroos are shot and killed in Australia every year under licence. Many more are shot illegally.

Whether they die humanely is open to conjecture. And while this practice continues to draw condemnation from some fringe groups, it usually escapes public scrutiny.

This was not the case when 617 wild horses were shot by the National Parks and Wildlife Service last month in a government-sanctioned feral culling program.

The emotive image of helicopter gunships in action added to the spectre of wholesale and allegedly necessary slaughter.

The difference between these two culls is stark – not for the number of animals involved – but for the fact that one is a species that rose from and became incorporated into the Australian landscape over millions of years.

The other was introduced as a slave animal 150 years ago and released into the wild where it became a feral pest. Yet it is the introduced animal that people flock to protect. Never mind the kangaroo is on this country's coat of arms.

Different animals evoke different emotions and it seems horses evoke the most passionate.

Benson went on to write about the threats to the integrity of the Australian environment posed by feral animals and closed his piece by arguing that in another 20 years, 'we could be overrun by vermin'. Hardline opponents of brumbies in the High Country would today consider those words remarkably prescient.

Debus was cornered. Notwithstanding the odd article like Benson's, as well as support from environmental groups such as the Colong Foundation for Wilderness, which called the cull a 'mercy killing', and the Total Environment Centre, which issued a press release headlined 'NPWS Feral Animal Control – Damned if They Do, Damned if They Don't', the public mood had reached a point where something had to give. Less than two weeks after the cull, Debus acted. 'I have listened to the community on this issue and I have banned all aerial culling of feral horses in all national parks in this state permanently,' he announced at a press conference.

Bob Debus would go on to be Environment Minister for seven years in the NSW Labor government under Premier Bob Carr – still the longest tenure of any person in that position. In that time, he would increase the area of national parks in his state by a third while boosting funding for the Parks Service accordingly. Later, he switched to federal politics and was Minister for Home Affairs under Kevin Rudd. In total, he spent over 22 years in state and federal parliament and is rightly proud of his distinguished contribution to public life and policy. But in conversation with the man, it's clear that he considers the aerial shooting ban after Guy Fawkes his most difficult moment.

Technically, Debus placed a moratorium on aerial shooting, which in legal terms is closer to a suspension than a permanent ban. But the moratorium hasn't been lifted, which means it's as good as a ban until there's the political and/or community will to overturn it, which is unlikely any time soon. Can you imagine a politician of any political stripe hoping to increase or retain popular support by putting forward a proposal to make it easier to shoot horses?

Debus, a lover of Kosciuszko and of all wild places, knows that he made wild horse management more difficult, but then, what choice did he have in those frenzied hours and days? 'In recent times, I've checked in with several members of my staff and a number of NPWS officials of the time who I am still close to. Every one of them told me the political situation had become utterly untenable,' Debus says. 'I tried to hold the line for some time – I can't say how many days – but I've come to the conclusion that anybody in government would have at least done what I did. Every MP in the state had offices just overwhelmed by people complaining. Not just a little bit. Overwhelmed! People wrote letters and they made phone calls and I can tell you that plenty of offices were getting more than 50 communications a day.

'I was used to doing unpopular things in several portfolios and this would often happen with other issues, more often in the law-and-order context. I was in the portfolio of prisons almost as long as the environment, and long after Guy Fawkes I would tell people that it was easier to go on talkback radio and defend the installation of condom machines in prisons than it was to defend National Parks against the aerial shooting of horses.'

Debus made another important decision soon after the cull. He commissioned leading Sydney University veterinary science expert Dr Tony English to write an independent report. The English Report was completed within weeks, but before it dropped, the Guy Fawkes situation ignited again when a horrific and unexpected discovery was made.

Dr Chris Shirley is a Dorrigo vet who moved to the area in 1988, two years after finishing his vet science degree at the University of Sydney. As the cull furore raged, he was invited to inspect the area for himself by a local RSPCA member who was seeking Shirley's professional opinion to help decide whether there were grounds to prosecute the NPWS. What Shirley saw from the helicopter, and then from the ground, wasn't pleasant.

'It was pretty blinking warm and by the time I got there, the horses were in a reasonably advanced state of decomposition,' he recalls. 'Carcasses were rotting and falling to bits and had maggots crawling through them. There were a number of cases where it was plainly apparent the horses didn't die quickly, or die as good a death as they might have. The idea when you shoot a horse with a high-velocity rifle is to hit the chest cavity. The bullet then goes through the chest and the shockwave ruptures the great vessels – the aorta, the pulmonary artery. There were a few horses where the first or second shot may not have gone through the chest cavity.'

Then the men in the helicopter saw it – a horse still alive. 'This horse was obviously unwell,' Shirley says. 'It was quite lame and in a fairly poor body condition. The area it was in was burnt out, so there wasn't much feed in there.' But the horse was moving at a disjointed trot, so the pilot landed the helicopter. On closer inspection, it turned out to be a chestnut mare. The RSPCA man dispatched it with two shots from his service revolver. 'The original projectile had hit the horse on the right-hand side of the fourth thoracic vertebrae, the top of the rib basically,' Shirley explains. 'The bullet must have hit it at an angle where it skewed away from the chest cavity. I'm pretty sure it would've dropped the horse initially and it would have collapsed. The positioning of the entry point was perfect. It's just in some ways unfortunate that it hadn't penetrated the chest cavity.'

Despite the discovery of the distressed, wounded horse, as well as everything else he saw, Shirley is at pains to point out that he was satisfied overall with the cull. 'In my experience, there is no pretty way to kill something when you're doing a mass cull. In the vast majority of cases, I thought the horses were well destroyed. My report essentially said that the vast majority of animals were destroyed in accordance with guidelines and protocols at the time. Not every shot was perfect and that is to be expected, but I came away from this thinking, "Oh, they were good, those shooters. You wouldn't want to try to escape from these guys on the ground." On an overall basis, I thought the shooting was done very well.'

The RSPCA didn't agree. The gruesome spectre of the horse that refused to die pushed them to prosecute Parks on 12 charges of animal cruelty relating to 226 horses, and they did it with overwhelming public support. They even flew Greg Everingham to Sydney to give evidence. Some people in Parks believe the RSPCA took advantage of an unprecedented fundraising opportunity with its legal action. Others feel they were just doing their job. Some think it was a bit of both. Whatever the case, only one charge stuck. Eleven charges were dropped in exchange for one guilty plea, which centred on the chestnut mare found alive. The plea bargain meant that Everingham's photographs couldn't be seen in court or considered in a judgement, which pisses him off to this day. The magistrate recorded no conviction but ordered the NPWS to pay the RSPCA's legal costs of $50,000. He told the court that while people felt 'revulsion' for the cruelty, evidence pointed to the cull having being carried out professionally.

When the English Report was published, it reached a similar conclusion, exonerating Parks and its shooters. 'I'm absolutely confident that the professionalism and the commitment and the intention of the staff of the service will be shown to be fact,' NPWS Director Brian Gilligan had confidently predicted when the English Report was commissioned. And so it proved.

Tony English listed 22 conclusions in his report, the first of which was that 'the use of aerial shooting in Guy Fawkes River National Park was an appropriate technique under the circumstances'. His second conclusion was that 'the shooting was carried out in a humane way, under approved protocols designed to kill the horses as quickly as possible'. Indeed, the first 20 conclusions supported both the reasoning behind the cull and the manner in which it had been carried out.

For the professional shooter, it was a bittersweet vindication. He was angry that Minister Debus had jumped the gun, so to speak, with his aerial shooting moratorium on horses, which was announced before the English Report was completed. 'At the end of the day, Bob Debus made that decision on the outcry from the public,' he says. 'The English Report clearly said there was nothing wrong with the cull, but Debus made that decision before facts had been investigated. He could have said, "Nup, I'll wait until the inquiry" but he didn't.'

The report didn't let Parks off the hook in terms of the way it had conducted itself. The 21st conclusion noted, 'It would have been prudent for the Service to have sought the involvement and cooperation of the RSPCA in planning and carrying out the operation, with emphasis on both the welfare of the horses and the significant ill-effects of the large horse herd on native flora and fauna if nothing was done.' The final conclusion said, 'Local land owners should also have been involved in some way from the outset, to ensure that they knew what was happening and why.'

Greg Everingham reckons that's too bloody right. 'Total load of bullshit,' he says of the whole unseemly episode and the justification for it. Both he and Erica Jessup still maintain that the horses weren't doing as poorly as Parks had claimed. They believe the animal welfare rationale behind the cull was exaggerated, and that a hardline horse eradication agenda was at play. Everingham will go to his grave believing the English Report was about as independent as a newborn foal without its mother's milk.

Bob Debus's last significant action on the matter, as recommended by Tony English, was to commission a study into the heritage value of horses in Guy Fawkes River National Park. A few months after the cull, he directed a Heritage Working Party to be established 'to provide an opportunity for a thorough investigation into the view of many locals in the area that these horses are of historical significance'. So the people in the area sat down and started a serious discussion about what wild horses meant to them.

The Heritage Working Party started things rolling with a crowded meeting in Dorrigo, which Erica Jessup and her partner, Graeme Baldwin, attended. 'That's when Parks realised locals were so passionate about the horses,' Jessup recalls. She soon moved back down from Toowoomba and would end up playing a significant role, alongside Baldwin and others. 'I wanted to make sure this would never happen again,' she says.

The Guy Fawkes River National Park Heritage Working Party canvassed key issues which mirror present-day debates over brumbies in NSW and Victorian national parks. When is a wild horse a heritage horse? How can wild horses be managed within the parameters of the NSW *National Parks and Wildlife Act 1974*, whose primary stated aim is 'the conservation of nature'? Another stated aim of the act is the conservation of 'objects, places or features of cultural value within the landscape'. But do horses fit into that category? There's no mention of them but they're not explicitly excluded either. It's an area as grey as Elyne Mitchell's titular brumby. But Jessup has done much to point the way forward.

It's not easy to catch Jessup on a quiet day because there's rarely such a thing in her world. But while she prepares beef curry and chat potatoes with garden spinach, and apple crumble, and chocolate self-saucing pudding, and orange and almond cake, and boiled fruitcake prepared to her mother's old Dutch recipe, and Anzac biscuits ('because you can't ride a horse without Anzac biscuits') on a Friday morning for one of the weekend horse treks she runs, she finds time to tell her personal story. She was born in Parramatta, the fifth of six children of poor World War II immigrants from Holland. Her dad drove trucks but his business went belly-up because of excessive road taxes. When his truck got repossessed, her parents bought a caravan and ended up parking it at Ebor Falls on the Guy Fawkes River. They lived there a while until her dad snared a job at Guy Fawkes Station, just up the road. The station manager had two daughters the same age as young Erica and invited her to learn to ride horses alongside them.

A few years on, when she was just ten or so, a neighbouring property owner called Charles 'Chilla' Menzies asked the girls if they wanted to go for a ride and 'have a look at the brumbies'. 'We didn't know anything about these brumbies,' Jessup recalls. 'I didn't even know that wild horses were a thing, but we nagged our parents to death and off we went. I can still picture that mob of horses flying off through the trees then coming back to have a look at us.' So began a lifelong love affair.

The Heritage Working Party's 150-page report was published in 2002. One of its key findings was that the Guy Fawkes horses 'are important in the cultural history of the Guy Fawkes area' and 'have a special association with a group of persons of importance in the cultural history of the Guy Fawkes area, namely the Light Horse regiments', and that they therefore 'have significant local heritage value, sufficient to warrant their being managed on this basis'.

A connection to horses that served in war is often claimed on behalf of Kosciuszko and Victorian High Country brumbies, but such claims are tenuous at best. The Guy

Fawkes connection appears to have far greater legitimacy. As late as World War II, local wild horses were captured and broken in by members of some of Australia's last Light Horse regiments. Those horses that didn't make it to the theatres of war were often released into the Guy Fawkes River valleys by servicemen who had neither land to house nor money to feed them. The 606 horses killed in the 2000 cull undoubtedly included descendants of those horses, but not every Guy Fawkes horse died on those fateful three days. At least 100 are believed to have survived in areas close to private property or inaccessible to the helicopter marksmen, and those horses passed on their historic bloodline, which lives on in today's herd of 1000 or so horses.

No one was marching in the streets of Dorrigo to protect the military heritage of Guy Fawkes brumbies before the 2000 cull. Pre-2000, locals had a relationship with their wild horses that was more mercenary than misty-eyed, but times change. Today, the horses are valued for different reasons.

Erica Jessup says she's not a 'brumby hugger'. It's a bit like conservation-minded farmers who shy away from calling themselves 'greenies' or 'tree huggers' because of the connotations of activism from afar. But if you were to find anyone hugging a brumby within a 500-kilometre radius of Guy Fawkes River National Park, that person would more than likely be Erica Jessup.

'They're more like dogs than horses,' she says. 'I've been in horses all my life. How do you go from high-end thoroughbred yearling preparation to playing with brumbies? It's easy! They're not flighty and snorting like thoroughbreds.

They're absolutely better-natured, they're intelligent and soft and self-sufficient and easy to work with. The amount of times I've called a vet for a brumby … it's not many. You don't have to do their teeth, don't have to do their feet, none of that stuff.'

In 2004, Jessup set up the Guy Fawkes Heritage Horse Association. It takes horses that have been passively removed from Guy Fawkes River National Park after being lured into portable trap yards with a combination of salt and hay. The association is the only group that takes them and they manage to rehome 80 per cent, with only 20 per cent going to the slaughterhouse.

The association deliberately avoids using the word 'brumby'. That might seem a minor point, but it holds the key to Jessup's greatest joy, and greatest sacrifice. 'When you use the word "brumby", it implies a preconceived idea that you want it left in the national park,' she says. 'It's a brumby when it's capering around the national park doing what it does. Once it's in my paddock or tied to my fence, it's not a brumby anymore.'

To many brumby advocates, a brumby not being a brumby (as in a wild horse) anymore is a bad outcome. But Jessup makes no apologies for domesticating the Guy Fawkes brumbies and turning them into plain old horses, one horse at a time. 'The park is not the place for them,' she says. 'Most of the Kosciuszko people I've dealt with, they don't want the horses out of the park. They like them on park so they can do all sorts of wild "Man from Snowy River" shit. We don't do that here.'

Life on the land is filled with tough decisions and Jessup has made hers. She loves the horses so much, she will save their lives even if it means extinguishing their wildness, the very essence of their 'brumbyness'. 'It will be an unfortunate outcome if they're bred out, but if Parks get their way and there's zero population, then unless people take mobs on and breed them off-park, they will be lost,' she says. Jessup says a good percentage of the horses that come out of the Guy Fawkes River National Park are good-looking, strong horses, 'not these inbred little things' as many Kosciuszko horses are. 'There's been nothing added to our horses for a long time. The original stock was really good,' she adds. To her, that stock is worth saving, even if it means the last Guy Fawkes free-running brumby ends up as someone's pet or working horse or equestrian pony.

But Jessup has an ace up her sleeve. It's no secret she and locals like Greg Everingham don't have the highest regard for Parks' attempts at horse management over the years. Jessup can't afford to get Parks offside, because her Heritage Horse Association has forged a solid working relationship with them. But you sense she's got a big, hearty laugh bottled up inside her when she says, 'The reason that I don't get too bent out of shape about it is I don't think Parks are capable of getting rid of all of them'.

Jessup once mentioned to Parks the idea of fencing off a few thousand acres and keeping a few breeding mobs as a tourist attraction. 'That would keep everyone happy, but they just went, "Pfft, no way,"' she says with a shrug. Greg Everingham also believes a sanctuary of sorts could be the answer. 'They've spent all this money managing them over 20 years, why not come at it from another way? Leave some horses there, keep everyone happy and the problem is solved.'

Alan Jeffery is retired from Parks, but he firmly believes sanctuaries within national parks are not the answer. He lists the damage that wild horses do to the ecosystems within Guy Fawkes River National Park – soil erosion, accelerated gully erosion, trampling native vegetation, fouling the waterways, even chewing tree bark that has minerals in it, the overall effect of which he says can be like ringbarking a forest. 'The big-picture take-home message is that national parks are not the place for large populations of roaming horses,' he says.

'If you want to have a sanctuary for horses or goats or pigs or whatever it might be, then don't call it a national park,' he says. 'The legislation is there to set these areas aside for nature, for culture and for appropriate recreational use. I've got no problem with the concept of horse sanctuaries but do it on land that isn't managed for its conservation values, because that's what parks are set aside for. They're not horse farms. We need to decide what we do with populations of feral species in our national parks. We're in the midst of a native wildlife crisis in Australia. Australians generally love their national parks, places that should provide refuge for the many iconic native animals and plants, but these refuges are suffering significant damage from feral horse numbers that are out of control when there is an effective and humane technique – aerial culling – available to control them and which should be used. Do we really value them more than the iconic Australian animals and plants that rely on these precious places?'

Dorrigo vet Dr Chris Shirley has a similar view. 'I remember thinking that if National Parks had shot 600 pigs, people would've been up in arms about how they let the feral pig population out of control in the first place. People have some sort of romantic attachment to horses, and what we have to discuss is, how much do we value romantic ideas? How much do we value environmental protection? How much do we value animal welfare?'

Shirley, like the professional shooter, feels Bob Debus was wrong to ban aerial shooting of horses in national parks before the English Report came out. He says he is 'cranky' with Debus now that the park has similar horse numbers as before the cull.

And Debus himself? He says he 'deeply regrets' the outcome of Guy Fawkes. But he remains hopeful that aerial shooting could be an option again one day in New South Wales 'as a last and carefully negotiated resort'. His assessment of the chances of that happening?

'You need your stars to align. You need some people in government who are committed to a rational solution. You need key people in the opposition willing not to take advantage of it. You need the RSPCA to continue to support the idea on humane grounds. And you need massively strong briefing of the media before you go into a shooting. In all of those circumstances, I think it still might be possible,' he says. For now, that seems unlikely. Alan Jeffery says that one of the contracted helicopter pilots on the 2000 cull told him that he'd been involved in an aerial cull of 30,000 horses in and around Katherine Gorge in the Northern Territory just months before Guy Fawkes. Needless to say, it began and ended without controversy as nobody blinks twice at outback culls, whether it's horses, camels, whatever. 'Your problem is you're too close to Sydney,' the pilot told Jeffery.

* * *

And in the heart of Sydney, in a spacious, sunlit corner suite overlooking Sydney Harbour on the ninth floor of the state parliament offices, NSW Deputy Premier John Barilaro, the architect of the *Kosciuszko Wild Horse Heritage Act 2018*, knows he owes much to Guy Fawkes.

'Guy Fawkes is the reason I can actually campaign on this issue of protecting brumbies, of not shooting them from the sky and letting their carcasses rot in the forest,' he says. 'It's just unacceptable, you know? At a time when Australians and people in general want to see kindness to animals, you're not going to get away with it.'

If only there was an effective way to control wild horses in national parks that's not as violent as shooting or as laborious as trapping.

Well, now. If you talk to a High Country brumby runner, they'll tell you the answer is lying right under our noses.

CHAPTER FIVE

THE RUNNING OF
THE BRUMBIES

A skier knows that feeling. There's snow in the mountains and your tank is full of petrol. There's a lift pass loaded on your smartcard and a bacon-and-egg roll in your belly. There are spots in the car park and the chairlifts are humming. Your phone is off: not here, leave a message. The mountains are yours.

Lewis Benedetti knows a similar feeling. Substitute for a pair of waxed carving skis a fit, healthy horse, swap glistening winter slopes for a frost plain with nervous brumbies whinnying under the cover of snow gums, switch the swoosh of skis on chalky winter snow for the thud and clop of hooves on the run … the feeling of anticipation and adrenaline are the same. Not here, leave a message. The mountains are yours.

Benedetti, 31, is a brumby runner, or buck runner as they also call themselves. Chasing and catching brumbies is what he does best and what he loves doing. Of Italian heritage, Benedetti was raised in Buchan, population two hundred and something, which is where you end up if you drive south from Jindabyne through the Byadbo Wilderness and pop out on the Victorian side, where the Barry Way becomes the Snowy River Road.

Home was a cattle farm and Benedetti was comfortable on horses from a young age. He caught his first brumby when he was 17, which is about par for a young bloke in that part of the world. 'Everyone sorta gets into it,' he says. 'It's more like a bit of a hobby, like a sport. We did that as well as rodeo. It's all sorta part of the same thing.' But for Benedetti, brumby running became more than a sport. It became his livelihood. He did it full-time until he was 25, and now does it part-time while running a horse-breaking and training business. Up until recently, he was paid a token $50 per horse by Parks Victoria as part of their horse removal program. That never came close to paying for fuel and horse feed and other essentials, but the real money was made selling the captured brumbies at the horse sales in Bairnsdale, the large regional centre of 15,000 residents on the Princes Highway, an hour south-west of Buchan. 'A really good type of brumby would sell for about $500,' he says.

Benedetti is a tall, wiry character, all muscle, comfortable in his skin and even more comfortable on horseback in the mountains. Like Erica Jessup at Guy Fawkes, he's proud that the horses he captures gain a second chance in life, even if they're no longer running wild and free. 'I've never taken a brumby to the fucken knackery,' he says. 'When locals picked them up, I made sure they were not going to the meat market.'

Despite such noble intentions, Benedetti would sometimes still be harassed at the sales. 'People didn't want brumby runners operating. We were frowned upon a bit because people didn't want any horses removed from the High Country,' he says. 'I had people come up to me and say, "Leave 'em alone. They should be in the wild." These people, they were just uneducated.'

There are those who believe brumbies should never be taken out of the mountains under any circumstances, end of argument. But those voices were drowned out in the autumn of 2020 when, virtually overnight, Benedetti was inundated with people begging him to catch them a brumby. 'All of a sudden, greenies started calling us brumby runners saying, "Can you catch as many as you can?" I had 30 people wanting a brumby at one stage.'

The sudden upsurge in demand for brumbies – some from unusual quarters – came after a surprise announcement by Parks Victoria in May 2020 that it would soon commence ground shooting brumbies in Victoria's Eastern Alps. That decision came as a shock to almost everyone. Though shooting wild horses is not banned in Victoria, as it effectively is in New South Wales due to the events at Guy Fawkes River National Park, Parks Victoria's 2018–21 Feral Horse Strategic Action Plan, released in 2018, had clearly stated that 'shooting will not be used to control free-ranging feral horses'. The policy backflip made it an excellent time to be Lewis Benedetti. With High Country brumbies suddenly in the gunsights of Parks, the only way to save as many as possible, and quickly, was through brumby runners. Benedetti was about to get very, very busy.

* * *

Why the sudden change in Parks Victoria policy from trapping-focused to trigger-happy? To understand, you need a sprinkling of history and geography.

The Victorian High Country is different to New South Wales' Snowy Mountains. Kosciuszko National Park is a vast, mostly contiguous expanse of terrain above the winter snowline, the exception being the Byadbo Wilderness. Victoria's High Country is more fragmented, with broad, deep valleys between areas of snow country.

Partly thanks to strict management protocols but mostly due to topography, Victoria's mountains have fewer brumbies than the mountains in New South Wales, and those brumbies are largely concentrated in the so-called Eastern Alps, which lie east of Benambra and Omeo. The 2018–21 plan had called for 1200 horses to be trapped and removed. According to the May 2020 announcement, these horses were now to be shot because Parks Victoria wanted to reduce their numbers.

Victoria also has a few smaller herds elsewhere, the most celebrated being the mob of 100 or so on the Bogong High Plains, the highest and most ecologically sensitive part of the Victorian Alps, which is similar in appearance and ecological character to the Main Range in the Snowy Mountains. The Bogong High Plains brumbies would not be shot, according to the May 2020 announcement, because they had already been slated for complete eradication (by trapping and removal) in the 2018–21 plan.

To many people, that was unthinkable. The Bogong High Plains horses had a direct lineage to cattleman and horse breeder Osborne Young, who ran as many as 1900 horses on the

Bogong High Plains in the 1880s, which he sold to all manner of buyers. Some of those horses were sent to the Boer War and other wars, and while none returned to preserve the war-horse bloodline, the cultural connection to the Osborne Young horses was significant in the minds of many. Others prized the Bogong High Plains brumbies for their distinctive look, typically dark in colour with white socks and a white blaze or star. For reasons emotional, historic and aesthetic, many people loved those horses, none more so than Jill Pickering, founder and president of the Australian Brumby Alliance.

Pickering, 74, was born with polio. She grew up in England and rode horses every couple of weeks. 'Horses were my lifeline in a very real sense,' she says. She moved to Australia as a young woman, settling in Richmond, and continued to ride regularly at a friend's place on the edge of Melbourne. One day in the late '90s, she decided to venture further afield. 'I've never been able to walk much, and I wanted to sit on top of a mountain and look down and see everything,' she recalls. Pickering got in touch with Steve and Kath Baird, who today still run Bogong Horseback Adventures. They told her she could expect to see brumbies on her horse trek. 'I said, "What are brumbies?" and they said, "Are you serious?"'

Pickering saw her first brumbies on that trip, a small mob of four skittish horses in the distance. It was barely a glimpse but it was enough: she was instantly smitten.

In the early 2000s, Pickering extensively toured Australia, observing brumby mobs as far afield as South Australia and Western Australia. Assorted brumby associations were beginning to pop up around this time. In 2007, at a meeting in Armidale, not far from Guy Fawkes River National Park, Pickering brought some of the disparate groups together and formed the Australian Brumby Alliance (ABA). It incorporated in 2009 and effectively became the peak body for all matters brumby. The ABA's umbrella status continues today alongside the explosion of brumby groups on Facebook, all fighting their own fights and often fighting with each other. But it still has eight member groups and considerable clout as a lobby group.

In 2018, when Parks Victoria announced plans to remove the Bogong High Plains mob, Pickering and the ABA took Parks on. This was a deeply personal struggle. This was her mob, the horses that first drew her to the cause. She would do whatever it took to save them, as well as the 1200 Eastern Alps horses slated for trapping and removal. The ABA lawyered up and took Parks to court for an injunction to prevent the cull. She contributed $450,000 to the fight, about 90 per cent of her life savings. Because Parks is always obliged to defend natural heritage values, the ABA had to frame its legal argument around horses comprising an irreplaceable part of the High Country's natural heritage. In essence: how could Parks destroy its own natural heritage?

The case ran for nearly a year. When the Federal Court of Australia's decision came down on 8 May 2020, Justice Michael O'Bryan said, 'I am not satisfied that the Action, involving the removal of brumbies from the Bogong High Plains and the reduction in number of brumbies in the Eastern Alps, will have or is likely to have a significant impact on the National Heritage values of the Australian Alps.'

Pickering points out that the judgement noted, 'the brumbies are one physical reminder of the historic activities and, in that sense, contribute to the social connection of the pastoral community to the Australian Alps'. But overall, the language employed in Justice O'Bryan's judgement was sweet music to those who prize the ecology of the High Country above all other values. Directly quoting the National Heritage Listing and the National Heritage Assessment Report of the Australian Alps, Justice O'Bryan said the aesthetic value of the High Country 'is reflected in "The mountain vistas, including distinctive range-upon-range panoramas, snow-covered crests, slopes and valleys, alpine streams and rivers, natural and artificial lakes, the snow-clad eucalypts and the high plain grasslands, summer alpine wildflowers, forests and natural sounds ..." The brumbies are not referred to in those descriptions.'

'She was absolutely trounced,' one anti-brumby figure says.

Financially depleted but undeterred, Jill Pickering vowed to keep fighting for the brumbies because they were an 'irreplaceable part of Australia's cultural heritage'. But it was clear that the days of the High Plains mob were numbered, and that the Eastern Alps herds would be significantly thinned out. Then came the really bad news. On the afternoon of 8 May, the same day as the Federal Court ruling, Parks Victoria issued a press release. Like an obituary published immediately after a well-known person dies, the release smelled strongly like it had been sitting in the bottom drawer awaiting this moment. It started innocuously enough.

Parks Victoria welcomes the decision from the Federal Court today which recognises the severe impacts of feral horses on the iconic Alpine National Park and allows horse control programs to resume.

Over the past 18 months, the injunction led to Parks Victoria suspending the majority of the alpine feral horse management operation. Trapping and rehoming programs that were previously implemented were put on hold, subsequently limiting the effectiveness in significantly reducing the feral horse population and environmental damage to the fragile wildlife, plants and habitats in the Victorian Alps.

The real shock for brumby supporters was buried down in the eleventh paragraph.

Parks Victoria is authorised by the *National Parks Act 1975* to control exotic fauna and to efficiently remove feral horses from high-conservation priority locations. Parks Victoria will also be moving to targeted ground shooting of free-ranging feral horses to control ongoing environmental damage occurring in high conservation value areas in the Victorian Alps.

As justification for its about-face on shooting, the press release cited the results of the 2019 aerial survey of horse numbers across the Australian Alps, which had recently become available. The survey estimated that Australian Alps combined horse numbers had risen from 9000 to 24,000 in just five years. Damage to fragile ecosystems from the Black Summer bushfires of 2019–20 also played a part in Parks Victoria's new policy direction. But brumby supporters didn't give a fetlock about the rationale behind the decision. All that mattered to them was that brumbies were going to be shot. Even people with no previous skin in the game suddenly wanted to save the brumbies – or even just one brumby – by any means possible.

That's why Lewis Benedetti's phone started ringing like crazy. And it's when a self-styled hero called Phil Maguire, with a Driza-Bone for a cape, rode in to try to save the day.

Phil Maguire has voiced some highly controversial views on numerous topics over the years and has made enemies in the mountains. But give the man his dues. Phil Maguire loves the High Country. He also knows how to whip up support. In recent years, Maguire has been the loudest champion of the brumbies on the Victorian side of the Murray, mainly through his Rural Resistance website and Facebook group. He is also frequently quoted in the media, sometimes by naive journalists who come across his name when researching the issue and see the big man in the big hat with the horse, possibly unaware of the radical views he's been known to throw out there.

Maguire lives on a neat property in Gippsland but also co-owns a property in the Bundarra Valley, a small patch of grassy cattle country surrounded by mountains, bordered on its western and northern flanks by the Bogong High Plains. At one point, he held High Plains grazing leases. Today, he perfectly fits the portrait of a disgruntled former leaseholder denied access to summer pasture for whom the brumbies have become an avatar of the grazier's hoof print in the mountains.

That's one reason why he loves the brumbies. He is also a horse lover.

When shooting plans were announced for horses in the Eastern Alps after Jill Pickering's unsuccessful legal challenge with the Australian Brumby Alliance, Maguire stepped in. First, he organised a protest at Nunniong Plains in the Eastern Alps – territory favoured by Lewis Benedetti for his brumby runs. Maguire urged people from various brumby groups to go into the bush, effectively as a human shield because Parks Victoria would never start shooting with people wandering around. By all accounts, the event was a bit of a shambles, and some people even got lost. But Maguire secured an injunction to stop the shooting, then launched his own case. He lost. He then went to the Victorian Supreme Court to appeal the decision, with funds raised by Rural Resistance supporters. His argument was that Parks Victoria was using wild horse management methods that were not set out in the existing 2018–21 plan. Chief Justice Anne Ferguson ruled that the applicant, Maguire, 'lacked standing' and threw the appeal out.

If Maguire felt humiliated, he cloaked it in fury while portraying himself as a martyr. 'I think it's a corrupt political decision, absolutely corrupt,' he said. 'If we have to sell our property to finance a High Court battle, that's what we will do.' Maguire entertained the idea of taking the matter to the High Court in Canberra, before pulling out for reasons which are unclear. While he'd lost in court, he had still won in two ways. First, his appeal had delayed proceedings for a crucial month. It was now winter, and mass horse removal by any method is impossible in the snowy months. Second, Maguire had become a conduit for public outrage at the impending cull, and harnessed the moment.

Maguire had been a newspaper journalist in Melbourne for a while, back in the day. He knew how the media worked and decided to make it work for him. He invited media to Anglers Rest, where the road into the Bundarra Valley meets the Omeo Highway. The plan was for Maguire and some mates to demonstrate how mountain horsemen muster and catch brumbies. And not just any brumbies: these would be Bogong High Plains horses, which he would hold on his property until they could be safely released, or perhaps until there was a change of government. Konrad Marshall from *Good Weekend* magazine was one of the journalists who went along. 'All the cracks had gathered to the fray,' Marshall notes drily, borrowing Banjo's line to illustrate what was in reality a bit of a media circus. 'I thought I was getting up to this remote spot where I'd find a roaring bonfire with 20 gnarled guys in Akubras and Driza-Bones waiting to get up at the crack of dawn.' What he actually found was about eight reporters and photographers, long-serving pro-brumby local Liberal party state MP Bill Tilley and no brumbies, despite Maguire's best efforts. One theory as to why Maguire had no luck capturing brumbies is that Gippsland councillor Sonia Buckley – another prominent brumby advocate who is trying to raise funds for a documentary about their plight – had organised a similar muster a few kilometres over the hill and had better horsemen.

Others say it's a good thing Maguire caught no horses as his fences are no good anyway. One way or another, the whole escapade was a bit of a pantomime and ended with Marshall and other journalists listening not to the snorting of entrapped horses, but to Phil Maguire snorting in disgust at Dan Andrews in a lengthy rant. This is perhaps the second most popular recreational activity in the Omeo/Benambra district, after brumby running.

Meanwhile, back at Anglers Rest in June 2020, Marshall was left in a bit of a spot. You can't write a magazine feature about brumbies without brumbies, so he returned to the mountains shortly afterwards for a second attempt at seeing how brumbies are caught. None other than Lewis Benedetti delivered the goods, chasing down and capturing a young colt without too much fuss. He had a productive few months that winter, did Benedetti. 'In the winter of 2020, I rehomed 22 horses – caught, broken in, rehomed,' he says with pride.

For the record, as of mid-2021, no Eastern Alps horses have yet been shot, nor the Bogong mob trapped and removed. COVID and one or two other things got in the way, so Parks Victoria had its excuses. Mind you, even its most ardent supporters concede that Parks Victoria is prone to bold statements followed by world-class bouts of procrastination.

* * *

If you're cyber-loafing on YouTube and you've got a spare two minutes and 21 seconds, you could do worse than watch the trailer of the 1982 movie *The Man from Snowy River*. 'Together, they fought, and struggled and loved, in a land as untamed, as beautiful, as they themselves,' the narrator swoons in his American accent and gravelly movie trailer voice. And, to be fair, if you had a hot young Tom Burlinson and Sigrid Thornton at your disposal, not to mention Jack Thompson and Kirk Douglas in supporting roles, you'd probably scoop words from the same vat of golden syrup.

But there's another video on YouTube that tells the story of brumby running like it really was, boots, chaps, spurs and all. It's an old ABC documentary called *Buckrunners* and it deserves to have been watched more times than 'Gangnam Style'. *Buckrunners* is an absolute gem of Australiana, filmed in 1965 but with a vibe more like 1865. It begins in Omeo, a town of about 400, whose main street is not a whole lot busier now than it was then, give or take an eatery or two catering to passing traffic en route to the ski villages of Dinner Plain and Mt Hotham.

'The horse and the history of this town are forever linked,' the not-even-slightly swoony or gravelly narrator says in the half-British, half-Australian accent typical of newsreels of the day. The documentary introduces Mervyn Pearson, a stoic, sun-bronzed local with a face like a crinkle-cut chip. He stands with one hand on his hip, the other holding a pipe, and speaks with unusually long pauses between words, as though reading from a stuck teleprompter.

'For over 100 years ... horses have played a major part in the development of Australia ... Apparently some of these early station horses ... strayed into the bush very early in the piece ... because ... some of our earliest stockmen ... were known ... buck runners.'

Old Pearson then lists assorted stockmen down the years who were known to be buck runners. One of them was Jack Riley, as in the man often claimed to be the actual Man from Snowy River. The documentary cuts to wizened locals who knew and rode with Riley. Then comes the pub scene. Almost nothing happens in the pub in Omeo, and therein lies its charm. *Seinfeld* always claimed to be a show about nothing, when actually it was a show about the whacky escapades and peccadilloes of four quirky New Yorkers. But the pub scene in *Buckrunners* is almost two minutes of incredibly watchable, unnarrated nothing. It's just blokes bending the elbow while ashing Capstan Filter cigarettes on the floor and saying, 'You blokes' this and 'Bloody' that and 'Brumbies' this and 'Yards' that, and pretty soon everyone's chin is wet with dribbled beer and the black dog on the bench has fallen asleep and you understand that by the time the pub shuts and the men leave for the brumby run, there won't be a sober one among them.

Next comes the camp scene, with horses snorting and tools clanking and fire crackling and billies boiling and saddles saddled and horses shod. Buck runner Jim Flannagan is introduced. He sits on a low stool outside a rough timber hut with his beaten-up old hat and unshaven face, a lick of hair curling over his forehead and an unlit cigarette in one hand. With eyes narrowed into a squint, he explains how a brumby run is conducted in colourful, at times unintelligible, vernacular. But it's clear from his hand gestures and those words that can be deciphered that the run is a well-orchestrated operation requiring immaculate organisation, tactics and elite riding skills from each member of the party, all of whom are men, because brumby running circa 1965 does not appear to be women's business. Towards the end of his monologue, Flannagan's face lights up as he envisages the fruits of a successful chase. 'We usually hope there's about 20 at least ... There's a big cloud of dust and boys pulling up horses and saying, "Look at 'em! Look at 'em! These are beauties, we'll have some fun at this rodeo,"' he enthuses.

Lewis Benedetti rides solo, seeking only one or two horses at a time. His methods are considerably more streamlined. As he explains, success depends not on the number of pursuers; it's about knowing what you're doing.

'The most important thing is understanding wild horses. I see so many people go up there and start chasing when they see a wild horse mob. Some of them have gone up there for ten years trying to catch a brumby and never caught one. You've got to know the country, got to understand what they do under pressure and where they'll run. Unless you know the country really well and understand wild horses, you're wasting your time.'

Benedetti seeks brumbies in several different areas in Victoria's Eastern Alps. His preferred patches are places like Nunniong Plains, Cobberas, Native Cat Flat and Native Dog Flat. In quiet defiance of the ongoing ban on brumby running in Kosciuszko National Park, he's even ventured north of the Murray – or the Indi, as the infant stream is called in its High Country headwaters – into the brumby-infested Tin Mines area south of Thredbo. He's also sought his quarry in the vicinity of The Pinch, a narrow reach of the Snowy River in the southern part of the Byadbo Wilderness.

Preparation starts with his own horse, which is a stock horse or thoroughbred, depending on the roughness of the terrain. 'You've got to put shoes on correctly for the bush,' he explains. 'The toe in a little bit, and the heel in a little bit so the shoes don't throw when they're galloping across a rock bed. And your horse has got to be fit – not just fit, but bush fit. There's a big difference. You could work the shit out of them for months but they still wouldn't be right unless you rode them in the bush. You've also got to feed your horses accordingly. They're basically an athlete, so they need high-energy feed, good hearty feed like oats.

'During the run, you've got to have your wits about you. You've got to understand your horse and know what it can do. If you come to a boggy bit, slow down. If your horse is tired, pull up straight away. You can't keep pushing a tired horse. The most dangerous part is when your horse is tired. They start missing their step, getting lazy.'

Benedetti doesn't often get to that point. With his knowledge of the mountain landscape and the behaviour of individual mobs, he rarely works his horse to the point of exhaustion. 'Most brumbies aren't that healthy,' he says. 'Some of them are in pretty poor condition, full of worms, pretty skinny. But they're still tougher than any other horse. Most horses in their condition would die.'

When Benedetti takes off after a horse, he doesn't gallop at full speed like Tom Burlinson. 'As a young kid, I was always going too fast, hitting the bush too hard. There are heaps of hazards when you're riding pretty fast through thick bush. I've broken my leg, my hip, fingers. It's taken me years to work it out, but if you sit behind them and pick your path, you'll eventually come up beside one. They know they can't outrun your horses and they will give in to a dominant horse. All horses need a leader, they need direction. One horse even turned around and followed me. As soon as you put a rope over them, most of them will submit.'

No doubt there are times when the chase and capture are not quite the foregone conclusions that Benedetti portrays. In Elyne Mitchell's books, feisty horses flee and resist capture furiously, and there are doubtless real brumbies that behave that way. Like Mitchell's brumbies, many horses must deeply resent the rope around their neck and fight it. Roping is the main area of contention for opponents of brumby running. They say it's cruel, that the rope is too short, too rough, that it chokes horses. Benedetti strongly rejects these claims. He has argued the point often with horse rehomers who take and give away, or sell, horses that Parks have trapped. His blood boils like a billy on a bonfire when he talks about it. 'I mean, fucken hell, have you ever seen one caught in a trap yard? When you yard a mob of horses, you might have three stallions and nine mares and a few foals in the mob. When you lock 'em up, what happens when they start fighting? I've seen horses kill themselves in trap yards by galloping straight into the rails. A brumby runner creeps up, picks out a nice one, gives it to someone and makes 'em smile. How is that inhumane?'

Benedetti believes that brumby running is not only the kindest way of removing horses but the most effective, because runners prefer younger horses. Brumbies don't live long. Very few make it past about eight years, a cruelly short life span even Elyne Mitchell's fictionalised mobs couldn't avoid. That means that if you take the young colts and fillies, you disturb the breeding cycle and the mob has no chance of replenishing itself. 'Over the years, I've seen certain areas that were overpopulated become nearly free of brumbies,' he says.

The young ones also make the best sport. 'As a brumby runner, the rule is a two-year-old colt is a good run because they're the hardest to catch. They're also the easiest to break and train. If you catch a brumby and it's over five or six, don't even bother trying to train it.' Young brumbies also make the best pets or working horses. 'I've heard so many wankers say you can't train a brumby. Fucken bullshit. They're easy as piss to train. And when you have a brumby that's so nice and sweet and you think to yourself that the government wants to shoot them ...'

Perhaps Benedetti has exhausted his allocation of fruity language for the day. Or maybe the second half of the sentence writes itself, so why fill in the blanks? Either way, his point is made. Brumby running is his idea of a humane, workable wild horse management tool, and stuff anyone who disagrees. And if you home in on the young ones, it's win/win/win/win because they're the ones that are challenging to catch, they're the ones that can be trained, they're the ones people want, and they're the ones that ensure overall numbers are thinned.

At face value, it's quite the organic solution. Get the mountain horsemen to fix the problem of too many mountain horses. But there's a catch. There's always a catch in this game.

* * *

Ross Constable remembers the waste. The feeling of hopelessness and the shocking, shocking waste. Now retired, the long-serving Kosciuszko National Park ranger started his working life as a deckhand on fishing trawlers. 'My lasting memory of the fishing industry is the amount of stuff that was just thrown overboard dead,' he says. 'Trawling is akin to clear-felling a forest. The nets came up with a lot of animal organisms considered bycatch – shellfish, crustaceans, small fish – and anything that wasn't marketable got thrown back in. I can only imagine the damage it was doing to the bottom of the ocean. But I must say, it certainly didn't prepare me for some of the cruelty I saw with wild horses.'

Constable had a bent for the outdoors life and commenced his career with the NSW National Parks and Wildlife Service in 1974. He worked there for 40 years. From 1979 to 1989, he monitored brumby running within Kosciuszko with another young parkie, Paul Hardey. 'I witnessed horrific cases of animal cruelty in the so-called heritage sport of brumby running or buck running,' Constable says. The horrors are too numerous to mention. But a few incidents stick in his mind, gristle in his teeth that no toothpick will remove. There was the juvenile horse down near the Tin Mines that was folded up under itself, its leg broken after being chased. He euthanised that one with his rifle. He found another horse with its entrails hanging out, which he reckons had been impaled through the stomach after being chased. He did away with that poor creature too. And those were just the horses the runners left behind. There were enough awful sights among the herds with or without help from runners. Horses teeming with parasites, flyblown, emaciated, all skin and bones. 'Horses are not native animals and they really can't survive out there,' he says.

Constable's colleague Paul Hardey saw sights just as terrible, and what really irked him was the complete disdain for animal welfare. He recalls a colleague coming upon a horse tied up to a tree that had just been left there to die of thirst and hunger. He couldn't bear that, so he untethered it and let it run free. 'Some people had a complete lack of concern for what happened to those horses,' Hardey says in the sort of tone reserved for a person who kicks dogs.

Hardey grew up with horses. Home was a wheat and sheep farm near Junee, a couple of hours north of the mountains. He was a whippersnapper of five when he learned to ride. His first horse, a chestnut called Star because of the star on its forehead, threw him one day when he was out rabbit shooting. But he got back on that horse, because idioms are often to be taken literally in the bush.

As a parkie, Hardey was different. Unlike many Kosciuszko National Park staff from then or now, he knew farmers on the fringes of the mountains and understood the way they think. He knew many horse lovers among them who understood the damage that wild horses wreak in the High Country. But he says those people have long stayed silent on the brumby issue for fear of retribution and bullying, and that they remain zip-lipped to this day. In late 2018, when anti-feral-horse protesters organised a walk from Sydney to the summit of Mt Kosciuszko to protest John Barilaro's brumby legislation,

Hardey thought maybe the moment had come when they would be moved to speak out. He asked some of his farming friends and locals with horses to accompany the trekkers on a section of their final leg. It would be a powerful act of solidarity, a clear message that true horse people understand the damage ferals cause. Crickets. *Breep-breep. Breep-breep. Breep-breep.* Pretty much everyone he approached told him they'd love to help but feared the backlash. Intimidation, ostracisation, lies spread in the community, doctors not accepting appointments, mail not being delivered, all the usual.

Hardey himself became familiar with intimidation early in his career. It was all part of the daily routine. Get out of bed, don your uniform, do your work, grab a knock-off beer in the pub, have someone threaten to beat the crap out of you. In the 1970s, it was largely to do with the impounding of stock which were grazing illegally in the park. After the abolition of snow leases, limited grazing was allowed in parts of Kosciuszko until 1972. Thereafter, it was strictly forbidden. At first, penalties were small. Then they upped the fine to $10 per head of cattle. One parkie impounded 1000 head of cattle that were grazing illegally up on Nungar Plain near Adaminaby. Hardey says the cattlemen came for him and were 'halfway over the bonnet to grab him' before they realised a policeman was on hand. 'I avoided the pub after hearing about that incident when I'd done an impounding,' Hardey says. 'If I walked in, everyone would swing their heads around and stare like a scene from a western.'

Monitoring brumby running also kept him busy. Back in the '70s and '80s, brumby running was legal in Kosciuszko, with a permit system in place. But that didn't mean it was always done with proper regard for animal welfare or the alpine landscape. 'It was a slab of beer and a few horses on the truck and "we'll go out and chase a few bucks",' Hardey recalls. 'Most of them were pretty good riders, but there were always some among them who didn't worry too much about what they did to the brumby. My records show that the horses with injuries tended to come from the same names. Certain families were definitely crueller than others. And unfortunately the good horsemen were not prepared to report the bad horsemen, because I don't recall ever receiving any reports of mistreatment of brumbies from buck runners.'

The horses caught in wire snares were the worst. Horses would often be garrotted around the neck, their skin cut, their deaths slow and agonising. All too often, Hardey had to euthanise horses. Some of the half-mutilated horses the runners took out of the mountains would turn up in local sale yards. Pet food suppliers were the only interested parties. 'Eventually, we recommended that the brumby running permit system cease due to cruelty and other issues associated with buck-running camps,' Hardey says.

The ban was in force by the end of the 1970s. But ranger Dave Darlington – who in the year 2000 would be the driving force behind the first Kosciuszko Horse Management Plan, and who would go on to become chief ranger of Kosciuszko National Park – continued to see illegal brumby running well into the 1990s and beyond. 'It was quite common,' he says. 'To be fair, a lot of the people were not the type to harm horses and they probably had a lot of respect for the horses they were trying to catch. There would have been those that quietly rode in, hardly took anything with them, took a horse or two, then rode out.'

Not everyone had such reverence for the horses or for the park itself. 'We would come across brumby runners' camps and there'd be things like steel bunks and metal chairs that they'd just left there to come back to,' Darlington recalls. 'We'd pull all that stuff out and take it to the tip, along with the bottles. You can't imagine the amount of grog bottles we took out. We had an old International four-wheel drive truck which was designed to carry a load of three or four tonnes. We filled the entire tray with grog bottles, cans and assorted rubbish that had been building up for a long time. This was at a spot called Ingeegoodbee Hut and it was like a rubbish tip out the back of the hut. There was a fair bit of social drinking that obviously went along with brumby running.'

Lewis Benedetti concedes that the combination of young men and alcohol and the thrill of the chase on a brumby run is not ideal. 'Yeah, I've seen young blokes going up there and getting on the piss and doing the wrong thing. But you'll see that no matter what you do.' Benedetti also says that not every horse tied to a tree is a horse abandoned and left to die a slow death. 'I've caught horses and tied 'em to a tree and come back the next day and someone has cut the rope because they thought it was there for days. No, it wasn't! It was only there for 12 hours. There are so many people who think they're a horseman.'

Paul Hardey today believes the practice of illegal brumby running is 'as much about retribution against Parks and greenies for basically stopping what they used to do in the mountains'.

And he remains unconvinced that the practice is, or ever was, done humanely by the majority of brumby runners.

'This is where there's been conflict between me and Leisa Caldwell,' he says. 'On social media she'd be calling for the return of local brumby running as a safe and humane way of horse management, but I'd reply, "You know that's not true, Leisa."'

There's an old document floating around the mountains which is pretty much the last word on brumby running and cruelty in Kosciuszko. It's a 1972 report from an anonymous Parks employee, entitled, 'Abuse of Wild Horses and Permit System'. The document details numerous instances of appalling cruelty and indifference to the suffering of brumbies, all of it inflicted by the sort of people who today would claim heritage status for the horses, and who would have been the first to join street marches against the purported cruelty of the Guy Fawkes cull.

The atrocities noted in the document don't make easy reading. Savage dogs were used to chase horses and to drive terrified foals from their mothers. Wire noose snares were suspended at horse-head height on horse tracks, and the carcasses of wild horses were found hanging in snares. Other horses were found tied to trees or hobbled to logs or left in yards for days without food or water. Some horses were severely injured during capture. Others escaped after being roped then slowly choked and starved or died of thirst after the trailing end of the rope became entangled in logs, trees or rocks. In summary, it wasn't a bloodbath out there. It was much, much worse. But this was 1972. Is it also 2021?

* * *

Ted Rowley is a transplanted West Australian, via Papua New Guinea, who found a little slice of paradise for himself and his wife, Jo, on the Mowamba River out the back of Jindabyne, near where the Moonbah Valley joins Kosciuszko National Park. Around 2012, not long after he'd moved in, he was out picking mushrooms with his hat as a basket when he came across a bunch of fellas in his cattle yards, all saddled up and ready for what looked like a brumby run that could last a few days, judging by the amount of gear.

Rowley is a jovial fellow with a booming voice. Growing up on an orange orchard in Pinjarra, his dad died suddenly when Ted was 12. But the old man had instilled some key life lessons before he departed. 'If I didn't hold the door open for my sisters, my father would belt me,' he says. With his old-fashioned good manners, Rowley was never going to cause a scene at the unexpected sight of intruders. He casually leant over the fence and said, 'Oh, g'day! What are you doing?'

'We're just going riding up in the wilderness,' one of the men answered.

'Oh, really. Have you talked to the person who owns the farm?' Rowley countered. Slowly, the reality of who they were speaking to dawned on them. And that particular brumby run ended before it started. Rowley later sought advice from a neighbour on how to handle the matter, should it happen again. He also checked with the previous owner. 'He was pretty clear in his message,' Rowley recalls. 'He said, "Tell 'em to fuck off and shut the gate.'" Some doors you hold open, others you don't.

'Now they park down the road on other people's properties and ride around us,' Rowley says. So they're still brumby running in Kosciuszko in 2021, even though it's been banned for more than 30 years.

In Victoria, the practice has clung to its legal status by a thread. Victoria even has a famous club – the Benambra Buck Runners (BBR) – named after the small town just north of Omeo, which one High Country local jokingly describes as 'the last hold-out of all the mad bastards left in the mountains'.

The spiritual leader and co-founder of the BBR was Ken Connley, who died aged 74 in 2020 and who co-owned land with Maguire. Connley was Jack Thompson's riding double in *The Man from Snowy River* and is said to have roped more brumbies than anyone in the mountains, a number believed to exceed 1500. Second on the list, with 964, is Craig Orchard, the current president of the BBR, himself a star of the screen, having featured with his wife, Tahnee, in the 2005 ABC series *Wild Valley*, which includes stunning winter scenes of brumby running in the snow. Despite his brumby-running prowess, Orchard believes trapping is the most humane and cost-effective way of reducing horse numbers, and that he and his Benambra Buck Runners could do a far better job of it than the parkies and their contractors.

Benedetti sees it differently. He reckons he and a handful of his brumby runner cohorts could get numbers under control without the need for the painstaking steps that go along with trapping – building temporary trap yards, luring horses in with hay and salt and/or molasses, then hoping like hell that they don't self-harm or attack each other when trapped. 'Half a dozen blokes could do the job in Victoria,' he says. 'If we worked too hard, we'd wipe them out. We'd definitely have the population wiped out within about three years.'

If only there were enough people like Benedetti and Craig Orchard who could be relied upon to chase and rope brumbies without overt cruelty, and without leaving a Hansel and Gretel trail of beer bottles and worse. And perhaps there are. But it's possibly all academic now, because on 26 March 2021, Parks Victoria's new Draft Feral Horse Action Plan dropped. On page 27, it said:

> Following a reconsideration of the safety risks associated with roping and the duties held by Parks Victoria to ensure a safe workplace, Parks Victoria can no longer include roping as part of the suite of feral horse control methods used in National Parks by staff, contractors or volunteers, especially as other techniques of feral horse capture and removal, with lower levels of risk, are available for reducing environmental damage caused by feral horses. Roping does not comply with the standards for health and safety.

Here's your headline: 'Occupational Health and Safety killed The Man from Snowy River'. It is a very 21st century death.

Benedetti was in Queensland on a stint managing an outback cattle station when the news reached him. It was hardly unexpected but, needless to say, he didn't think much of it. Nor, it seems, will he heed it. 'Well, we will still do it', he said via text message. 'Where we go, it is no man's land.'

With the death of Ken Connley, the elder statesman of brumby running in Victoria is now unquestionably Jim Flannagan – the same Jim Flannagan who starred in the 1965 documentary *Buckrunners*. Journalist Konrad Marshall interviewed the then 87-year-old at his home in mid-2020, as part of the *Good Weekend* cover story with Phil Maguire and the dysfunctional brumby muster. 'He's still strong,' Marshall says. 'I think I interrupted him in the middle of building a long farm fence by himself on a rainy cold day in the middle of an Omeo winter, and that's six months after he'd been kicked off a horse.'

Old Jim Flannagan is still strong of mind as well as body. He'll go to his grave convinced that brumbies are not the pests all those parkies and greenies say they are. 'They are not doing the damage and they do not create the erosion that a lot of people seem to think they do,' he said in a recent YouTube video, one of a series created by the pro-brumby activist and Gippsland councillor Sonia Buckley to help raise awareness and funds for her brumby documentary.

Most brumby advocates repudiate the science around brumby damage to some degree. Some dismiss it completely, while others believe it's overstated. When you meet the scientists and ask them about the attacks on their work, on their credibility, on their character, you discover that they have a wide range of responses, from defiance to despair to everything in between.

CHAPTER SIX

THEY EAT HORSES, DON'T THEY?

In 2007, incumbent Australian of the Year Tim Flannery said it would never rain again and the dams would never fill. Except he didn't. Or not exactly, anyway. But if you read certain newspapers or online news portals and blogs, and the comments underneath the stories, oh, he said it all right. And he has been mocked for it ever since.

Flannery, a palaeontologist, environmentalist, and several other 'ists', became a figure of national renown around the time of his award-winning 2005 book *The Weather Makers*, which predicted all sorts of coming catastrophes due to climate change. He was named Australian of the Year in 2007 and in 2011 was appointed chief commissioner of the Climate Commission, a government body the Abbott government promptly disbanded upon its election in 2013. In these years, he became a go-to commentator on climate change matters.

One day in 2007 on the ABC's *Landline*, in response to a question about what climate change would mean for farmers,

Flannery explained how winter rainfall was already in a long-term decline in many areas of southern Australia, and if you coupled that with decreased run-off, 'the rain that falls isn't actually going to fill our dams and our river systems, and that's a real worry for the people in the bush, particularly for irrigation'.

It was a broad, factually based overview of the problem of a warming climate as it relates to water management. And while it contained that phrase about the rain that fell struggling to fill our dams and our river systems, the comment was laid out in context. Flannery certainly never said, explicitly or even implicitly, that 'it would never rain again'. But that interview would haunt him for years.

Good communication is a vital aspect of science. Without it, science has little chance of changing the public dialogue or breaking through to the policy realm in a meaningful way. But as the Flannery example shows, even the tiniest imprecision in science communication – perceived or otherwise – can be distorted and weaponised against the communicator. Dr Don Driscoll knows this better than anyone.

Driscoll is 52 and sports a decent Ned Kelly beard, slightly greying at the front. He's Professor of Terrestrial Ecology and Director for the Centre for Integrative Ecology at Deakin University, as well as one of Australia's most accomplished researchers into the impacts of brumbies in the Australian Alps. He is also a loud voice in the fight to rid the High Country of brumbies. In bygone eras, scientists quietly did the science then shut up. Not in Driscoll's world. To him, the dual roles of researcher and advocate are inseparable.

'There's no point having powerful observations if you don't also communicate them in a powerful way,' he says. 'I think a lot of science communication fails because it's held back by scientists wanting to provide all the caveats and concerns first without telling what the actual story is.'

After a High Country trip in 2014, Driscoll had one hell of a story to tell.

At the time, he was working at the Australian National University in Canberra. One August weekend, he and a colleague, Sam Banks, undertook a backcountry ski trip on the Rams Head Range. They drove past Thredbo through to a spot called Dead Horse Gap, so named for some brumbies which died way back in the day, frozen solid in deep snow after a heavy blizzard. As they climbed through the snow gums on the lower slopes of the Rams Head Range, they soon started seeing horse tracks that cut deep ruts in the snow. At one point, the tracks all seemed to converge, and that's where they saw it. A grotesque apparition, half embedded in the snow: an emaciated dead horse.

'We walked over to have a look at it and found that its abdominal cavity was totally open and all the insides were pretty well gone,' Driscoll recalled in a video he released shortly after the trip. 'I really didn't know what would have done that. Maybe foxes or something like that. It was surprising to see the insides gone like that.'

The two men moved onwards and upwards, camping in a snow cave which they dug high on the treeless plateau of the Main Range near Mt Kosciuszko. The morning brought bad weather and limited visibility. Snow gums are a godsend in those conditions, lending definition to the landscape and shelter from the mountain gales, so Driscoll and Banks descended as quickly as the latter's novice skiing skills allowed. Returning the same way, they noticed three horses standing in the snow around the dead horse they'd found the day before, nuzzling its body. At first, it looked like the horses were pining for their dead mate. Eating it, more like. The brumbies had their heads almost up to their ears in the dead horse's intestinal cavity.

'They were eating out the entrails of this dead horse. These feral horses had turned to cannibalism,' Driscoll said in the video.

Banks and Driscoll understood perfectly well that horses are herbivores, and that the three horses were after the semi-digested or fully-digested grass in the intestinal tract. But they had actually eaten the intestines, to the point where pretty much the whole tract was gone.

'When I saw that horse, I knew it was pretty bizarre,' Driscoll recalls. 'It made me think, "What are the extreme circumstances that these horses are living in up in the Alps?" Why are they in such dire straits that they are prepared to eat their fallen comrades, as Sam put it? It was a long way from the imagery of streaming manes and tails.'

Driscoll posted his four-minute YouTube video a month later. He called it 'Cannibal Horses in the Australian Alps'. To this day, he's still copping a Flannery-type backlash for the title of that video, and everything it implies.

After the snow had melted that spring, Driscoll and Banks returned to Kosciuszko. This time, they were on mountain bikes instead of skis and they headed south on fire trails from

Dead Horse Gap instead of north on the Rams Head Range, down towards a distinctive conical peak near the Victorian border called The Pilot. The trip was in the name of recreation, not research. 'I hadn't really engaged in the whole horse issue and it wasn't something I was going to follow up in a big way,' Driscoll says. He had been a High Country lover from the age of 16, when he climbed Victoria's highest peak, Mt Bogong, in a white-out at Easter time. The enclosed, intimate mood of the alpine landscape in fog entranced him. Being based in Canberra, just a couple of hours from Kosciuszko, Driscoll wanted to explore as much of the NSW Snowies as he could.

But the tone of the trip changed when Driscoll and Banks saw the sheer number of horses in the country south of Dead Horse Gap. This country is known as The Cascades and is immortalised in Elyne Mitchell's books. Thowra, the eponymous Silver Brumby, defeats impressive stallion The Brolga in a fight to the death and becomes king of the Cascade Brumbies. In Mitchell's works of children's fiction, the brumbies seem to live in harmony with the environment. Driscoll discovered a very different reality.

The Cascades is an area of sphagnum-lined creeks babbling their way through open frost hollow valleys, where cold air drains on winter nights preventing the growth of snow gums. It's gorgeous, rolling country, each valley more sheltered than the last as you journey south. This is not the dramatic high alpine terrain of the Rams Head Range, with its granite tors and views of distant blue ridges extending to the horizon. This is Australia's snow country at its most intimate, easy on a walker or mountain biker's eye, and their legs too, with complex plant communities thriving in boggy wetlands supporting all manner of native creatures.

Or, at least, that's what it's like where the horses haven't trampled and trodden the delicate alpine plants and fouled the waterways. Driscoll couldn't believe what he and Banks had found. 'On this trip, we really saw the impact horses were having on the environment,' he says. 'There was horse dung – the biggest piles I've ever seen – and the smell of horses everywhere. The landscape was dominated by these enormous animals and we saw almost no native animals. There were broken shrubs and pathways everywhere in the bush. In frost hollows where you would normally have a lot of native tussock grasses and a range of other natives, there were weeds and an invasive grass, *Holcus lanatus*, also known as Yorkshire fog. All of this disturbance was clearly caused by horses.'

Driscoll returned a changed man. The dead horse on the first trip up the Rams Head Range had been more of a curiosity than anything else. While it had opened his eyes to welfare issues around the brumbies, this was different. Now he was concerned about the welfare of the landscape itself and its plant and animal communities. 'After that trip, I was thinking that clearly there has been a massive management failure,' he says. 'And I thought, to fix this up, all we need to do is point it out.'

Ah, such sweet naivety. Looking back, Driscoll knows it. 'We had no idea it was so controversial,' he says. 'We had no idea there would be such vehement opposition and the issue would be used as a political football, as it has been.'

Driscoll learned fast. And as he came to understand the passions of the pro-brumby people, he knew what he had to do. In the face of what he saw as the irrelevant and, to a large extent, false claims of heritage, he began compiling as much evidence of horse damage as he could. When he started his work in 2014, there were numerous scientists working on the issue, researching the impacts of horses on everything from waterways to individual creatures like the corroboree frog, Guthega skink, mountain pygmy possum and more. But the information was strewn in a hundred different locations, and often confined to obscure corners of the internet only academics could access.

Driscoll did his best to collate information and make it more accessible. He set up a website which links out to studies and papers on feral horse impacts. He began writing on the topic himself in a straightforward, accessible voice on platforms like the popular academic website *The Conversation*. Always in his articles and papers, he used the term 'feral horse' rather than 'wild horse' or 'brumby', in order to negate the emotional connection. As the science of feral horse damage began to filter in the public consciousness, the snowball effect kicked in and new researchers began working in the area. Driscoll was the man who rolled the initial snowball.

In 2018, Driscoll helped commission and edit two extremely significant publications on the horse question. One was an entire issue of the journal *Ecological Management & Restoration* devoted to the matter of feral horses in the Australian Alps. The other was a collection of abstracts from the Kosciuszko Science Conference on Feral Horse Impacts. The conference, held in November 2018 in response to John Barilaro's *Kosciuszko Wild Horse Heritage Act*, was co-convened by Deakin

University (where Driscoll works), the ANU's Fenner School of Environment and Society, and the Australian Academy of Science. The Academy already had skin in the game. It had issued a sternly worded statement before the bill went before the NSW parliament. Signed by 14 scientific heavy hitters including Driscoll, it stated that, 'The Heritage Bill places a priority on a single invasive species over many native species and ecosystems, some of which are found nowhere else in the world.' The effect of that statement was like a slap with a wet paper towel. The bill became legislation as the Liberal–National Coalition gained the support of the Shooters, Fishers and Farmers Party and the Christian Democrats.

But the Academy wasn't done. The conference was a key moment. For the first time, researchers and other stakeholders had come together to present information on the damage caused by horses to the High Country. For the first time, their research was collated in one document. It was out there. It was rigorous. It was something you could hold. It was something concrete you could give to politicians, especially if a government more sympathetic to environmental concerns ever came along. The cherry on top was the Kosciuszko Science Accord, signed by 90 scientists, which stated, 'We agree that scientific evidence shows that there is a clear and present threat to the natural water catchments and the natural ecosystems of Kosciuszko National Park and other Australian Alps national parks caused directly by thousands of feral horses.' The Accord went on to make six demands of the NSW government, including repealing the *Kosciuszko Wild Horse Heritage Act*.

Reading through the bound collection of conference abstracts is a sobering way to spend an afternoon. There's a paper on horse damage to the Byadbo Wilderness by Ian Pulsford, Jessica Ward-Jones and others. Damage to the alpine bogs of the Bogong High Plains is documented by a suite of Victorian scientists, four of them with doctorates. The impacts on corroboree frogs are laid out by young researchers Dr Ben Scheele and Dr Claire Foster. News on that front is not good: the frogs lay their eggs in and around pillows of sphagnum moss and rely on vegetation cover to protect them. Scheele and Foster found that horse grazing is severely compromising these habitats. And for the benefit of the voluminous army of brumby supporters who say, 'Yeah, but what about the deer?' they noted that no tracks or scats of deer or pigs were found in the areas studied.

There was more. There was much more. Emeritus Professor Geoffrey Hope, one of the most eminent natural historians of the High Country, presented clear, concise information on how horse trampling destroys the water-holding capacity of alpine bogs and peatlands. Freshwater ecosystem experts Associate Professor Jamie Pittock and Professor Max Finlayson doubled up on those findings in the broader context of how river systems across south-east Australia could become imperilled by the muddied, eroded, silted-up, increasingly intermittent High Country streams.

Dr Hayley Bates explained how the current growth in horse numbers and their ever-expanding range would start to pose a serious threat to mountain pygmy possum habitat. The pygmy possum is an interesting case. It's one of Australia's smallest and cutest marsupials which, ironically, requires a thick blanket of snow to keep warm during its winter hibernation, because a dense snowpack insulates against severe cold. With climate change and thinner snowpacks, the possums have already got problems. The last thing they need is competition for food or their ground cover trampled or eaten.

Dr Martin Schulz and Dr Ken Green presented their bleak findings on another small native mammal, the broad-toothed rat, which has been wiped out in large parts of the plains of northern Kosciuszko National Park. It too relies on vegetation for protection from both predators and the elements, and its favoured habitat is a few hundred metres lower in elevation than the pygmy possums, in areas already heavily populated by horses. The tussocky snow grass meadows the rats prefer have been mowed down to the height of lawn by hungry hoofed herbivores, leaving the rats nowhere to hide, nest, breed or live.

Then there was the story of the stocky galaxias, a critically endangered fish whose precarious fate was covered in a paper by freshwater scientist Associate Professor Mark Lintermans of the University of Canberra and one of his students, Hugh Allan. You might wonder who else but a couple of researchers cares about a small, semi-translucent fish half the size of your little finger. But galaxias are one of the marvels of the mountains. Mountain galaxias, a close cousin of the stockies, are easily spotted in the shallow cold mountain streams that are barely deeper than puddles on the walk to Mt Kosciuszko from the top of the chairlift at Thredbo. It's one of the wonders of the mountains to see fish thriving so high up. Indeed, they're the only Australian fish that survive underneath ice in winter. But both the mountain and stocky galaxias have an introduced enemy – trout. The mountain galaxias of the Main Range are lucky to live in streams too tiny to support trout. The stockies of the lower streams have had no such luxury. So successful have the trout been in their predation that stocky galaxias now live only in a three-kilometre-long section of Tantangara Creek in northern Kosciuszko. That's it. A three-kilometre stretch of one creek. And the only reason they're still around is because that creek has a six-metre waterfall that acts as a natural trout barrier. But a small waterfall in rolling country is no barrier to horses. The Tantangara area has the highest density of brumbies in Kosciuszko, and those brumbies are now silting up the creek when they cross it and drink from it, destroying the habitat of the last remaining stockies. The clock is ticking fast.

Helping to provide platforms for stories like these is a large part of Don Driscoll's mission. But he is more than a conduit. Driscoll is an active, often provocative voice who directly addresses the arguments put forward by brumby advocates. Through his papers, seminars and on social media, he refutes what he calls their 'whataboutism' – What about the deer? What about the damage caused by excavation work for Snowy 2.0? What about ski resorts? – with hard facts about the extensive and cumulative horse damage. He also does an exceptionally fine line in myth-busting their pseudoscience.

The pro-brumby people have circulated mountains of information of dubious scientific worth, arguing that brumbies not only don't damage the environment but that their presence is actually good for it. Leisa Caldwell's heritage report is just one source of these sorts of claims. Driscoll is far from the only scientist whose work directly debunks such misinformation, but he's definitely the most fun to ask about it, because he gets good and worked up talking about this stuff.

So, then. Let's start with one of the classics: 'grazing prevents blazing'. It's a neat phrase, bandied about for years by cattlemen and enthusiastically adopted by brumby supporters, which encapsulates the belief that introduced grazing animals reduce the fire risk in the High Country by keeping the fuel load in check. It's an attractive, elegantly simple argument which, at first glance, appeals to logic. Does it stack up? Over to you, Don.

'Cattle and horses graze the least flammable part of the landscape. The snow grass they eat is much less flammable than shrubs, which is the part of the landscape that really drives fires and determines how severe and intense they are. A really important part of this is the perceptions that graziers have. They'll be standing in the Alps and see fire stop at the snow grass and say, "See, it stopped because my cattle were grazing there!" But it stops there whether they were grazing or not, because snow grass is not particularly flammable. I'm not saying it doesn't burn, just not anything like the shrubs.'

For additional evidence that grazing does nine-tenths of bugger all to prevent blazing, look no further than the largest fires in the recorded history of the Australian Alps. Those were the Black Friday fires of 1939, still the only fires that have swept through the entirety of the High Country in New South Wales and Victoria in the heart of the era of mountain cattlemen. Meanwhile, the fires in January 2020 burnt a third of Kosciuszko – the largest national park in New South Wales – at a time when more brumbies grazed than ever before due to a lack of horse removal immediately before and ever since the Barilaro legislation.

Despite such obvious, in-your-face examples that disprove the 'grazing prevents blazing' theory, cattlemen and brumby supporters cling to it like the last snow patches of January cling to the south-eastern slopes of the Main Range, defying the midsummer heat. Supporters have a Plan B too: blame the parkies. Ignoring, often wilfully, the effects of climate change, which helped produce the hottest, driest summer on record in 2019–20, they argue that the fires were a result of mismanagement by National Parks. That seemed like a claim worth putting to the NSW Department of Planning, Industry and Environment, which manages Parks. Their response:

> The Independent Bushfire Inquiry Report determined the 2019–20 bushfires were caused by extreme weather and climate change, not elevated fuel loads.
>
> The Independent Bushfire Inquiry also cited research that finds: '... typical grazing practices have limited potential to alter fuel loads in native forests in ways that will significantly alter bush fire behaviour across the landscape'.
>
> The 2019–20 Fire Season involved over 11,000 fires – only 236 started in national parks.

That last point is important. Landholders adjacent to national parks will often blame Parks for enabling (through mismanagement) fires that impact their properties. In summers like the Black Summer of 2019–20, fires can start almost anywhere. And the idea that grazing animals like brumbies can mitigate the risk is like arguing that M&Ms keep tooth decay in check. It's something which would be really, really cool if it were true ... but it's not. The truth is that fire dynamics are complex, especially in the mountains. Leading expert on High Country fires, Dr Phil Zylstra of Curtin University and the University of Wollongong, has proven with mathematical modelling of millions of data points, as well as on-the-ground research, that areas of the Australian Alps that haven't burnt for the longest time are the least likely to burn in the immediate future. This might seem counterintuitive but, in simple terms, it's because scrubby bushes grow back in a thick and highly flammable state in the decade or so after a major fire, then thin out over time.

Mountain cattlemen used to burn their leases every year to promote fresh shoots, which gave them the sense that they were keeping the landscape trimmed like a well-kept beard, keeping large bushfires at bay. In actuality, they ended up making a scrubbier, more flammable landscape. They also caused terrible erosion, both by hooves and by the scars of too-regular fires on delicate soils. High Country grazing, romanticised in literature and cultural mythology, is in many ways some of the worst ecological vandalism ever wreaked upon Australia.

Another claim put forward by brumby advocates is that horses help prevent fires by making tracks through the landscape – known as pads – that act as natural firebreaks. Driscoll dismisses that one like a bushman swatting flies.

'Brumby pads or a bushwalking track through a snow grass area might stop a fire under mild conditions. But a mild fire is probably going to peter out anyway. Under conditions when it matters, when there's no humidity and the wind is 50 kilometres per hour or higher and there's been a drought for a year to two, a fire will leap over a two-lane highway.'

Leaving fires aside, what about the oft-repeated claim that brumbies help disperse seeds through their droppings?

'The idea that there is some benefit to horses spreading native species is laughable. Those species have evolved over thousands of years. They don't need horses.' Driscoll doesn't add, 'I mean, seriously, how stupid could you be?' but the tone of his voice suggests he might be thinking it.

In August 2020, Driscoll presented a webinar, simply entitled 'Feral Horses in the Alps', which tackled these and other furphies. One of the pro-brumby Facebook groups tried to sabotage it by flooding it with members. That's how much they hate Driscoll. In the brumby wars, the bloke has a target on his back. Partly that's because he takes the time to debunk junk science and irrelevant and/or overblown heritage claims. But it also stems from that episode up on the Rams Head Range. The phrase 'cannibal horses' brought him to the attention of people who've never much cared for scientists or paid serious attention to their work. One such person is Peter Cochran.

Cochran, though relatively short in stature, is a towering figure in the brumby wars and in the Snowy Mountains of New South Wales generally. The former three-term state member for Monaro and local mayor has a cattle property on the upper Murrumbidgee in a beautiful grassy valley called Yaouk (pronounced 'yayak' as in kayak), which is ringed by snow-capped peaks in winter, near where Kosciuszko National Park meets the southern border of the ACT. He also runs Cochran Horse Treks, on which paying customers are promised the chance to see brumbies. And when he's not running cattle, or horse treks, or his BUGSPRAY Facebook group, Cochran runs his mouth. This is perhaps his greatest talent.

'This type of academic terrorism undermines the credibility of the author and therefore the ANU, presumably at taxpayers' expense,' Cochran thundered in 2014, as the story of the cannibal horses gained traction.

In person, Cochran is just as combative. He litters his speech with phrases like 'corrupted scientific community' and 'politically influenced science' and 'perpetuation of bloody lies' and 'predetermined agenda'. There are numerous people like Cochran across Australia, landholders who would shake their heads in disbelief at Richard Swain's comment 'Show me the square millimetre where they looked after [the land]'. Farmers and cattle folk who'll tell you that they, and only they, understand land management, and that parkies with their green-left agenda are ruining things for everyone. But few are as bellicose as Cochran, or have the political nous, or are as well connected, or half as outspoken. And his followers love him for it.

As for Driscoll, he doesn't flinch when he's accused of 'academic terrorism', or when anyone on the brumby side of the fence calls him anything. Let them play the man, not the ball, in their game of political football, even if the man they're playing is him. He can take it. All the same, you can't help wondering whether he awarded the brumby supporters a free kick with the way he framed the cannibal horse incident. Did that phrase not invite them to question how much a man who believes horses eat horses could truly understand about ecology?

'We could see a horse eating a horse,' Driscoll says bluntly. 'And while some people have taken it out of context and jumped to the conclusion that we thought that horses were out there stalking other horses and tearing their insides out, that's not what we said. That's their interpretation.

'The video we made clearly says that what we saw was horses nibbling the edges and the insides of the open abdominal cavity. My only regret about that video is that I didn't link it more explicitly to animal welfare issues. If I made it again, I would add more to the story about how horses starve above the snowline. It's something that the horse people don't want to talk about.'

* * *

Tick, tick, tick, tick, tick, tick, tick, tick, tick …

That's the sound of the stopwatch on the TV show *60 Minutes*, ticking out to the ad break after an interview subject just said something unbelievably profound that condensed the whole segment into a few key words. It would be a mistake to think such grabs are easily obtained. It's incredibly rare that you put someone on the spot and out pops a succinct, pithy, perhaps even witty synopsis of an issue, and you pack up your gear and hit the pub for an early schnitzel and beer.

It would of course be lovely if things happened that way, but when you drive five hours from Sydney to Narooma on the south coast of New South Wales and sit down with Dr Alec Costin AM on the back porch of his rambling house, you soon realise you're going to be there a while. Which is fine. There are views across expansive lawns to Narooma's teal-blue Wagonga Inlet, there's baklava from the best Lebanese pastry store in Sydney, there's strong black tea, there's a hungry magpie warbling for its daily snack, and there's no real time pressure. So you might as well settle in and shoot that cool breeze wafting across the inlet.

Besides, it is an honour to be in Costin's company. The pioneering soil scientist is the godfather of Kosciuszko ecology. His groundbreaking work on ground that was well and truly broken led to grazing eventually being phased out in the NSW Snowy Mountains. The Australian Academy of Science describes Costin as 'an international authority on the ecology of high mountain and high latitude ecosystems'. Deirdre Slattery and Graeme L Worboys describe his legacy with considerably more panache in their book *Kosciuszko: A Great National Park*:

> For ecological scientists, the mountains are a 'storehouse of evidence' of the natural history of the continent. This treasure trove had barely been touched until Alec Costin's research and resulting report in 1954 established primary descriptions of the vegetation communities and soil types of the Monaro region. Doing this was like setting down the warp and weft in a richly patterned carpet: these

underlying threads hold the carpet together – an essential foundation supporting a beautiful and complex design.

In a sense, the *60 Minutes* line writes itself here. Costin brought to a nation's attention the terrible damage that hard-hoofed grazing animals inflicted upon the humus soils of Kosciuszko. Those soils are far richer than similar soil types in most of the world's montane regions, supporting 212 flowering plants and ferns, 21 of which are endemic. Costin catalogued them in his most famous work, *Kosciuszko Alpine Flora*, published in 1979. His life's work was documenting the ecological wonderland of Kosciuszko, protecting it, restoring it. Getting sheep and cattle removed was key to that. That was in the mid-20th century. Yet here we are in the third decade of the 21st century and brumbies are undoing all his work, and the work of many of his colleagues. Can he believe it? And how does it make him feel? A good line or two in response to those questions and we've got our grab. *Tick, tick, tick, tick, tick, tick, tick, tick, tick* …

But here's the thing. Almost a century of High Country history is ensnared in the steel trap of Alec Costin's mind. So many names. So many places. So many jobs. So many bosses. Though Costin is 100 per cent lucid, his mind meanders like a mountain pathway. He's telling you how he became a soil scientist after a school visit by senior public servants, then he's off on a tangent about some old bloke called Tom or Clancy or whoever. And though the names sound like they've been drawn from a hat of typical 1950s Aussie bloke names, they all turn out to be *really* important people. The effect that Costin had on those people, both personally and politically, was remarkable.

One of them was the late Sir Garfield Barwick, a minister in the second Menzies government and later Chief Justice of Australia for 17 years. Barwick was a skier and High Country lover who served as a trustee of Kosciuszko State Park for 20 years from its creation in 1944. He was neither pro- nor anti-grazing to begin with. A dose of Costin charm and persuasiveness changed all that. 'Barwick was a key person because of his status, and he was always negative, he wasn't satisfied with the evidence of damage. Because of his legal background, he had to be convinced. He was always saying, "You've got to prove it."' Costin recalls.

The first place where grazing had been banned after the creation of the state park was the Main Range. Cattlemen had set fire to the coarse snow grass each autumn and early spring, but the grass on the highest peaks had never previously burnt, nor had it been eaten or trampled by ungulates. It bears repeating that small native mammals were the heaviest animals to graze above the tree line before Europeans arrived. Under the weight of sheep and cattle and the wax matches that stockmen used for lighting fires, the landscape collapsed. Denuded, rocky slopes replaced alpine meadows. Delicate high alpine streams became erosion ditches. You could have fought a war there and left it looking better.

But within a few years of grazing being banned, the land showed signs of recovery. In his role as a member of the Kosciuszko State Park Advisory Committee, Costin escorted Barwick on a trip from the summit of Kosciuszko through to the valley of Whites River and a high peak called Gungartan, about 30 kilometres to the north-east, where grazing was still happening. 'It was so obvious how the grass was coming back,' Costin says. 'And as we went along towards Whites River Hut and Gungartan, you couldn't see the new grass at all because they were still grazing in that area. Barwick couldn't deny the evidence. From then on, he was against grazing.'

One of the things that helped sway Barwick was a delicate flower with semi-translucent white petals – the anemone buttercup. A painting of that very flower holds pride of place in Costin's home today, the artist his second wife, Beryl. His discovery of a large patch of anemone buttercups on the trip with Barwick was incredibly significant, as it was one of the plants that cattle had almost eaten out of existence. 'Well, okay, this is getting to the crux of the matter,' Costin enthuses when you ask him about the selective grazing preferences of cattle. 'See, you and I or anyone with a good appetite for food, we just pick what we want. And that's exactly what animals do. They are highly, highly, *highly* selective grazers. So much of the alpine and subalpine vegetation is unpalatable, but then there are the ice cream plants.'

Costin often uses the term 'ice cream plants' in his published works. It refers to plants high on the Main Range whose leaves cattle and sheep would devour before anything else. Examples include billy buttons, a gorgeous long-stemmed perennial with tightly bunched globular yellow flowers, and alpine celery, a sprawling herb with stems like celery stalks. But if one particular ice cream plant was a rich Belgian chocolate flavour, then it was the anemone buttercup, the near extinction of which was a largely undocumented ecological catastrophe. The anemone buttercup mostly grows near late-melting snow patches, relying on their icy trickles to flourish. This makes it an unbelievably improbable plant in the Australian context. Name another plant on the world's flattest, hottest continent that relies not just on snow, but on summer snow. And cattle were eating it like hay.

Sir Garfield Barwick saw the anemone buttercups and understood. And you have to ask: would today's version of Sir Garfield Barwick accept such evidence? Would a politician on the conservative side of the fence (as Barwick was) be moved by a flower? Costin even moved a politician to tears on one of his tours across the recovering Main Range. His name was Clancy Kingston and he was the mayor of what was then called Monaro Shire. 'Bloody Clancy was tough as nails,' Costin says. 'But I took him out on the range and he started weeping. He was a dyed-in-the-wool grazier and he said, "Alec, I've never seen the country look so beautiful."'

As a soil scientist, Costin did stints with both the NSW Soil Conservation Service in Kosciuszko and the Victorian Soil Conservation Authority on the Bogong High Plains. But his focus was as much on water as soil. He talks at length in his circuitous way about the miraculous hydrology of Kosciuszko, and how hard-hoofed animals destroy its drainage lines, bogs, and the subtle substrate network of springs that ensures water flows regularly in all seasons. 'Water can be regarded as a crop,' he wrote in 1957 in 'A Report on the Condition of the High Mountain Catchments of NSW and Victoria', published by the Australian Academy of Science. That crop was in the process of being harvested by the Snowy Mountains Hydro-Electric Scheme, construction of which had begun in 1949. Decision-makers took notice. Why undertake the largest engineering project in Australian history – a project relying on a steady inflow of pure mountain water – if the quality and quantity of that water was compromised? Thus did economic concerns lead to a full grazing ban not just on the Main Range but, eventually, across Kosciuszko National Park. It was a bit like arresting Al Capone on tax evasion, but no matter. Costin's tireless ecological advocacy and field work had done the trick.

If Alec Costin sounds like some sort of ecological Superman, swooshing through the mountains in a green Lycra suit, converting cattlemen and politicians and anyone he met into staunch environmentalists, it should be noted that his successes were hard-won and the hours he worked were long. In the mid-1950s, when working for the CSIRO, he was stationed at the temporary Snowy Hydro scheme town of Island Bend, just downstream from Guthega. Each day, he would rise well before 5 am. His first job was to handwash the nappies of five of his six young children, allowing his wife, Margaret, some precious sleep-in time before her long day of childcare. He'd then take his pack – which today is housed in the National Museum of Australia – and drive his old Land Rover up past Charlotte Pass to begin his day's work on the Main Range. In this phase of his working life, he wasn't just chronicling the damage as a scientist; he was actually helping to repair it, stabilising precious slopes one straw bale and roll of wire mesh at a time. It was Costin who discovered that the high alpine plants are sensitive to the zinc in the galvanised iron that prevented the mesh rusting. Today, the immensely popular untreated steel mesh walkway from Thredbo to Mt Kosciuszko is heavily rusted, all thanks to the wind, snow, rain, and Alec Costin's work. His legacy in the mountains is everywhere.

But the man also had his failures and his enemies. He never came close to establishing a cordial working relationship with the prominent cattleman Tom Barry, or with Peter Cochran. His first run-in with Cochran was back in the day, when Costin's old boss in the Soil Conservation Service, Sam Clayton, sent him up to the Cochran family property to borrow a horse for a few days' work in northern Kosciuszko. 'I arrived there and round the stockyard, there were blokes all over the place,' Costin says. 'I couldn't work it out. And there was a bloke much younger than I was, who looked like he was in knickerbockers. That was Peter Cochran. So they had this horse standing and I was to take delivery of it. And as soon as I put my foot in the stirrup, that bloody horse just took off like a jet. It was a set-up and everyone had been waiting for it. It was sheer good luck that with one foot in the stirrup I was able to swing myself over and put the other foot in the stirrup.'

Cochran, 20 years younger than Costin and possibly too young to remember the incident clearly, does not accept this version of events today.

'That is a blatant fucking lie!' he says. 'And that's why Alec Costin wrote the books that he did, he was a fabricator.

'Almost every book he wrote about the ecology of the park – we've got a whole string of students that have been through universities using AB Costin as the basis of their studies, and you've got this perpetuation of bloody lies. I would never do that to anybody, I've never had AB Costin on my property ever. Nobody bloody liked him. Costin is a bare-faced bloody liar!'

Cochran's reaction illustrates the animosity certain mountain folk hold towards scientists perfectly. The scientists don't have to go out on a limb as Don Driscoll did; merely doing their job is all it takes. Reading Costin's works, you can see how he cultivated enemies. He called grazing 'exploitative'. He argued that it made no economic sense because even tiny reductions in water yields played havoc with the economics of the hydro-electric scheme. But Costin also showed compassion. He suggested compensation for a small minority of cattle families. He wasn't out to hurt anyone. But to him, Kosciuszko always came first. It still does.

He's actually quite the pessimist when it comes to the future of the mountains, and the world generally, is old Alec. 'We're like a lot of mountain cattle, getting more and more numerous, just overrunning the beautiful environment,' he says as he reaches for his third piece of baklava. His daughter Acacia Rose, also an accomplished ecologist as well as a Thredbo-based backcountry adventure guide, said he had a sweet tooth. She was right. 'And people don't give a damn about the beautiful environment. It's all about whether they've got a TV to switch on. I think the human race is going down the drain in a big way.'

Eating baklava on the back porch with Alec Costin while pelicans hover above the docking fishing boats, you feel grateful that the human race hasn't slid all the way down the drain yet, even if we're clinging to the metal grille. 'You can see the pecking order there,' Costin says, gesturing towards the pelicans. 'There are a couple of bosses always at the front, the tailenders at this end, the ones in the middle are getting pushed around a bit. So many memories ... I hope we get some rain ... The woman next door is feeding the local sea eagle ... Can you see the sea eagle? Do you see those ripples? That's a big wave that's come through. These things are happening all the time and one never thinks to notice them.'

Alec Costin's 95-year-old scientific eye sees more than most. He's three kilometres from the open ocean, but the shape and size of ripples on the glassy inlet at the foot of his garden tell him what's happening way out at sea. His work in Kosciuszko did something similar. From studies of soil and alpine flora arose a much bigger story of a landscape ravaged. The ripples of Costin's life work continue to be felt in Kosciuszko today.

But what about the big question: are the brumbies undoing it all? Costin will offer no *60 Minutes*–style answer to that question. Not that he needs to. Some things are implicit. And anyway, it turns out he wrote his answer in his preface to the Kosciuszko Science Conference on Feral Horse Impacts:

It took a long time – 26 years – and millions of dollars to heal the soil erosion in the summit area. This was a big cost to the community that should have been avoided. In the stock-free Kosciuszko National Park, I have personally witnessed its gradual recovery, though some of it will take generations to heal to a stable state. Kosciuszko was on the mend: the catchments were healing and ecologically based catchment management was being implemented.

So why change this? Why legislate through the *Kosciuszko Wild Horse Heritage Act 2018* in favour of a known agent of environmental damage to the mountain catchments, the feral horse, undoing 75 years of catchment-healing investments by multiple governments? Thousands of feral horses will continue to impact water catchments and water delivery of national economic importance for so many people downstream. Endangered Australian species will also be impacted. There is a need to repeal this regressive Act.

Tick, tick, tick, tick, tick, tick, tick, tick, tick ...

* * *

'I hope you're sitting down.'

David Watson, Professor of Ecology at Charles Sturt University, has a truth bomb to drop, and wants to make sure the blast force doesn't blow you away.

Watson is no stranger to dramatic announcements. In 2018, after John Barilaro's Kosciuszko Wild Horse Heritage Bill passed, he protested by quitting his position on the NSW Threatened Species Scientific Committee, which he had held since 2015. He didn't just hand in his ticket quietly: Watson penned a letter to then NSW Environment Minister Gabrielle Upton. 'Clearly, our advice has been ignored and I can no longer continue to justify committing my time, energy and professional insight,' part of his letter read. Its final line said:

The wilful disregard that you and your government colleagues have for science diminishes our collective future, relegating our precious national parks and priceless environment to political playthings.

He then posted his full letter on Twitter and sat back and watched as all hell broke loose, which was exactly what he'd hoped would happen.

Watson first heard rumours about the proposed legislation only a few weeks before it was tabled. Normally, there would be rumblings for months or even years about a proposed law of such magnitude, but it blindsided the majority of the scientific community. When a colleague said to Watson, 'Oh God, have you heard what the Nats are doing?' his response was 'Really? Nooo. That's not real. That can't be real.' But it was real, and as Watson explains, he was incensed. 'I talked to the chair of the committee, Marco Duretto, and said, "Listen, mate, in good conscience I can't continue contributing to this forum if this gets up. Do you see a problem with me resigning publicly if this bill is supported?" We had a good chat about it, and in a follow-up phone call he said, "Look, I'd be thrilled if you did."

'Then, blow me down, the bill not only gets up but it's unanimous. The environment minister speaks in strong support of it, and I'm like, "Fuck that. That is fucking bullshit. I am not. Cannot. Nope. No."'

Watson lives in Burrumbuttock. You read that right: Burrumbuttock. It's a one-pub, one-shop map speck in the Riverina region of New South Wales, about a 25-minute drive north of Watson's university campus in Albury, which

Watson reckons is just the amount of time he needs to take off his husband/dad/woodworker hats and put on his professor/ committee member/mentor hats. The Burrumbuttock area was originally native grassland and box eucalypt country. Now, it's some of the most productive agricultural country in Australia that's not irrigated, with a predominance of wheat, canola and sheep farms. 'That productivity used to generate birds, quolls, possums and dragons. Now it generates oilseed, fibre, and cheap protein for humans,' Watson says.

Watson lived in Albury when he started at Charles Sturt. Then one day he was invited to give a talk at a place called Wirraminna Environmental Education Centre, a small area of restored bushland in downtown Burrumbuttock. He basically never left. Watson and his American wife, Maggie, bought an 1890s mudbrick house on acreage across the road from Wirraminna and have created their own little slice of paradise. These days, Watson regularly posts pics on Twitter of Burrumbuttock sunrises and sunsets and trees and ducks – huge flocks of ducks waddling right past his front door that seemingly stretch halfway back to Albury. He also posts daily pics of what he calls his #AquariumOfUnusualSize, which sits right in the middle of his living room. The aquarium takes up so much interior space, views of the outside world are filtered through it. Life seen through nature. There could be no better analogy for Watson's world view.

Back in 2018, as he agonised over his position on the NSW Threatened Species Scientific Committee with the passage of the Wild Horse Bill looming, Watson called an impromptu family meeting. 'I was sitting in the TV room next to an open fire, wrestling with it. My two older boys were still awake, the youngest asleep. I said, "This is what's on my mind, I'm not too sure where to go from here. Am I better to suck this one up and learn from it and just keep chipping away because that's the right thing to do and apply my knowledge to this important public process? Or do I say, 'No, no, no. Line in the sand, I can't continue'?" I wasn't convinced either way. I was unhappy with both outcomes. I didn't want to fall on my sword, I didn't want to make a big spectacle about it, but then I thought if I did, it could call attention to this and help catalyse the public to go, "Ooooh, that's not right." That was probably the clincher, that's what Maggie really convinced me of. She said, "If you're going to do it, you're going to do it publicly.'"

Scientists don't often make overtly political statements on their own. It's one thing for 14 scientists to condemn the wild horse legislation on Australian Academy of Science letterhead, or for 90 of them to sign the Kosciuszko Science Accord. Safety in numbers and all that. Watson was taking a huge risk by posting his complete and utter disdain for the government's actions on social media. It was the sort of act that could threaten his future job prospects, his ability to secure grants, his very credibility. But screw all that. A man has his principles. He also had the blessing of both his wife and the chair of the NSW Threatened Species Scientific Committee.

'You have to understand, the committee speaks with one voice and they do it in a very formulaic way,' Watson explains. 'Any committee business has to go through the chair, then through various channels, then through the minister's office before it's released for public comment. So whenever controversial things pop up, the committee is a completely toothless tiger. It cannot bite at all. So the only way, really, for this to get out was for someone to go, "Nup, I'm taking my footy, I'm going home and I'm letting you all know why."'

Watson sent out his tweet in the morning, forgot about it because he wasn't hugely into social media back in 2018, and got on with his busy day. That night, he checked in on Twitter. 'Ooh, that seems to have struck a nerve,' he said to himself. Apart from one or two messages calling him a coward, the response was overwhelmingly positive. Doubtless the lack of vitriol was partly because brumby supporters tend to live on Facebook rather than Twitter, but still. Watson was even contacted directly by several self-described 'horsey people'. 'They were universally praising,' he says. 'They said, "Thank you, thank you, thank you. We love horses, we love the High Country, we love enjoying the High Country, but we're in fierce agreement with you that feral horses have no place in a gazetted national park." That took me aback.'

Watson tweeted the next day that the positive response showed that people care about the role of science in society, and about the need to base policies on evidence, not emotions. He later wrote a piece for *The Guardian Australia* about the episode. Its last paragraph contained a stinging slap to those who would base land management decisions on the literary fictions of Banjo Paterson:

Putting horses, mountains and the complexities of feral animal management to one side, this issue brings into very sharp focus the disdain our government shows for science.

Being a 'clever country' necessarily involves listening to our scientific community. If governments continue to ignore considered advice from the very panels they sanctioned specifically to give them considered advice, a lesser Australia awaits. An Australia where sharing quiet moments with your kids, wading along a crystal clear mountain creek, is no longer possible. Our rivers fouled, our mountains choked with weeds. Maybe they'll tell stories about that instead. Or write poems.

Watson is the first to point out that he is not a trained expert in Australian alpine ecology – his specialty is mistletoes – but he has spent plenty of time up in Kosciuszko and the Bogong High Plains. He fell in love with the High Country on a Year 7 trip, more or less forgot about it as he worked in the tropics in Central and South America, and the red deserts of outback Australia, then renewed his love affair from Burrumbuttock. One day, he was driving along the Snowy Mountains Highway, which cuts diagonally from his part of the world to the NSW south coast via northern Kosciuszko. 'The light was gorgeous so I stopped to get a picture,' he recalls. 'Sunlight on looming rain clouds, an ashen sky, sunlit snow gums, and I was like, "Oh this is a moment."'

Watson pulled over, stretched his legs, and there they were. 'Bloody horses! And I was like, "What?" And all the pugging, all the marks on the ground. And this wasn't some spot where I'd stopped expecting to see horses, it was just some random roadside spot. And I had a look at the grass by the road and I thought, "Gosh, you're up against it, you're just hanging on, you're a deep-root perennial. It's late autumn and you're basically on hold right now, and here are these hungry mouths." That's bullshit. That is not cool. Just at a time when plants are straining to survive, they get smashed. And this was just one random moment of many.'

David Watson, like Don Driscoll, believes it his responsibility to speak truth to power as part of being a scientist. 'Yes, I'm a scientist; yes, I do communicate my own science and the science that I think warrants a broader view.' Also like Driscoll, Watson has no hesitation trashing junk science. He knows enough about High Country ecology to understand that horses are no good for it, and he knows a myth worth busting when he hears one. The old 'grazing prevents blazing'?

'That one really sticks in my gob.'

What about the idea that brumbies are good for the High Country because they disperse seeds?

'I'm happy to call that out and say that it is utter, unadulterated, ocean-going, fur-lined garbage.'

If everyone in Burrumbuttock speaks so colourfully, it must be a hell of an entertaining place at closing time in the pub. But back to Watson.

He had something important to say at the start of this, something best heard while sitting, not standing. Hit us with it then, Dave; let the cat out of its ocean-going, fur-lined bag.

'Okay. This might be a mind-blowing moment, but the reason I get up in the morning, the reason I do what I do, is to maximise the raw material of biodiversity for after humans have gone.'

Um, what? What do you mean *after* humans have gone?

'Oh, we're fucked. There's no tiptoeing around that. We're in freefall now. We are over the precipice. If you were to wave a magic wand and fix every environmental issue we've ever made, we'd still be in freefall. So let's just look a little bit down the road. We're doing everything we can to accelerate our own demise, so what motivates me is to maximise biodiversity for whatever comes next once humans are gone.'

Hang on. We're not even fighting for a fingerhold anymore? We're gone? We're talking about whatever comes next?

'And, specifically, how will I know if I've been successful? If mistletoes outlive humans, that's how. And that's what motivates a lot of the science I do. If I do my job properly, mistletoes have a long, rosy future and we won't consign them to the fossil record.'

Speaking of records, let the record show that Watson doesn't hate horses. Quite the opposite. 'People say to me, "Oh you scientists, you just hate horses." Not true! We've got a horse, OK? I don't hate horses, I love horses! They're a special, worthy intelligent animal that's super important in the story of the human species. But not up there. Anywhere else, pretty much. Go for it, fill your boots. But not on the rooftop of Australia that's already dealing with a litany of issues. This is one lever we can pull. We can pull the no-horse lever.'

In conversation with Watson, it's clear that the brumby issue stuck in his craw because it was one of those moments when the inevitable demise of the natural world was unnecessarily pushed one step closer thanks to a lever pulled by John Barilaro.

And if you speak to John Barilaro, he'll tell you exactly what he thinks of people like David Watson, Don Driscoll and Alec Costin, or any scientist.

'The scientists have got their head up their arse, mate … Mr Flannery, he said our dams would never be full. You know the only fool here is Flannery.'

CHAPTER SEVEN

SHIFTING THE GOALPOSTS

A lot of people have called NSW Deputy Premier John Barilaro a lot of things, but for creativity and sheer volume of insults, comedian and journalist Jordan Shanks surely takes the cannoli. Shanks, better known by his performance name friendlyjordies, released a 27-minute YouTube video called 'bruz' in September 2020. In it, he ridiculed Barilaro, including for his brumby legislation: 'If he's stupid enough to pass that, he'd be stupid enough to pass a bill preserving the lice on his head. Brumbies are basically majestic rabbits.'

The 'bruz' video has now been viewed over 700,000 times. That's comfortably more viewers than the combined nightly audience for the 6 pm news on the leading commercial TV network in Sydney or Melbourne. Friendlyjordies has reach that most journalists can only dream of. Attitude and delivery too. He's also got many admirers in the mountains. And 'bruz' was by no means his first swipe at Barilaro. The war of words had started months earlier when Shanks called Barilaro and

NSW Premier Gladys Berejiklian koala killers. The duo were portrayed as the characters Mario and Luigi from the iconic Nintendo Super Mario Bros. video game series, stomping on koalas and killing them. Barilaro was none too happy with the accent in that video, calling it offensive and racist. So Shanks doubled down on both the mock-Italian accent and the slurs in 'bruz'. Barilaro took defamation action. It was a legal shot-over-the-bow which effectively warned Shanks to stop defaming him.

'He doesn't dispute the content of the video,' Shanks says. 'There are all these lines in my video saying he's responsible for destroying natural habitats for 27 species ... and he's not disputing any of that in his letter!'

Will it shock you to learn that Shanks brings out his finest Bruz accent while paraphrasing Barilaro's words? He can barely stop himself. He may not even realise he's doing it.

It's pretty much pistols at dawn between Barilaro and Shanks now. You might even say it's pizzas at dawn, and you might even go so far as to surmise that Shanks reckons Barilaro can go focaccia himself. And if you think these gratuitous Italian cultural references are in bad taste, you've probably got a point. However, if you feel that Shanks is straying into racist territory by lampooning the man born Giovanni Domenic Barilaro in Queanbeyan in 1971, the son of Calabrian immigrants, consider this: Shanks is not mocking Barilaro's ethnicity for its own sake. 'He's styled himself as Giovanni when he needs to be, as a bushie when he needs to be,' he says. 'But there's nothing bush about him at all! He's so much more at home in Rushcutters Bay than in Cooma. Nothing about him rings bush.'

That may be so. Barilaro's family home is in Jerrabomberra, basically an upmarket housing estate between Queanbeyan and the ACT border. If he ever made the oft-mooted switch to federal politics, which ironically could be possible thanks to the national profile Shanks has helped him attain, he could drive to work at Parliament House in about 15 minutes. But while his roots are suburban, John Barilaro has friends in the bush. Friends of expediency rather than soulmates, perhaps, but you take any friends you can get in politics. And he made legions of new friends at the 2019 NSW state election, when he won 25,868 votes, or 52.31 per cent of the primary vote in the seat of Monaro. He first won the seat by a narrow 2.1 per cent in 2011, the year the NSW Coalition ended Labor's 16-year reign. In 2015, he clung to power with a still skinny 2.5 per cent. In 2019, his margin blew out to an almost untouchable 11.6 per cent. Nowhere was he more dominant than in the Snowy Mountains. And when you meet him, he makes no secret of the fact he's extremely bloody proud of that.

'Jindabyne is my strongest booth. I got 70 per cent of the vote and that's where a lot of the National Parks staff live,' he says. To be precise, Barilaro won 65.61 per cent of the two-party-preferred vote in Jindabyne. But close enough. The man is locally popular despite all the parkies and greenies who would rather hard-boil their eyeballs than vote for him. No prizes for guessing the issue that has endeared him to locals. 'The community have this connection to these horses regardless of whether they're referred to as pests or not,' he says. Like Elyne Mitchell's silver stallion Thowra, who defeats all challengers with cunning, speed and might, John Barilaro has become king of the mountains. And it's good to be the king.

In person, Barilaro is a relentlessly upbeat, chipper sort of character. Maybe it's the weather. You'd have to be a properly miserable bastard to not feel chipper as hell on a March morning like this, the first blue sky day after Sydney's prolonged rainy spell. The sun is streaming through the north-east window of his ninth-floor corner office overlooking joggers in The Domain, commuter ferries ply Sydney Harbour, and it's a good day to be alive. An even better day to be the second most powerful person in the great state of New South Wales, even if with great power comes a busy schedule. There was a Treasury meeting over breakfast and a flood relief crisis meeting is imminent. But first, there's that appointment his people made a few weeks back. Some bloke writing a book about the brumbies. Important issue, that. Better squeeze him in.

'How are ya, mate? Where would you like to start?'

At the beginning, thanks, John.

Barilaro seems like the sort of person you call John. You wouldn't call Premier Gladys Berejiklian Gladys, but her deputy is definitely a John. So, anyway, John, how did all this come about? Quite a few scientists have said they were blindsided by the Kosciuszko Wild Horse Heritage Bill when it was tabled in May 2018. Even some parkies were shocked when they woke up one morning and learned that brumbies were about to be protected by law. Did you pull this thing out of your back pocket on a whim, or was it a while in the works?

'Anyone that says they weren't aware of it is talking rubbish,' Barilaro says without pause. 'For anyone in National Parks to say, "Oh, I didn't see this coming," well, I'm going to call bullshit and I'll tell you why. I had plenty of conversations with people in the park in those early days, and they were well aware of what was occurring. We made it very clear that we were going to legislate the heritage connection or the cultural connection of those horses, that was made very public. And many in the National Parks Association and even the National Parks came out publicly against it, so they weren't blindsided, they knew exactly what was coming.'

Which is fair enough. Barilaro was hardly coy about his love for the brumbies of Kosciuszko in the years leading up to the drafting of the Wild Horse Bill. In 2015, amid media reports of a possible cull, he delivered an impassioned piece of oratory on the Floor of the NSW Legislative Assembly:

> I ask the House to picture this image: a beautiful stallion running wild and free, his muscles bulging with strength. When he stands up on his back hooves one is overcome by his grace and power. There is nothing quite like seeing a brumby in the wild. It is an absolute thrill.

And on he went. If you'd been playing brumby bingo, your card would have been stamped in about 30 seconds as Barilaro brought up the Light Horse, the Sydney Olympics opening ceremony, the Guy Fawkes cull, Banjo Paterson, the deer and pigs – all the usual associations and whataboutisms. People in the mountains had clearly schooled Barilaro well. But give the man credit: he also formed his own feelings for the brumbies. He knew and loved Paleface, the fine silver stallion on the cover of this book, and even went to visit him after the bill passed in 2018, as a sort of celebration/photo opportunity. Nobody can deny that John Barilaro was banging on about brumbies long before he introduced his legislation, so if anyone was blindsided by the first law in Australian history prioritising an introduced species over native species in a national park, it's because they weren't paying attention.

Besides, as Barilaro rightly points out, the legislation had its genesis long before he appeared on the political scene. It all began in November 2006, in the lead-up to the March 2007 state election, when a memorandum of understanding was signed by NSW Liberal leader Peter Debnam, NSW Nationals leader Andrew Stoner, and three horse riding groups – the Australian Horse Alliance (AHA), the Snowy Mountains Horse Riders Association (SMHRA) and the Snowy Mountains Bush Users Group (SMBUG), whose president at various times over the years has been Peter Cochran, which is why the Facebook group he sponsors is called BUGSPRAY. The MOU was primarily about the rights of recreational horse riders, advocating for broader recreational access for horse riders within national parks, nature reserves, state recreation areas, state forests, and other public land. But buried down on the third of four pages was a single bullet point, which read:

The NSW Liberal–Nationals Coalition will ensure that through appropriate Government departments and ministries that 'Brumbies' are recognised as part of the cultural heritage of New South Wales and through Statutory instruments and Plans of Management and in consultation with the Australian Horse Alliance and local horse riding interest groups this heritage is recognised and protected and appropriate viable populations are protected in reserve areas.

It read like a throwaway idea, a thought bubble. An ancillary concern at best. But it was the first documented suggestion of a political move to protect brumbies. Peter Cochran naturally urged his network to get behind the MOU, telling them in typically firebrand language that, 'The ALP in 12 years, influenced by extreme "greens", have prohibited horse riding in the majority of National Parks and Public Lands.

'My business future AND THE SECURITY OF OUR STAFF depends on a change of Government in NSW,' Cochran thundered, punishing the Caps Lock button. But change didn't come. Not for four more years, anyway. The Liberal–Nationals Coalition fared poorly in the 2007 NSW election, defeated by the incumbent Labor government, both overall and in the seat of Monaro. Seems like the promise to improve the lot of riders wasn't enough of a vote winner in the mountains.

Then in 2011 the Coalition took power in New South Wales after 16 years in the political wilderness. A fresh political face called John Barilaro won the seat of Monaro for the Nationals. 'From that moment onwards, we've been having the conversation and the debate around these horses,' Barilaro says.

On 5 June 2018, a day before the Kosciuszko Wild Horse Heritage Bill passed, Labor MP Michael Daley put a question to Barilaro on the Floor of the Legislative Assembly:

> My question is directed to the Deputy Premier, Minister for Regional New South Wales, Minister for Skills, and Minister for Small Business: Peter Cochran, a donor to the Minister for Regional New South Wales' election campaign, says he drafted the legislation relating to brumbies in the Kosciuszko National Park. Is this the same Peter Cochran whose business, Cochran Horse Treks, stands to profit from the passage of this legislation? Will the Minister table the form of draft bill that Mr Cochran says he prepared for him?

Barilaro ducked the question, and a follow-up question, changing the subject to the legacy of Guy Fawkes. But it was indeed the same Peter Cochran whose business stood to profit from the passage of the legislation. You'll recall that a major selling point for customers of his business is the near certainty of seeing wild brumbies. 'We ... ride out among the brumbies on Currango Plain to visit Mountain huts or the tops of Mountains,' his website says. Cochran's prints were all over the Wild Horse Bill, from his initial support of the MOU all the way through to the legislation itself. Cochran actually stated on Facebook that, 'The bill was originally drafted under instruction from myself by pro bono solicitor Richard Smallwood, long-time campaigner for horse riders and a member of Australian Horse Alliance'. That's right – former

Nationals state MP Peter Cochran, acting as a private citizen, instructed his solicitor to draft a bill which would become state legislation. This may or may not be how the Parliament of New South Wales was designed to work.

As for the matter of the donation to the National Party, which amounted to $10,000 from the Cochran family, Cochran says it was $5000 each from his wife and from himself. 'Barilaro wasn't even preselected. You can check the dates out. It was declared in the electoral commission. It's all there on paper. The dates, the whole thing. Check it out,' he says with a flourish of his hands. Interestingly, he offers this nugget of information in response to a question that wasn't even about the money.

The question of political donations is of serious public concern, particularly where concerns might be raised that the job of governing might be unduly influenced to favour the interests of donors.

Barilaro's thoughts? 'No, not at all, mate. I owe Peter Cochran nothing. My career is my doing, I've worked my arse off ... People think somehow I'm in Peter's pocket. Yes, he made a donation to the National Party in 2011 before I was actually elected because he was a former member and a successful businessman who was campaigning for the party ... And people will say, "But that has influenced decisions around the legislation", which is garbage, right? Firstly, it was legal. He's entitled to support in a democratic process whoever he bloody wants, right?'

The relationship between Cochran and Barilaro is actually quite nuanced and complicated. 'We haven't always agreed,'

Barilaro says. 'Is he passionate? Yes. But that doesn't make him always 100 per cent right. But you know what? I respect people that are vocal, and sometimes Peter helps the argument, and sometimes he hurts the argument.'

If Cochran is argumentative, the genius of John Barilaro is that he *is* the argument. Now, a word like 'genius' might be anathema to friendlyjordies, or anyone who wears a lyrebird arm patch to work, or indeed any member of the public who'd like to see Australia's most ecologically significant and fragile inland national park without horses. But there's no denying Barilaro has worked the brumby issue to his advantage like a pro by keeping himself at the centre of it. Getting the legislation through was just the beginning. Since then, he has masterfully shifted the heritage goalposts, broadening the portrayal of brumbies from symbols of the grazing era in the High Country to icons of Australiana. He has even – in a brilliant outflanking of the political left – turned them into avatars of multiculturalism.

'My parents migrated to this country, right? And the mountains represent something very special to us ... It's the melting pot for multiculturalism, right? Go to Cooma, go to Jindy. That's what I love about the region. It's who we are. The Australian migrant story is absolutely captured in the Snowy Scheme and it's a positive story.'

This is true. The mountains are one of regional Australia's multicultural hotspots. Of the 100,000 workers who built the Snowy Scheme, more than 65 per cent were migrants from 30 different countries. Many remained after construction finished in 1974 and to this day, their descendants carrying

European surnames can be found throughout the mountains. So here's where Barilaro is going with this: the brumbies are the four-legged equivalent of the migrants who made their home in the mountains, and, like people from afar, they've become part of the fabric of the place. And that heritage deserves not just recognition but protection.

'There are a whole lot of introduced species in our landscape – brumbies, you name it – and that's the reality. But mother nature evolves, the environment evolves … If a brumby was a physical building, if it were bricks and mortar, there'd be protests out the front if they tried to pull it down because it represented a time 180 or 200 years ago. But because it's not, it's treated as a pest, let's shoot the bastards. And the same people that would be fighting for heritage on bricks and mortar are the same people that want to destroy our heritage brumbies.'

Heritage aside, the other way that Barilaro has made life exceptionally difficult for opponents of Kosciuszko brumbies is through some of the oldest political plays in the book: stalling. Obfuscation. Casting doubt on the facts with dexterity.

The *Kosciuszko Wild Horse Heritage Act*'s long title is 'to recognise the heritage value of sustainable wild horse populations within parts of Kosciuszko National Park and to protect that heritage'. It essentially enshrines the right of horses to exist in Kosciuszko, but that doesn't mean the wild mobs can just run free and multiply exponentially with no management. Even in the madhouse that is the NSW parliament, where they knock down perfectly good stadiums because … well, no one is quite sure why – yes, even at 6 Macquarie Street they still have standards, or something approaching them, when it comes to drafting the fine print of legislation. So even though the *Kosciuszko Wild Horse Heritage Act 2018* makes a mockery of the sections of the *National Parks and Wildlife Act 1974*, which state that parks exist for the 'conservation of biodiversity' and the 'maintenance of ecosystem function', the Act still has a few checks and balances, the main one being the requirement for a new plan of management to be implemented. Brumbies will be protected for heritage reasons, but their numbers must still be controlled.

But despite the gist of the legislation, a new management plan is nowhere in sight. A Community Advisory Panel and Scientific Advisory Panel were set up in 2018 to help formulate the new plan. After three years and many meetings, there's still no plan, Stan. So for now, Kosciuszko is still operating under the increasingly outdated 2008 Horse Management Plan, which allows for trapping and rehoming or trucking horses to the abattoir. However, virtually no horses have been trapped in Kosciuszko since 2016, when the draft plan Rob Gibbs and others worked on for three years was consigned to a small cylindrical filing cabinet underneath somebody's desk.

With Kosciuszko horse management effectively in limbo, Barilaro has talked the talk. At a public forum in Jindabyne ahead of the 2019 state election, he found himself in a room with a surprisingly large contingent of anti-brumby folk. Blowing with the breeze like any good politician, he boldly stated that his aim was a 50 per cent reduction in brumby numbers immediately. Hasn't happened. Hasn't come close to happening. 'He must have a different interpretation of the word "immediately" to the rest of us,' one activist says.

Meanwhile, aerial surveys of the entire Australian Alps show that horse numbers exploded in the five-year period between 2014 and 2019. Estimated numbers rose from 9190 in 2014 to 25,318 in 2019 – an increase of near 23 per cent per annum. As many as 19,000 of those horses were thought to be in Kosciuszko, with the majority in the north of the park where the elevated plains and loosely treed, gently undulating snow gum woodlands are perfect brumby habitat. Barilaro has frequently disputed the veracity of the count. So have all the brumby advocates in the mountains, not a single one of whom believes the Alps-wide number is anything remotely approaching 25,000. If bagging Dan Andrews is a favourite pastime among brumby advocates in the Victorian High Country, then contesting the horse count numbers is almost a full-time occupation for pro-brumby folk in the Snowy Mountains of New South Wales. The problem with the aerial survey data is it's difficult to explain how it's compiled and calculated. You can't just go *eeny, meeny, miny, moe* and count wild animals anywhere, let alone in mountainous, mostly treed terrain. In ultra-simple terms, the process involves helicopters flying along transects above the landscape. The animals counted along those transects are used to extrapolate the likely numbers elsewhere. To explain it in greater detail, you need brackets and little squiggly symbols and … forget it. Too hard to explain. And, therefore, all too easy for brumby advocates to dismiss. And despite the fact that the brumby counting technique is the same proven methodology used to obtain reliable estimates of wild animal populations the world over, brumby advocates say the numbers are pure parkie propaganda.

'It's not scientifically based but politically based because everybody who was involved in the count is anti-brumby,' Peter Cochran says of the semi-regular surveys, six of which have now been conducted since 2001. 'There is not one person anywhere in the whole process that is prepared to look at the practical aspects of the debate.'

For those seeking a breakdown of how the count works, the Australian Alps Cooperative Management Program does a good job of simplifying the methodology on its website. The Program is a small body jointly funded by the Federal, NSW, Victorian and ACT governments which deals with trans-border land management issues across the entire Australian Alps bioregion. One of its jobs is running the Alps-wide aerial surveys. The current head of the Program? None other than Rob Gibbs, who moved sideways within Parks after all the abuse he copped formulating the 2016 draft plan. The brumby issue seems to follow him. But then, there's no escaping it in the mountains these days.

John Barilaro has loudly demanded a recount on numerous occasions. There's always a good excuse for brumby advocates to demand a recount. The drought. The fires. The parkies have an agenda. It's Wednesday. And every time a recount is called for by Barilaro or anyone of standing in the mountains, doubt is cast over the survey numbers, and the army of brumby supporters on Facebook cry in despair that every last brumby is about to be wiped off the map because if we don't know the real number, how can we be sure that trapping and removing even a few hundred brumbies won't wipe out the whole herd? It's a ridiculous argument but then, abandon sense all ye who log onto Facebook. And so the horse management process remains stalled, like a snowmobile parked on a grassy ski run awaiting winter snows.

After the Black Summer fires, calls for a recount were, for once, justified. After the previous major blaze in the NSW Snowy Mountains in 2003, horses perished and the herds thinned out. Numbers were much smaller overall back then, but there was still a significant reduction. Who knew how many brumbies had been lost between the 2019 survey and the 2019–20 fires? Barilaro repeatedly advocated for a recount in the first few months of 2020. 'The brumbies perished in the fires and we need an urgent recount, simple as that,' he said. 'What does National Parks have to hide? What does the Environment Minister have to hide? A recount ends the battle. The facts will speak for themselves.'

It was far from Barilaro's first swipe at his own Energy and Environment Minister, Matt Kean, the man charged with implementing the new horse management plan. Kean is a small-l Liberal from Sydney's leafy upper north shore and no ally of Barilaro's nor of anyone on the pro-brumby side of the fence. The two Coalition heavy hitters have skirmished openly over environmental issues ranging from land-clearing to water management to brumbies. But their biggest brumby showdown came in mid-2020 after Kean gave the go-ahead for the trapping and removal of several hundred horses which had strayed into three sensitive new areas in northern Kosciuszko, after their regular haunts were burnt out in January 2020. A group with the extravagant name of the Snowy Mountains Brumby Sustainability & Management Group Incorporated, led by its president, Alan Lanyon, took the matter to the NSW Land and Environment Court. The State of New South Wales won – the trapping and removal could go ahead. Barilaro wasn't happy. Indeed, it's doubtful that any Deputy Premier of the State of New South Wales had ever been so displeased with a court case won by the State of New South Wales.

The court case was in July. In August, Kean surprised many by announcing on Sydney radio station 2GB that he would commission a recount. He was largely forced into this decision by the publication of a photo of old animal skulls, including some of horses, displayed outside a Parks depot in Jindabyne. In a classic political manoeuvre, he got on the front foot and turned bad news into good news, spinning the recount as a proactive, sensible move. Barilaro called the decision 'a win for our brumbies'. In truth, it was a win for both men. Barilaro could hold his head high, having achieved his precious recount, despite losing the battle of the post-fire horse removal. Kean had already established his pro-environment credentials by advocating for the emergency post-fire removal of horses, and now had a moral victory by appearing to be conciliatory. 'There are three very sensitive areas of the park where we want to manage some of the horses out,' Kean said. 'So we'll manage these sensitive areas ... but we'll do a full recount in the interim.'

The trapping and removal went ahead in late 2020. Several hundred horses were trapped – though, farcically, all pregnant mares or mares with foals were released back into the park, so the overall effect of horse removal was drop-in-the-ocean stuff. Then the recount happened, with the figures released in

January 2021. Post-fires, the number of horses in Kosciuszko was now estimated at 14,000, not 19,000 or thereabouts. 'We will always have wild horses in Kosciuszko but 14,000 is still too many,' Kean said. 'If we want to preserve this precious place and the plants and animals that call it home, we need to manage horse numbers responsibly.' Like Barilaro, Kean can talk a strong game, but he too is not always able to deliver. Where is the plan? Still no sign of it as this book goes to print. The process seems to have stalled.

Barilaro was also sending mixed messages after the recount. A petition from hardline NSW brumby advocates containing a relatively meagre 4231 signatures was put to the NSW parliament in March, calling for an end to horse trapping, culling and removal in Kosciuszko National Park, full stop. As mentioned, this was never the intent of Barilaro's legislation, yet it was soon revealed that the petition had been sponsored by none other than John Barilaro. Then, in a Budget Estimates Committee, Barilaro said he supported cutting Kosciuszko horse numbers by up to 10,000, which would knock the new estimated figure of 14,000 down to about 4000. Wait – does he want to manage horses or not? With his left hand Barilaro has swatted away the prospect of any reduction in horse numbers, while his right hand holds an olive branch with a number that would work for him. Help us out here, John.

'I've always said there was a figure around 3000, which most people believe was the right number,' he says. 'I've never backtracked. I was misquoted by the anti-brumby movement because they thought if they wedged me against my supporters, that'll play out later in a poll or in the debate. But I can make it clear to you my position has always been around the 3000 figure.

'The debate has been about this false number that was 19,000. Then we had bushfires, drought, all of that. And what we said was, "Let's have a stocktake". And to be able to come back and say there's 14,000, well, I would argue that it probably isn't 14,000. It's still probably exaggerated, but it's closer to the real number than 19,000. And that's why I welcomed those results, because they showed for the first time a reduction in 5000 horses from the previous survey. And remember, in the debate during the drought they were saying that the number of these horses was growing, like somehow they were unicorns and miraculously had a population explosion in the middle of the worst drought. I mean, you talk about science and data. These are the guys throwing that rubbish up at us, that's why I don't believe the scientists and the experts that have an ideological bent.'

That, right there, is pure John Barilaro. He's disdainful of science and scientists, like his mate Peter Cochran, but overall, he's a very different character. He wears a grin rather than a scowl, for one thing. He also knows there's a useful place in politics called the middle ground, and while he hardly gravitates towards it, he has been known to wind up somewhere near it, after posturing to his supporters. Barilaro actually cops abuse from his own supporters on social media when he talks of reducing horse numbers over time, yet he knows that whatever the eventual number, he will be remembered as the man who legislated to protect them. So he takes a little, gives a little. Blusters a little, listens a little. Digs in a little, compromises a little. 'I'm prepared to learn on the journey,' he says. 'I have changed my position on so many things in my political journey because I've actually engaged with the counter side, and that is actually being honest with yourself.'

Despite having welcomed the recount and the new estimated tally of 14,000 brumbies in Kosciuszko, Barilaro reckons the real number might be considerably lower. But he's willing to concede that there are probably still too many. 'Even if it was 10,000, most brumby supporters who are measured and balanced would say 10,000 is too many horses,' he says. 'So there is room to remove four or five or six thousand horses which should not cause any contention. Yes, there are those brumby supporters who don't want to remove any. Well, I'm not on their side.'

Irrespective of how many brumbies there are in Kosciuszko National Park and the rest of the Australian Alps, here's what we know with absolutely certainty: horse numbers have increased in recent years like never before. Even after the 2019–20 fires, there were still far more than in the days when cattlemen worked the mountains and habitually killed or removed them. Anecdotally, anyone who has walked or worked regularly in Kosciuszko over the last couple of decades knows there are now more horses. They're everywhere, and you don't need a helicopter or a PhD in algebra to tell you that. And if you really want to know how rapidly their numbers have grown within a generation or two, there's one person with a better handle on it than most.

* * *

Dave Darlington remembers the first time he set foot on the slopes of Mt Kosciuszko, back in the 1960s, when he was 11 or 12. In 1977, they would eventually close the road at Charlotte Pass, eight kilometres from the mountain, but before then you could drive straight through to Rawson Pass on the flank of the mountain. So the Darlingtons drove down from Sydney – a five- or six-hour trip these days which was more like two days on the rickety roads of the 1960s – and pulled up at Rawson Pass, right next to a huge snow drift. Summer snow drifts can be good fun for a spot of tobogganing, but they can also be frightening, with clefts and fissures in the stale remnant winter snowpack that look like mini-crevasses on a glacier. Young Dave's dad, who had never seen snow, warned his son not to walk on the drift in case he stumbled into a crevasse and was never seen again.

Some analogies write themselves. Dave Darlington would spend the bulk of his career in the National Parks and Wildlife Service in Kosciuszko, rising to the position of regional manager from 1999 until his retirement in 2013. And he spent every minute of that time watching his step, especially when it came to the contentious issues of wild horses.

Darlington first worked in Kosciuszko in temporary positions in the late '70s. 'Even then, it was obvious that some of the rural families were very antagonistic towards the Parks Service,' he recalls. 'They'd say, "Oh you work for bloody Parks." They had a view that their land or their cousin's land or their grandfather's land was "taken away" from them when the park was being established. But that negative feeling towards Parks had nothing to do with horses. Back in that time, some landowners saw the brumbies as a bit of a damn nuisance because they were putting pressure on their fences. I guess they viewed them in a similar way to kangaroos – the horses were eating their feed, the prime purpose of which was to support their cattle herd.'

As a young ranger in the mid-'80s, Darlington's patch was the area behind Thredbo through to the Victorian border – real Elyne Mitchell country. The first discussions about wild horse numbers started around that time. 'The issue didn't worry us greatly because we were still seeing what we thought were horses in relatively low numbers through the late '80s and into the early '90s, and there was a very dry period around 1987 to '88 with some big fires,' Darlington recalls. 'In the mid-'90s, we started to see noticeable impacts around the Ingeegoodbee River around Tin Mine Huts and down around Cowombat Flat, and by about 1997 we started noticing horses up on the Main Range above Thredbo. That wasn't good.'

To this day, even the staunchest brumby advocates concede that horses have no place on the Main Range. 'We noticed that just two or three horses would make lasting impacts in that true alpine area,' Darlington says. 'With horses in that true alpine zone above the tree line, it's a bit like someone going onto their local bowling green with football boots on. It's such delicate, soft ground up there. Sometime back when vehicles could still drive to Rawson Pass, someone tried to drive up Mt Etheridge [Australia's fifth-highest peak, just east of Kosciuszko]. Fifteen years later, you could still see the wheel tracks. So we became really concerned about that fragile alpine area where the heaviest native animal you ever see is the occasional echidna. The next heaviest is a copperhead snake.'

As the new millennium approached, Kosciuszko rangers had no idea of actual horse numbers, nor the capacity to do aerial surveys. But it was clear that horses had started to proliferate and spread. But why? Darlington reckons it was the combination of a few things. Some good rain years, a lack of other feral animals competing for grass – deer were virtually unheard of at the time – and the end of legal brumby running possibly played a small part, even though, as mentioned, Darlington would still find the piles of junk left behind by illegal brumby runners. Mostly, he puts the increase down to breeding. 'I was talking to a professor of equine studies and they were telling me that while the gestation period is 11 months, a mare can come on heat again a month after a foal is born. Some feral horses seem to have a foal every year, and while a lot of people say, "That's bullshit, it doesn't happen", even if they had one every second year, after 20 years a small group of horses can become very large. As an example, recently I camped on the Gungarlin River. Back in the year 2000, the population of horses in that area was about 18. Now, it's in the order of about 300.'

When Darlington was appointed regional manager of southern Kosciuszko in 1999, his staff told him they felt something needed to be done to control the horses. Darlington agreed. 'We looked at the option of doing a feral horse management plan for the whole of the park. My colleagues in the north said there were relatively few concerns there, so that first plan focused primarily on the true alpine area and the Pilot Wilderness area south of Thredbo. We worked with local people who could put out trap yards. Some of those locals worked as volunteers and some became paid contractors who were paid a certain amount per horse. In the early days, we held a great deal of hope. We thought if we could master this technique, we'd be able to manage the numbers. But as the years went by, it was like trying to bail out a boat with a teaspoon. The other thing we quickly realised is that the southern area of Kosciuszko National Park is so rugged, there are not many places you can drive a truck to. That made trapping and removal really difficult.'

By this stage, shooting was off the table as an option due to the events at Guy Fawkes River National Park, so the horse numbers just kept growing. There was virtually nothing Darlington and his team could do to stop them. By the early 2000s, Darlington reckons there were at least a couple of thousand and the impacts were increasingly worrying. 'Remember, some people today say they'd be happy if there were three or four thousand left,' he says.

Darlington bristles over the inadequacy of horse management methods that don't involve shooting. 'If you're going to have a big impact on pest management, you can't mess around at the edges by removing five per cent,' he says. 'You've really got to lower the numbers, otherwise within a few years, they're back.' Back, and then some. In good seasons, wild horse herds can reproduce at a rate of 20 per cent or higher. The surveys suggest that's what's been happening.

Because he's retired, Darlington is free to speak his mind. One of the changes that occurred towards the end of his time in the Parks was the muzzling of local parkies as communication became centralised through Sydney. 'As Parks officers, we were allowed to talk to the media,' he says. 'Bob Debus was a very considerate and sensible environment minister. He used to encourage us to talk about what we were doing. There wouldn't have been a week when one of our staff wouldn't have been talking to ABC regional or a local paper about park issues, whether it was fires or feral animals or restoring a mountain hut or a new walking track. We were encouraged to be a voice around the community. With the change of government in 2011 came a change of rules. This current government has silenced not just the Parks Service but the whole public service. These days, you hardly ever see a public servant on TV or radio. Governments like to hoodwink the public into thinking that the minister has done a thing when the bloomin' minister has done absolutely nothing except cut the ribbon.'

Darlington also laments the fact that the NSW government won't allow its staff to make comments if someone says something threatening or defamatory or plain wrong on social media. That's why Rob Gibbs copped so much flak while being powerless to do a thing about it. As for Darlington's views on John Barilaro, don't get him started. 'The time that our elected reps have in parliament is incredibly valuable. There are a whole lot of things that could be legislated, from people's education options to options for health care, to community safety, the list goes on and on. Those things are highly valued by the community, but to think that scarce parliament time was taken up by a bill to protect feral horses. Honestly, you've got to scratch your head and say, "Is that the sort of thing our government should see as a priority?" The same objective could've been achieved by having government direct a change in NPWS policy. You didn't need a brumby bill.'

Not that Dave Darlington would have welcomed such a directive in his day. Far from it.

'The area around Currango Plain in northern Kosciuszko is absolutely disgusting. It has been flogged to a dust bowl. You'd hang your head in shame if it was your own land. I never thought we'd see the numbers that we're seeing. It's just a horse paddock up there. And the streams throughout the park. What used to be pristine streams like the Ingeegoodbee, you'd swear someone had gone in with a plough where there used to be tall tussock grasses. I was never a fisherman but people would tell me there was always pretty good small trout in the Ingeegoodbee. Not anymore. It used to be fantastic broad-toothed rat habitat. Not anymore. It's just disgusting to see what has happened to that area. What used to be pristine bogs where the moss was a metre or more deep is now just mashed into a muddy pulp. And this is not just one or two spots. There must be many hundreds of kilometres of major and minor streams in Kossie that have had their banks trashed due to horses. When you start looking closely at areas heavily populated with horses, it's hard to see a square metre that hasn't got a hoof print on it. I see myself as a land manager and this is no way to manage land.'

A person looks back at their career and they have highs and lows, successes and failures. Dave Darlington is no exception.

But when he looks at Kosciuszko today, it's like a wound that won't stop bleeding.

'It's a real personal disappointment,' he says. 'I was a bloke in the year 2000 who said, "We've got a growing problem, let's start to do something about it." And all we've seen in 21 years is the problem get massively worse, and I mean *massively* worse. I've seen the politics creep into this more than it ever should have. Things like climate change are giving us enough challenges at the moment, you've got the rapidly growing problem of feral deer, and then they dump a major feral horse problem on top of everything. It's just a disaster. A disaster.'

* * *

Nev Barrass was 33 years old and had never been to the city. Or not into the heart of it, anyway. 'I was petrified,' the proprietor of Thredbo Valley Horse Riding says.

But there are times for a man to face his fears, and in August 2016, when the 2016 Kosciuszko National Park Draft Wild Horse Management Plan was open for public submissions, Barrass was one of 350 protesters who descended on Parliament House in Macquarie Street, Sydney, many of them on horseback. Peter Cochran and his Snowy Mountains Bush Users Group led the charge, and Cochran was the man quoted in most media interviews, expressing outrage at the recommended figure of 600 horses, as well as the potential to cull trapped horses on the spot, which were two of the details of the draft plan.

For Barrass, the day is all a bit of a blur. He rode William, his trusted chestnut half brumby, half thoroughbred, with two white socks and a white blaze. 'He's one of the most amazing horses that I've ever dealt with in my life. A beautiful boy.' Barrass had performed at arena shows on William, standing on his back and cracking whips, jumping through fire, all that sort of hoo-ha. Back on his property halfway between Jindabyne and Thredbo, he even skis behind William on occasion, with a special harness he has made. Horse stunts have never given him much cause for concern. But the city – that was a different story.

'I'm a bush rat,' he says. 'I'd never been in the city, or certainly never been that far in the city. Why would I go to the city when I've got this?' he says, gesturing towards Crackenback Peak and the subalpine bushland around him. It's far from the least sensible thing anyone ever suggested. But on that day in August 2016, Barrass had a reason to head to town. So he unloaded his horse down at Mrs Macquarie's Chair, where he saw the Sydney Opera House for the first time in his life, before riding up through The Domain then through what he calls 'the square where *Sunrise* is'.

Martin Place?

'Yep, and then straight up Macquarie Street with 350 protesters, and we stood outside Parliament House and had a good yell.'

Like the others, Barrass had turned up to protest the draft management plan. He says the disagreements he and other protesters had with the draft plan were 'vast and various', and he reckons it'd take him another couple of hours to run through them all. Spending a couple of hours in Nev Barrass's horse paddocks on a mild autumn afternoon is also far from the least sensible thing anyone ever suggested. He sits under a black sallee tree, its dappled bark nodding to every colour of olive in the supermarket deli section – yellowy-green, purply-black, classic olive-green and everything in between. He cracks open a couple of stubbies of cider. The sun shines. Horses munch hay. The wind can't be bothered. Ouch! Green ant bite! Never mind. One type of creature definitely not biting is the horses. Barrass keeps about 60 horses on his property. Many are rehomed brumbies or horses at least partly descended from brumby stock. There are maybe 30 in our vicinity this delightful afternoon. Like the weather, they are most wonderful, docile horses, though a couple are a little cheeky, sidling up for a bit of affection or nuzzling for one of the wild apples that Barrass stopped to pick from a roadside tree on his way home.

'You know when apple boy's coming, don't you? Gem, Gem, outta the way, love! Bubba, get outta the way. Thank you, darling.'

Nev Barrass and his wife, Linda, have no children but they basically have 60. The horses could ask for no better father. Barrass breaks in his own horses, though he shies away from the term. 'A traditional horse breaker would tie them up, strap a saddle on them, then get on them and kick the ears off them to stop them bucking. We educate them. If you go and break a brumby, you're an absolute moron because it'll never like you. Brumbies have grown up in a mob environment, so you've got to allow them the time to accept you. You can't force it upon them. You've got to form a relationship with them so they accept you as part of their mob.'

Nev Barrass is not a widely known member of the pro-brumby mob. That's because he tends to avoid the political side of things, give or take a Sydney rally. He's also too busy running his successful trail-riding business, which flourished during the COVID period of 2020 when the sort of people who normally went overseas for holidays sought domestic activities. But Barrass seems to sense he might be needed at some point. 'They've been fighting for 40 years and they're sick of fighting it,' he says of the long-term brumby campaigners. 'They've got a couple of little, tiny wins and thank God they did.'

You don't think the 2018 *Kosciuszko Wild Horse Heritage Act* was considerably larger than a 'tiny' win?

'Nothing has actually progressed from that.'

If Barrass becomes a more prominent spokesperson for the cause, they couldn't have a better man, not just because he loves working with his own domesticated brumbies and understands everything about the creatures from their bloodlines to their behaviour, but because he strongly supports their continued presence as wild animals in the mountains.

'I get goosebumps just thinking about the tradition of "The Man from Snowy River",' he says. 'The romance behind having brumbies in the mountains is something that is so ingrained in our history and in our culture,' he says. 'They're on the ten dollar note with Banjo Paterson, for crying out loud. No other country in the whole world has a feral animal on their currency.'

And when you're sitting in a paddock under the black sallee trees talking about Banjo's rivalry with Henry Lawson, and you mention how Paterson and Lawson basically traded barbs over their poetry in *The Bulletin* magazine back in the day – Banjo the romantic, Lawson the realist, each believing they were telling it like it really is – and you describe their rivalry as a sort of old-fashioned version of the rap battle in the Eminem movie *8 Mile*, Nev Barrass's bearded face cracks a broad smile, and he cracks another stubby of cider and the cracks in the brumby debate don't seem so wide after all.

* * *

The brumby folk aren't the only ones who can mobilise in protest.

Linda Groom is a Canberra-based retired librarian who has been walking in Kosciuszko since the 1970s and remains an active bushwalker. In the mid-2010s she had started seeing increasing horse damage in Kosciuszko and was wondering what she could do about it. 'I knew there was a problem, but I thought at that stage the government was going to fix it,' she recalls. 'The draft plan was a bit conservative but it was heading in the right direction.' And then the direction of the horse management debate pulled a massive U-ey. Groom had never been an activist of any sort but when John Barilaro pushed through his brumby bill in 2018, well now, that just felt like a book he had no business borrowing.

Groom wanted to protest – but how? As a member of bushwalking clubs, she knew how to lead walks. So she organised a 36-day, 560-kilometre walk all the way from Parliament House in Sydney to the summit of Mt Kosciuszko. 'I figure retired librarians can do anything,' she says.

The walk was quite the logistical and physical challenge. Five walkers trekked the whole way, but they were joined at various stages by many more. Support staff helped out with cooked meals and other necessities, and the walkers stayed in small-town pubs, in campgrounds and sometimes even on properties with the permission of the owners. They made it to the summit of Kosciuszko on a Saturday afternoon in reasonable weather and unfurled a banner. Its words were very carefully chosen: *Save Kosciuszko National Park From Wild Horses and Other Feral Animals.*

'We mentioned the other feral animals partly to avoid the "What about the deer?" line, and we used the words "wild horses", not "feral horses", because calling them feral horses shut people off from listening. We were gently trying to wean people onto the idea that wild horses were a problem.'

While Groom was on the walk, she got a call. A new group was forming to tackle the horse issue. She took a day off the walk and met with Richard Swain, his wife, Alison, and others. She was in. No convincing needed. Today, Groom is Reclaim Kosci's most dedicated volunteer. In the early days, she was putting in 60-hour weeks. These days it's more like 20 to 30 hours, all of it unpaid. One woman in a suburban Canberra home, giving everything she can to save Australia's most fragile and iconic inland national park. The Facebook comments are the worst. Groom has taken it upon herself to moderate comments on Reclaim Kosci's page. It's a tough struggle. Does she ever despair?

'No. I suppose I have a possibly innocent view that science and common sense will prevail in the end.'

Groom points out that in most environmental campaigns, environmentalists are pitted against some sort of economic argument, as is the case with climate change, or with a group trying to save a local park from a property developer who wants to put up apartments. 'Horses don't earn export income, they don't make Australia an innovative, clever country, they don't do anything,' she says. 'Lots of people say they earn a little bit of tourism money, but there are no studies to support that. But you could say that alpine wildflowers earn tourism money. This argument shouldn't be that hard, you know?'

And the cultural heritage claims?

'I don't think there's a cultural argument. There's a sentiment argument. Is there a difference? Yes. Culture is usually an agreed interpretation of the past by a community, and this is not agreed in any way.'

Defiant words. And Linda Groom has got some for John Barilaro too. 'I wonder if Mr Barilaro ever considered that it was his brumby bill that made me volunteer for Reclaim Kosci and decide never to stop?'

* * *

When you're 203 centimetres tall, or six foot eight inches in the old scale, aeroplanes are pretty uncomfortable places. And when it's hard to sleep on a plane, you get thinking time. So when Andrew Cox got thinking on a flight back to Australia after a year out of the country, it shaped the course of his life, and would also eventually help shape the fight over brumbies in Kosciuszko.

Cox had studied maths and computer science at university, and his first job was as a computer trainee for an insurance company. But his real passion was the natural environment. By the time he was five years old, Cox reckons he had 'climbed' Pigeon House Mountain – a distinctive, rocky pinnacle on the NSW south coast – as many as three times, riding in his parents' backpack. At Sydney Uni he joined the bushwalking club. A six-week trek through Western Australia's Kimberley region in his student years helped him realise that the outdoors was in his blood. In his soul too. To Cox, the natural world was more than a setting for adventure. It was a place of wonder and nourishment with its own intrinsic value.

In that plane, Cox realised that simply loving the outdoors wasn't enough. 'What am I giving back?' he asked himself. 'That's when I resolved that I would commit time to conserving the places I was visiting and enjoying.' The first step was a graduate diploma in environmental studies at Macquarie University. Then came volunteer work for the Wilderness Society, where he worked to save wilderness areas which he knew better than many of the seasoned campaigners. In his first paid job, with the National Parks Association of NSW, he wrote a brochure called 'Burning Questions' after Sydney's deadly 1994 bushfires. The brochure rebutted claims that environmentalists were responsible for the fires because they didn't support hazard-reduction burns. One of the loudest voices airing such misinformation was none other than Peter Cochran, then the member for Monaro, who was using the fires to whip up anti-environmentalist sentiment. It was not the first time and would be far from the last time Andrew Cox locked horns with Peter Cochran.

Their next clash came during Cox's first full-time job in the environmental sector in the late 1990s, when he was working for the wilderness unit of the NSW National Parks and Wildlife Service. Bob Carr had been elected NSW premier in 1995 with a promise to increase the number of national parks as well as the area of designated wilderness in New South Wales. Cochran, sometimes wearing his horse rider's hat, but always with an antagonistic hat the size of a sombrero, was one of the chief opponents of wilderness. Cox had his first taste of the horse issue around this time. He went to Cowombat Flat, at the source of the Murray, to talk about the access for recreational horse riders (which has since been revoked) and saw the impacts of the brumbies. While the wild horse issue wasn't yet a huge concern, Cox had the foresight to understand that would change after the moratorium on aerial shooting put in place after the cull in Guy Fawkes River National Park. 'I could see the ban would lead to bad things,' he says. His next job, working for the National Parks Association of NSW, began just before the 2000 Guy Fawkes cull. Cox watched as the 2003 then the revised 2008 Kosciuszko horse management plans were released with little effect. 'You could see that the plans were already heavily influenced by those who found culling horses offensive,' he says. 'Those parts of the plans that were good – that sought to reduce horse numbers – were going to fail.'

Throughout the 1990s, Cox had gotten to know Kosciuszko better. In 1994, he undertook a five-day walk through the Pilot Wilderness south of Thredbo. 'The walk was just about all off track and I just couldn't believe how many horses I saw,' he recalls. 'I could see a meandering clear, beautiful river called the Ingeegoodbee being ruined. I don't want to go there now, and I don't want to go to northern Kosciuszko either. I feel like I'll be trampled in a tent at night. It's not a pleasant experience anymore and I advise people now not to go there. I tell them, "You're going to be afraid at night and you'll be surrounded by all this mess." It's an embarrassment and definitely not a place to take a young family, or to take someone who wants to enjoy a national park.'

In 1999, biologist Tim Low published an important book that opened a lot of people's eyes. Entitled *Feral Future*, it told the story of the invasive plants and animals that had colonised Australia and outlined the need for a strategy to do something about the problem. *Feral Future* covered everything from cane toads to fire ants to exotic fish to numerous weed species to larger quadrupeds. In 2002, on the back of the book, an NGO called the Invasive Species Council (ISC) was born. Low was one of eight members of its foundation committee. In 2010, after he finished working for the National Parks Association of NSW, Cox worked his way up through the ISC and was appointed CEO in 2013. He still holds that job.

In June 2018, with the passage of the Kosciuszko Wild Horse Heritage Bill imminent, Cox worked with Richard Swain and others to try to stop the legislation going through parliament. When the bill became law, they regrouped. The Invasive Species Council put aside some funding, the ACT National Parks Association kicked in some cash, people like Linda Groom got involved, and in November, Reclaim

Kosci was officially born, as a joint campaign hosted by the ISC. Its mission statement, as per its website:

> Kosciuszko National Park is for all Australians. Feral horses are muddying its clear streams, trampling its unique plants and destroying animal habitats. Reclaim Kosci aims to stop the damage.

Its slogan: 'It's a park, not a paddock!'.

Ultimately, Reclaim Kosci seeks a repeal of the Barilaro legislation – an unlikely goal with the Coalition in power, but a possibility if Labor is elected. For now, Reclaim Kosci measures its success in more modest terms. It has lured some big names like Peter Garrett on board, and has been most effective when inviting notable people into the park to see the damage for themselves. In December 2020, Federal Environment Minister Sussan Ley visited Kosciuszko with Reclaim Kosci.

'It's quite extraordinary that the wild horses have put the pressure on the park that they have over the recent years,' she said during her visit. 'I remember the park when this area was my electorate when I first became a member of parliament and clear differences between then and now, and the pressure of horses is a call to action I think for agencies, state government, and people who care about the environment, and agriculture and farming and the balance between the two.'

Cox reckons Sussan Ley was saying publicly what numerous politicians say privately. 'What's heartening is you have a minister who gets it. She's brave enough to use her authority when she doesn't need to and I guess that's what leadership is about. She didn't need to say that, but she's someone who understands horses, who understands the area and who understands that something needs to give here. We're stuck in a rut and she's trying to get us unstuck.'

Reclaim Kosci can't yet claim any major victories, but they're in the fight, and that's something. 'It's all about little steps,' Cox says. 'The fact that today we have all the players saying we have a problem and that it needs to be addressed is significant at the state level and the federal level. We've put the park back at the centre, where it should be. We've outlined what would be lost and we're having a proper debate now based on facts not false cultural heritage narratives and false claims. There's still a long road ahead. Even getting a new plan is only part of that road. But it is now accepted that there are too many horses in the park. We have set out the path for them to follow, and politicians usually follow. And those that advocate doing nothing have been revealed to be a small, noisy minority, which reassures me I'm on the right path.'

Small, noisy minority? That sounds like the sort of thing friendlyjordies might say about his old foe John Barilaro. And, in a sense, Jordan Shanks has cut through at a level Reclaim Kosci can only dream of. Towards the end of his 'bruz' video, having dished out every insult under the electric candelabra, Shanks reveals himself to have filmed the video at Barilaro's exclusive country estate about 200 kilometres south of Sydney, which is advertised at $1850 a night on Airbnb. He also reveals that he had sex in at least two locations on the property and finishes his eff-you by placing Mario plush toys at strategic locations on the premises. The sheer audacity of it all has made Shanks a hero to many in the mountains. For all the hard work on a shoestring done by Reclaim Kosci's small team of consultants, staff and volunteers, in the minds of many Kosciuszko lovers, the giant middle finger raised by Jordan Shanks is the most meaningful action yet against Barilaro, even if it won't remove a single brumby.

CHAPTER EIGHT

THE TROJAN BRUMBY

If you're going to bang on about the number of brumbies in Kosciuszko, at some point you'd better go take a look for yourself. That's assuming you can make it to your destination at the end of Pockets Saddle Road in northern Kosciuszko National Park without slamming into one.

On the flanks of Mt Nungar, two healthy bay horses dart onto the road, narrowly missing the car. They defiantly gallop ahead, kicking up dust for a good kilometre or so before veering into a bush clearing. Driving along the eastern side of Tantangara Dam, there are a couple of small mobs near the road among the lightly spaced snow gums. When you arrive at the locked gate at Gurrangorambla Creek and gaze out across Currango Plain, it's like arriving at an open range horse zoo. Welcome to Brumbytown. Population: a bloody lot of them.

We strap on our gaiters, throw on our packs, and stride out across the plain. The other half of 'we' is Stefan De Montis, a 32-year-old Canberran who has been walking Kosciuszko since his late teens, and who walks a different section of the park most weekends. Sometimes he guides walks with the Australian National University Mountaineering Club, though these days he mostly walks solo or with his partner, Phoebe. With legs like ladders, Stefan covers exorbitant distances quickly with a minimum of exertion, gliding as he's striding, as effortless in motion as a champion long-distance runner. Keeping up with this Gurrangorambla rambler is quite the challenge. Before long, we're halfway across the plain towards our morning tea target of Old Currango Homestead, a speck starting to take shape on a low hill to the west. The scene around us is both beautiful and disturbing.

Brumbies. Mob after mob after mob. They are, it must be said, magnificent. Many of the horses south of Thredbo are stocky, scruffy, shaggy, bony, and not much bigger than ponies, but these horses are lithe and leggy like thoroughbreds, and just as full of themselves. One mob of a dozen brumbies, including at least three foals, gallops towards us, led by the intimidating stallion. 'This is our territory and don't you forget it' he appears to be saying. And he's right. Brumbies own this place now. The ravaged creeks and grassland are proof. This plain should be tussocky but instead it's mown like a bowling green. The creek should flow narrow, swift and clear, a metre or two wide at most, and lined by overhanging bushes with tiny white flowers. Instead, it's several metres wide and bare. Everywhere along the creek's banks, chunks of turf have subsided because of the pressure of half-tonne beasts that need to drink every day. With each subsided chunk, the creek widens, its banks becoming walls of mud rather than cushiony, richly vegetated embankments.

Nowhere is there sphagnum moss. Horses rarely eat sphagnum, but they eat grass and other plant species that grow around it, killing it until the moss literally just blows away. Denuded of what Rob Gibbs calls 'the big sponge', Gurrangorambla Creek has become a long, winding stormwater drain. Nowhere are timid wallabies or friendly kangaroos to be seen. In the context of how this place should look, it's like a forest turned into a savannah, or a bleached coral reef. Or, to borrow the sort of architectural analogy which John Barilaro employs in support of brumbies, it's like a soulless modern apartment building erected on the site of a row of razed Victorian terraces.

'The damage is as plain as day,' De Montis says.

It is. Nor is the recent brumby damage the first assault on this place by ungulates or their keepers. When you look closely at the landscape, there are echoes of the cattle era everywhere. Here and there, the ground is strewn with the rusty remnants of old wire fences. At a bend in the creek, an old opaque brown bottle juts out of the muddy embankment, just below grass level. That bottle tells a two-pronged tale of scorn for the land. Presumably it was discarded beside a cattleman's creek-side campfire somewhere, back in the day. Over time, it was covered by vegetation and soil. Then, as the horses eroded and broadened the course of the creek, it ended up lodged in the bank, its bottom end poking out over the water. Eventually the bottle will tumble into the creek as the banks inevitably erode further. Can horses really pollute creeks with beer bottles? You'd better believe they can. On Google Maps satellite view, does Currango Plain look different from the almost horse-free

Happy Jacks Plain 30 or 40 kilometres south? You'd better believe that too. Can you, therefore, see brumby damage from space? That's the kind of statement that's open to ridicule like Don Driscoll's 'cannibal horses'. It could travel through Facebook groups forever, decontextualised, weaponised, mocked, memed and mudslung. But you can. You can actually see how different two subalpine Kosciuszko plains look when one has vast herds of resident brumbies and the other doesn't.

'When I plan a walk, the first thing I do is use satellite imagery to find a viable route,' De Montis says. 'So I'm looking for bogs and water courses and I want to avoid steep hills, that kind of stuff. And it's crazy when you look at Currango. It's bare, and it's absolutely threaded with horse tracks. It's shocking.'

Leaving aside the damage visible from ground level or above, the broader issue with disturbed landscapes like Currango Plain is nothing less than the hydrology of the Australian Alps, upon which so many depend. An April 2021 paper called 'Feral horses (*Equus caballus*) increase suspended sediment in subalpine streams' that was funded by the NSW Department of Planning, Industry and Environment, found that 'damage to stream banks by feral horses potentially degrades water quality and affects aquatic ecosystems'. The three scientists who wrote the paper published in the CSIRO journal *Marine and Freshwater Research* – Peter Raymond Scanes, Adam McSorley and Adrian Dickson – used motion-sensing cameras near subalpine streams in northern Kosciuszko to quantify how often horses interacted with creeks. The short answer is often. They found that stream turbidity peaked at

50 times the national guideline because of horse activity, and that the suspended sediment in creeks leads to a high risk of loss of aquatic diversity and impairment of ecosystem function. They found that the damage was 'unequivocally caused by horses' as opposed to other animals like deer and pigs.

So horses do two things to Kosciuszko streams. First, by trampling sphagnum, they destroy the capacity of stream banks to hold water and release it slowly. Second, they ruin the quality of the water itself. The miracle of a High Country stream, which runs clear in even the worst drought, is destroyed. Many Kosciuszko streams are now like the creeks found on farmland across Australia that run muddy when it rains and dry up between wet spells. This is a hydrological disaster with the potential to impact millions of Australians. The Murray–Darling Basin needs the uninterrupted flow of pristine alpine streams to fill its irrigation storages. The Snowy Hydro scheme, and its offspring Snowy 2.0, also need regular, clear water. The High Country itself needs its ecosystems unsullied.

But did a single pro-brumby person see that report and go, 'Hmmm, maybe we should thin out the herd?' It's unlikely they know the report exists. And if they do, and if they'd bothered to read it, it's unlikely a single heart or mind would have changed. The old saying that you can lead a horse to water but you can't make it drink? If scientific evidence was water and brumby advocates were horses, you couldn't even lead them out of the stable. All of which frustrates the hell out of De Montis in a way he could never have expected when he started walking Kosciuszko almost 15 years ago.

'I don't know how anyone could not want this place to thrive,' he says. 'This is just what I think about when I'm out here. It confuses me. After all these years, I'm still confused by this whole horse thing ... You can walk into the National Museum in Canberra and there's a whole exhibit on rabbits and the destruction they've done and the lengths that Australia had to go to in order to get rid of them. Yet here we are repeating that same thing.'

At least we have a momentary reprieve from the unfenced horse paddock. Horses avoid extremely boggy ground, so it's almost a relief to find a stretch of swamp in a low-lying part of the plain as we near Old Currango Homestead. Normally you'd resent the slog through thigh-deep reeds and sludge, but we revel in the richness of the undisturbed wetland. A low ridge on the western edge of the swamp provides firmer footing, then it's back into the gloop before a longer incline leads up to the homestead, which in truth is just a hut. Old Currango is one of hundreds of huts in the High Country of New South Wales and Victoria, many of which have been preserved by groups like the Victorian High Country Huts Association and the Kosciuszko Huts Association (KHA).

De Montis is the huts history officer of the latter organisation. He says that Old Currango was built in 1873 by an old grazier called Tom O'Rourke and is the oldest remaining building in Kosciuszko National Park. The huts are prized today as refuges against the weather by summer hikers and winter cross-country skiers, but they're more than emergency shelters. They are historic relics of the grazing era and structures of beauty in their own right. In the 1970s, parks authorities were seriously considering destroying the lot of them, but the publication of *Huts of the High Country* in the 1980s by Canberra-based Kosciuszko historian Klaus Hueneke changed all that. Today, they are treasured by all. But it does beg a question of the KHA huts history officer. Since the huts are relics of the cattle days, and since brumbies are in effect living symbols of the same age, is it not hypocritical to say that the huts should be treasured, renovated, celebrated, while the poor old brumbies should be carted away in horse floats, or shot? De Montis's answer to that question is one of the most thoughtful responses imaginable. So let's go there. Stefan, is it hypocritical to champion the huts and reject the brumbies?

'No, it's not. Firstly, the huts are there. They don't move and their history is built into their foundations and can be linked back to the grazing families. But there is no set history to an individual horse. I'm not denying that there isn't some cultural heritage attached to the horses, but how can we say that a particular horse out there on the plain came from some lineage when for all we know it just ran out of somebody's property in Yaouk? For me, that's one key difference.

'I also think there's an interesting distinction between the cultural heritage of a horse and the history of a hut. Cultural heritage is a thing that people choose from history and assign to their identity, and the history of the horses is leaning very directly on a very white, very conquistadorial history. It feels like the idea of cultural heritage that's thrown around with the horses is the heritage of a white man with an Akubra chasing them down. The cultural heritage of the horse is a vestige of stockmen on the land, even though they never owned this land – they leased it, they borrowed it. But the huts are accessible to everyone here. I've got this guy that I've taken out on all my ANU Mountaineering Club trips. He's an Asian student studying in Australia and he loves the huts because he doesn't feel excluded from the heritage side of things. He feels welcome in the huts. The huts are neutral.'

But not all huts are neutral. Some feel like they belong to the horse folk.

After cheese and salami at Old Currango Homestead, plus a bit of satay jerky from a Sydney Asian grocer because we do, after all, live in a multicultural nation, we walk north on the Mosquito Creek Trail, winding our way through a low range of hills in beautiful old snow gum forest. You can tell your elevation in these mountains by the trees. At elevations from about 1400 metres to 1600 metres, the snow gums are white-barked and slender-limbed. Closer to the tree line between about 1700 and 1900 metres, they become short, stumpy and gnarled with bark that turns vivid orange and red when wet. Here, at about 1300 metres, the snow gums are a bit of both – thick-limbed but tall. They're also not too close together, which makes this forest perfect shelter for horses at night or in a storm. We glimpse a horse here, a horse there, and then we're through the hills and out on Cooleman Plain, just east of Bill Jones Hut. If Currango is the oldest remnant cattleman's hut in the mountains, Bill Jones could well be the newest. It was built in 1952 by William Travis Jones, who held a grazing lease in these parts from the 1930s to the 1970s, and is believed to be the last hut built for grazing in the area. The dirt-floored corrugated-iron hut is far from the prettiest or most welcoming in the mountains. And the scene outside it is nothing short of a disgrace.

Recreational horse riders and commercial horse trekkers regularly stop here, and the signs are everywhere, from the piles of horse poo beside the hitching rail at the front of the hut to the creek beside the hut. The creek is a mud pit. A filthy, stinking mud pit. What once must have been a babbling, joyous little streamlet is now a chain of near-stagnant puddles. If your cattle or horses had reduced a creek on your private property to that state, you'd be embarrassed to show your face in town. 'I always wanted to take John Barilaro up to a clear stream that comes out of a rocky surface where horses don't go, and then take him here to Bill Jones Hut where the creek has just been obliterated,' De Montis says. 'I think this is the best example of destruction by horses in the mountains.'

In fairness to the brumbies, the nameless little creek outside Bill Jones Hut may have been trashed by domesticated trail horses more than wild ones. That said, Stefan and Phoebe camped here one night and a mob was galloping around the hut during the night, including an angry stallion that was none too pleased at the tented intruders. Either way, the creek, or what's left of it, is a stark example of what horses do to Kosciuszko waterways. Right there, in plain sight. But do the recreational horse riders see it? They must. Surely they see it. Surely they have water bottles to fill. Surely they have eyes.

De Montis reckons it's perfectly possible they see nothing amiss. 'I don't have any ill will towards people riding horses as a form of recreation, but I honestly think they don't see it,' he says. 'Horse riders ride to where other horse riders ride. Many come to Bill Jones Hut via an old bridle trail that comes over the hill from Cooinbil Hut on Long Plain. To them, this sort of damage to the environment probably seems normal.'

Maybe they see it, maybe they don't. If there was a horse rider on hand, we'd ask them. And there's another question you'd like to ask. Even if they see it and recognise the damage, do they care? Maybe they don't. Maybe they write it off as a casualty of their recreation. If so, you could argue they're no worse than the skiers and snowboarders who think nothing of riding smooth slopes that were created by felling magnificent old-growth snow gums and blasting grand old granite boulders to smithereens. Then there are the unsightly lift pylons, the sewerage, the vast bitumen car parks, the run-off, the roads and the rest of it. One of the reasons the Australian Alps National Parks and Reserves are Australian National Heritage–listed but not a World Heritage Site is that they are disqualified because of the volume of commercial activity. There are many who have modified, commercialised, desecrated this landscape. You can't blame everything on horses. That said, the ski resorts sit within strictly controlled leasehold areas, whereas brumbies know no boundaries. Brumbies can, and do, wreak damage on streams, subalpine grasslands and alpine meadows across the mountains. Some brumby supporters say the damage is grossly overstated. These people are beyond reason. You could show them a brain tumour and they'd call it a pimple. The more rational ones seem to have a sort of cognitive dissonance, which is a fancy way of saying they just don't give a stuff.

The good news on this fine but breezy afternoon is that Cooleman Plain has much less horse damage than Currango.

It's different underfoot too. Drier. Firmer. A little rockier. Much better walking. We've crossed into limestone country and are heading north to Blue Waterholes, a dramatic series of pools on Cave Creek, a broad and quite remarkable stream that disappears underground, leaving dirt and round river stones, only to reappear a few hundred metres downstream as the limestone miraculously regurgitates the underground water half a metre deep. This is karst or cave country. The creek runs through a series of deep gorges with towering cliffs and De Montis knows all the little holes in the gorge walls that lead to caverns the size of a basketball court. He knows the best spots to photograph creeks that spring out of the rock walls like artificial waterfalls in an upmarket shopping mall. It's incredible, magical country, although when you get to the main Blue Waterholes campground, the spell is broken.

The campground is accessible by two-wheel-drive vehicles on a dirt road via nearby Long Plain, which means there are strange creatures called humans there, whom we've not seen all day. There are no horses in sight but they've caused all sorts of trouble here in the recent past, intimidating campers by stomping and trampling around their campsites. In 2010, Parks recorded 124 horses within a five kilometre radius of the Blue Waterholes campground. In 2018, twice that number were counted. In 2019, a ten-year-old boy at a nearby campground on Long Plain was hospitalised after being kicked in the shoulder by a brumby. Majestic brumbies running across the plains are a fine sight from a safe distance, but wild horses and humans don't mix.

They don't mix with cars either. The Snowy Mountains Highway in northern Kosciuszko is dotted with diamond-shaped yellow signs with a picture of a horse instead of the kangaroo with which Australian motorists are so familiar. Numerous road accidents have occurred around Kiandra, and on the road up to the Selwyn Snow Resort. On occasion, brumbies have been killed in motor accidents, and it's surely only a matter of time before a motorist or passenger is killed. Brumby advocates know it too – they discuss it on Facebook, fearing the public relations backlash.

We've walked a long way today, but we press on because we have important business. Two pieces of important business, actually. The first is to make Oldfields Hut by twilight. It's De Montis's favourite hut and having once visited it, it's easy to understand why. The second piece of business is a meeting we have in the morning with an important person in these parts.

We climb out of Cave Creek at the start of Clarke Gorge, hoof it over the hill, and circle Cooleman Plain in a wide arc. We stop briefly at Pockets Hut – large, clean, well-preserved, but far from the most charismatic hut in the Alps – then tackle the climb up and over the Gurrangorambla Range on the Murray Gap Trail. Because De Montis is powered by a battery that never runs out, he goes ahead. It's good to be alone in the forest on the Gurrangorambla. The Black Summer fires mostly missed this range. A few moments of uphill trudging with the squeaky-gate soundtrack of gang-gang cockatoos never hurt anyone. But wait. What's that noise? It's two mountain bikers. They're fit young guys trying to pedal up the hill, but the incline is just too steep, so they de-bike and push.

We talk briefly. They're doing some kind of circuit from the southern suburbs of Canberra through to Adaminaby. It's at least 100 kilometres on rough bush tracks and they'll probably finish in darkness.

'Did you see all the brumbies?' one of them asks. 'Beautiful!'

Something new is happening in the mountains that hasn't yet been well documented, and these two fellas embody it. In the old days, cross-country skiers and walkers understood the mountains. The High Country was their adventure playground but it was also their cathedral and they treated it with due reverence. Such people of all ages are still out there in the skiing and walking community, but in the social media generation, a new breed has emerged who use the mountains as a kind of giant outdoor gym without engaging in the landscape, its history, its ecology, its song. At their worst, the new breed leave beer cans and toilet paper in the snow on backcountry ski and snowboard trips. Or they mountain bike off track on the incredibly delicate snow-patch feldmark vegetation on the Main Range and post about it on Instagram, as a famous Australian adventurer who really should've known better did recently. Mostly they're not ecological vandals. They're just oblivious to the fragility of the landscape, to what Richard Swain would call the song of country.

De Montis made a good point out on the plains today. He said he hates the word 'hiking' and prefers 'walking' or 'bushwalking'. For one thing, it sounds less American. But there's also a sense of engaging with landscape when you 'walk'. A 'hike' doesn't quite have the same connotation. This might be splitting hairs. But there's no doubt that many among the new wave of hikers, mountain bikers, trail runners and assorted outdoors fitness freaks are no different to the recreational horse riders who don't see, or won't see, the desecrated muddy creek outside Bill Jones Hut. More people visit Kosciuszko and Victoria's Alpine National Park every year, yet how many truly understand the High Country? How many even try? One reason why the movement to manage brumbies finds it so hard to get mainstream traction is that even its target audience is largely disengaged.

From the crest of the Gurrangorambla Range, it's a quick downhill walk to Oldfields Hut, a classic tin-roofed slab hut with a long, timber verandah. The place is like something out of a book of bush yarns. From the verandah, you look north-east to Mt Bimberi, the highest peak in the ACT at 1913 metres. Though just 315 metres lower than Kosciuszko, Bimberi is almost invisible on Canberra's western skyline, barely protruding above lower, closer ranges. But it's an impressive lump of a thing from this side, glowing orange then dark purple in the setting sun. De Montis made a fire while the mortal half of our walking party huffed and puffed over the range. We sit sipping a frothy can or two, solving the problems of the universe while kangaroos and wallabies stand guard. A quick stroll across the tussocky meadow to fill water bottles down in the Goodradigbee River reveals a metre-wide stream with an overhanging arch of bushes and water as clear as the mountain air itself. De Montis has only ever seen one horse in this valley, and it shows.

Sitting with De Montis, it feels like big things lie ahead for him in Kosciuszko. He's walked virtually every valley, ridge and summit, and not just in the popular areas. He has also taken amazing photos along the way. Most Kosciuszko photographers whose work fills local shops and galleries are cliché merchants. A perfect rustic hut. A summit at sunset. Snow gums laden with snow. But Stefan has the eye. He walks and records the park in a completely original manner. It's all there on his Instagram page, and maybe that will be his legacy. Or maybe the people he's inspired through guided walks are his great legacy. Maybe his gift to this place will be more along the lines of his advocacy with groups like the Kosciuszko Huts Association and National Parks Association. Then again, maybe one day he'll publish books filled with his exquisite photos and become the great modern chronicler of this place. In a sense, his weekly traverses of Kosciuszko are already an artwork, a mind map of inestimable intricacy and beauty which, for now, only he can see. But imagine if he could share it. Imagine if he could translate to the page not just the images but the understanding, the longing, the belonging, the fear of loss, all of it. Whatever the future holds, Stefan De Montis is already an important person here. When a man covers the ground of Kosciuszko so forensically, so respectfully, so lovingly, that man should be listened to.

And what's on his mind right now is that the park is going to hell in all sorts of ways. He wishes they'd declared more wilderness back in the 1990s, especially in the north of the park. Unfortunately, Peter Cochran fought it when he had Barilaro's job as the local member. It annoys De Montis that they've recently blazed a walking trail up Hannels Spur on the steep western flank of Kosciuszko, one of the wildest areas of the mountains, and he resents the fact that some adventure tour operators have licences to take people up it. He wants the wildest parts of Kosciuszko left well alone by commercial operators of any kind. The way he sees it, everyone from Snowy 2.0 to the horse riders to the wilderness sports folk wants a chunk, and none of those chunks is leaving the park as it should be. He worries about the legacy of Barilaro's brumby legislation, not just because of the damage caused by horses themselves, but because it sets a dangerous precedent. 'What happens to the next single-interest group that looks at the way the brumby people whipped up a frenzy?' he says. To Stefan De Montis, brumbies are the proverbial Trojan horse.

* * *

If you're going to go visit Darth Vader, you don't want him showing up in his tennis whites. You want him in the black cape, helmet on, heavy breathing through the big black grille. You want him in the sort of mood he'd be in before he's had his morning cuppa, and uh-oh, a stormtrooper just took the last coffee pod.

So it is that we wake early at Oldfields, pack up our tents and gear, and hoof it back over the Gurrangorambla Range down to Old Snowy Campground, one of the designated campsites for horse riders in Kosciuszko. Our meeting is with Peter Cochran, who is in a very Peter Cochran mood. The first thing that's gotten him offside is our arrival time. We're on time to the minute but he seems to think the appointed hour was last night. The text message exchange on the old iPhone tells a different story. Right here, Peter. 9.30 am. Anyway, misunderstandings happen.

The second thing that's turned Cochran good and cranky is the cap.

'You know what's blown me out of the water? You've arrived here with an ABC cap on.'

For the record, the cap is black and says *ABC Jazz* with the squiggly logo. Its provenance is unknown. It's just one of those random accoutrements that was sitting on top of the clothes dryer, and who knows how it got there. Probably a visitor to the house left it. In the mad scramble between work and household duties and packing for this trip, it was the only hat lying around so it got thrown in the backpack. There was actually speculation around the campfire last night that it would piss Cochran the hell off. Took him all of about five seconds to rise to the lure.

So here we are in a campground full of trailers and tents made of heavy canvas that look unlike anything a modern bushwalker ever carried on their back. It's a scene out here. There are people grooming horses and checking gear, and there's even what looks like a solar-powered shower down by the creek. Cochran's always banging on about the things a real bushman would do. The short answer is they'd splash the cold, refreshing mountain waters on their body, not warm it in a shower that looks like a circus tent.

Anyway, best to keep such thoughts inside their bubble. Cochran doesn't have much time here. Best to let him speak. Cochran is accustomed to being lauded by his supporters. His BUGSPRAY Facebook group is full of people cheering him on. 'Up and at em, Peter!' one supporter urges with a hand-clapping emoji. 'Super hero Cochran', another says. 'The brumbies need you', swoons a third. He's the big man out here at Old Snowy Campground too. So, then. Up and at 'em, Peter.

'You've got to remember that people like Leisa and I have been fighting a battle over the management of Kosciuszko National Park – and this relates not only to brumbies, it relates to grazing in the High Country, the fuel management, bushfires, the whole thing – for 50 friggin' years, right? And we've had a multitude of people like yourself come by, all with good intentions and a predetermined agenda, and we get sick of it, righto?'

Thought bubble: You agreed to the meeting, but ... okay.

'We get sick of the shit being put on us time and time again, so if you want to see damage in the park, go and look at the bloody destruction through the whole fucking park now. It's burnt to a cinder for the second time in 17 years and go and write a story on that, then you'll be doing something worthwhile. That's my attitude. So what I'm saying to you is that I don't really want to talk about it, for the reason that we have been blocked out totally from the ABC, totally from some of the Fairfax media for 50 years and we've had a gutful of it. Journalists have no place in my life at the moment, to be frank.'

Thought bubble: Again, you agreed to meet a journalist. The impression forms that journalists serve a very useful place in your life as fodder to chew out in front of your paying guests. Which is fine. We weren't expecting tea and scones.

'If we're going to have an interview and go into a discussion and you have a predetermined view on the number of horses and the situation that exists at the moment, I'm going to have a lot of difficulty talking to you. The brainwashing that's going on with the horses with the issue over 30 or 40 years has distorted not only the political debate but the science, and I don't believe the science is based on anything else than a political agenda.'

Thought bubble: Come on, mate. You've been arguing the line about scientists with a political agenda for a long time now.

'So if you've been convinced that there are 25,000 horses in the park by the science that has been presented to you and you're convinced that the science that we've seen already is right, then there's not much point in you and me talking. And I'm surprised that Leisa didn't tell you the same thing.'

Thought bubble: Whoa, take a look at that brumby. It just bolted straight past the campground. Loud whinny. Not sure if the whinny came from the brumby or one of Cochran's horses. A bloke in an Akubra would probably know. A bloke in an ABC cap? Forget it.

'I thought about this after you rang, and I can't see any point talking about this at all because I think you've come with a predetermined attitude towards the issue. And I think you're going to have difficulty writing the book.'

Thought bubble: Sixty thousand words and counting. Many articulate, passionate brumby supporters have made invaluable contributions.

'I don't know what Leisa said, but we just get tired of it. You're bashing your head against a brick wall, and all I ask you to do, if you want to be objective, go and have a look at this bloody park at the back of Kiandra, take a walk through to Tabletop, walk down into Tumut River, take a look at that country and tell me that this park is well-managed. Then I'll believe you.'

'I have walked through there recently,' De Montis says. Because of course he has. Because there's barely a Kosciuszko tussock he hasn't stepped lightly upon.

'What do you think?' Cochran says.

'It's total devastation,' De Montis replies.

'It *is* total devastation,' Cochran echoes. 'And we're talking about 2000 brumbies? Really? *Really?* And people are going on about brumbies? Fucking hell, come on. No, I'm sorry, I can't do it. I get bloody angry even thinking you're writing a story about brumbies when that up there is total devastation – wildlife killed, vegetation destroyed totally, and we're talking about brumbies. Anyway, I have to go because I have people here paying money to ride.'

Thought bubble: Questioning the aerial survey numbers to downplay the effect of horse damage. Why focus attention on a few wild horses when the fire damage is so bad? Cochran is warming up now.

'If you go and look at the destruction of those bloody mountains now, you can understand why we're as distressed as we are now because it's the second time in 17 years we've been fucked by idiots.'

Actual question here, not a thought bubble: Fucked by idiots? Were the 2003 and the 2020 fires really the fault of Parks?

'Partly. The bureaucracy generally, the influence of the Greens on Parks management ... there's a political influence, there's a corrupted scientific community who perpetuate the same bloody stories about the management of fuel, a really hot year, all that sort of thing. We are now having the coldest spring we've had in my lifetime. We had a frost here this morning, it was minus four. All I'm saying is that the information the management of the park was based on, including Costin and others from the very outset, much of it was based on scientists who had their origins in Europe, and the management of the ecosystems in Europe is entirely different to what it was in Australia obviously, they didn't understand the eucalypt, they didn't understand that the eucalypt is a flammable plant and it has to be managed. Talk to foresters about it.'

So, then.

There is much to unpack here. Let's start with fire management, or what Cochran sees as mismanagement. He claims Parks have stuffed it up, that we're fixated upon a few wild horses when infinitely worse ecological damage has been inflicted upon Kosciuszko by two megafires within 17 years. Here's the thing: fire authorities undertake hazard reduction burns in Kosciuszko, just as they do in other national parks. Kosciuszko fireys won't speak out because they're trying to raise families and live peacefully in the mountains and fear reprisal, but they'll tell you what the scientists tell you, which is that burning on a broad scale too regularly creates dense regrowth that actually makes forests more flammable. This is especially true in the alpine ash and snow gum forests of the High Country, where fire dynamics play out totally differently from other Australian landscapes. And those fireys will tell you that nothing, absolutely nothing, will prevent a megafire when conditions are as hot and dry as they were in the Black Summer of 2019–20. If you read accounts from old cattlemen who worked the land, you'll see that even they understood High Country fire dynamics. There's a paper called 'Fire History of the Australian Alps' written by a really interesting bloke mentioned earlier, Phil Zylstra of the University of Wollongong, a former shearer and anti-parkie who pulled a 180-degree turn in his thinking as he came to understand the alpine landscape, eventually becoming a Kosciuszko ranger himself, then a leading fire dynamics expert. In the paper, he quotes an old cattleman called Roy Hedger, who held snow leases, and said, 'We would never burn bush country as it would make it worse.' Yet Cochran consistently claims forests should be thinned out, and even suggested that we 'go and talk to foresters about it'. Maybe he should take his own advice. Maybe he should go and say that to Ian Dicker, chief fire officer for the region and a former forester. That'd be a tea party worth bringing a plate of scones to.

As for Cochran's meteorological claims, presumably he didn't know he was speaking to a journalist who writes about weather for a living, but even the most cursory Google search reveals his claim that the spring of 2020 was the coldest in his lifetime to be industrial-grade gobbledygook. The spring of 2020 was in fact the fifth warmest on record overall across New South Wales, with daytime maximums well above average and the warmest average minimum temperatures in 106 years. That's state-wide data, but the local readings reveal a similar picture. There's no weather station at Old Snowy Campground, more's the pity, but the nearby stations at Cabramurra and Cooma Airport both recorded average temperatures well above normal in the spring of 2020. And that night of minus four? Well, a freak cold pool of air must have mysteriously descended upon Old Snowy Campground, because over the hill at Oldfields, which sits in a classic frost hollow valley at a similar altitude, the dew on the tents never came close to freezing.

It seems likely that Cochran is dog-whistling an anti– climate change narrative with his misguided meteorological assessment – it's not the warming climate's fault, it's the parkies! And it sometimes seems like half the mountains are in on the game. In Adaminaby, just down the road from Cochran's place at Yaouk, there's a display in the window of a local gallery at the shops. In a large typeface, it says: *Climate change NO Climate Phase YES*. Beside those words is a *Canberra Times* article from 1939 that reads: 'An unparalleled hot spell was experienced in Canberra during the weekend when for the first time on record, temperatures of more than 100 degrees were recorded on two consecutive days. The maximum on Saturday was 101.7 degrees and on Sunday 102.8.' The inference is clear. What climate change? We have always had record-breaking hot spells. There's just one little problem. Those Fahrenheit temperatures translate to 38.7°C and 39.3°C respectively, and consecutive days with higher temperatures have occurred numerous times since then, while in January 2020, Canberra registered its hottest recorded temperature of 44°C. Indeed, December 2019, when the Dunns Road fire which roared through Kosciuszko National Park started, was Australia's warmest and driest month on record. This 'phase' just keeps getting warmer, year on year on year.

How does all this tie together? The climate denial, the fire blame game, the downplaying of brumby damage – where does it all lead? To answer that, there's no better source than Cochran himself. In January 2021, he told the *Tumut and Adelong Times*, a local newspaper serving the valleys north-west of the mountains through which the Black Summer fires passed en route to Kosciuszko:

> There are other areas where the brumbies are, where the fuel levels were kept down – particularly the northern end of the park – where there is minimal damage. There's a message there for park managers and those responsible for managing bushfire in this country, and it's all about fuel levels ... They need to spend more time actually monitoring the fuel and managing it on an annual or bi-annual basis, not a ten-year cycle, and take advantage of wind conditions for fire and take advantage of drought conditions where livestock can be put into the park to reduce fuel levels during times of drought.

Boom. That, right there, is what it's all about.

Put livestock back in the park. Use cattle and brumbies to help minimise the fuel load. Brumbies are good. Cattle are good. Brumbies and cattle help prevent fires because they are magic like unicorns. But as discussed in Chapter Six, the grass and small plants that cattle and horses eat are not what fuel major fires. This cannot be stated often enough. Large, introduced grazing animals in the Australian Alps do not, repeat, *do not* stop the mountains burning. The old 'grazing prevents blazing' argument is a myth, and anyone who argues it has not read (or properly understood) the literature or is wilfully ignoring it.

For Stefan De Montis, brumbies are a Trojan horse because they give interest groups a precedent to organise and push for whatever it is they want that Kosciuszko probably doesn't need. To cattlemen, brumbies are the Trojan horse that open the door for a potential return to cattle grazing in the High Country. That's unlikely to happen anytime soon, but times change and governments change and no one pays attention to scientific evidence anymore, which people like Cochran know as well as anyone.

Before we leave Cochran, let's pay the man his due: as John Barilaro says, he is undeniably passionate. But here's the thing. His mood changes like the mountain weather, curmudgeonly one minute, you-beaut the next.

A few months before we met at Old Snowy Campground, he unloaded on his BUGSPRAY Facebook page, calling me a 'dick', a 'fraud' and a 'boofhead'. This is not necessarily the sort of language you'd hope to see in the public domain from a man who'd served three terms in state parliament, but there it was. And didn't his supporters hammer the laughter emoji in approval. For the record, the outburst came after a radio debate in which we'd discussed the brumby damage at the source of the Murray at Cowombat Flat in southern Kosciuszko. Visiting that place in December 2019, in the heart of the drought, was heartbreaking. The infant Murray wasn't its normally clear, babbling self. Instead, it staggered into life in a series of stagnant brown pools pugged by hoof marks and fouled by brumby poo. With a dry creek bed upstream, the only option for fresh drinking water was to search downstream. This had all been explained on radio. But Cochran didn't listen or knew better. Because Peter Cochran always knows better. Here's what he wrote in full:

> Greenie bushwalker this morning claimed he was walking north from VIC border, came to headwaters of Murray River on a hot day and couldn't get enough clean water for a drink (because of brumby shit). So he walked DOWNSTREAM for a km to get fresh water! What a dick! A bushman would have walked upstream 50 metres for clean water!! This boofhead traded under the name of Sharma. I'm calling him out as a fraud! What do you think?

As explained on the radio, there was no water upstream. *None.* It was a drought, and the Murray at Cowombat is so close to its source that its upstream reaches turn to dirt in a drought. But five or six hundred metres downstream from the first muddy pools at Cowombat, the Murray meets Pilot Creek, renowned for always flowing because it's fed by healthy sphagnum bogs in forest gullies where horses rarely tread. Abundant clean water was indeed to be found there – downstream.

The best local bushmen and women get their water there every time.

CHAPTER NINE

THE YORTA YORTA, THE WATER, AND THE HORSE SLAUGHTER

Poor old Scruffy the brumby never stood much of a chance. With the forest floor bare of grass and her mother's milk drying up to a trickle, the bedraggled little bay filly was as small and skinny as a three-month-old foal, even though she was probably six months old. As if she didn't look rough enough, Scruffy had a massive haematoma on her shoulder, likely the result of a kick from another horse, perhaps even from her mother. Scruffy the brumby appeared destined for a short, brutal existence.

Scruffy was born in the Barmah Forest in Victoria. Together with the Millewa Forest on the NSW bank of the Murray River, it's Australia's largest remnant river red gum forest, about half an hour north-west of the famous paddle steamer port of Echuca. The Barmah Forest has been home to a small population of brumbies for as long as anywhere in the High

Country. The herd has generally totalled somewhere between a few hundred and a thousand or so, and it is loved by many locals, even without 'The Man from Snowy River' mythology to whip people into a cultural frenzy. But ecologists claim that the Barmah brumbies do just as much damage as High Country horses, and the local Indigenous people, the Yorta Yorta, are also strongly opposed to the presence of horses in the forest. It's like the High Country fight on a smaller scale, except for one key difference: until recently, there had never been any planned trapping or shooting of horses in Barmah by Parks. But that has changed. And many locals are ropeable.

In January 2020, Parks Victoria released its Strategic Action Plan 2020–2023 for the Barmah National Park and Barmah Forest Ramsar site. A Ramsar site is one that's in accordance with the Ramsar Convention on Wetlands of International Importance, so named for the Iranian city on the shores of the Caspian Sea where the convention was signed in 1971.

'The long-term aim for feral horses in Barmah Forest is to reduce their numbers to zero, thereby alleviating the total grazing and trampling pressure caused by this introduced species,' the plan stated. The horses, estimated by Parks Victoria to number around 750, wouldn't all go in one hit. They would remove 100 per year over four years, then a revised plan would be produced, detailing how the remaining horses could be eradicated. As in the High Country, that got a lot of people very angry indeed. And as in the High Country, the horses earned a stay of execution in 2020 due to the COVID pandemic and other factors. But, before then, nature was doing a pretty good job of thinning the herd on its own.

In the drought of 2017 to 2019, huge rainfall deficiencies were experienced throughout the Murray–Darling Basin across New South Wales, Queensland and Victoria. With scarce feed in the Barmah Forest the brumbies began to die, one after another after another. For Scruffy and her whole family, the outlook was somewhere between bleak and hopeless. And then along came the Barmah Brumby Hay Angels.

* * *

Renée Neubauer is the daughter of a motorcycle speedway racer but her passion has always been four legs, not two wheels. For most of her childhood she lived on properties with horses. For the last 20 years she has thrown herself into horse welfare issues, mainly through Project Hope Horse Welfare Victoria, which is said to be the longest-running group dedicated solely to equine welfare in Australia. Neubauer's kids are young adults now, but in the early 2000s, when they were barely hip high, she and her husband, Scott, started taking them on camping trips in the Barmah Forest, a couple of hours north of their property just outside Melbourne.

'It was the perfect place,' she says. 'We loved the Murray River and we loved the fact that there were brumbies up there. Both our girls rode, and for them the brumbies were the biggest hook. We knew a couple of isolated spots on four-wheel drive tracks, and we tended to camp near brumby tracks that went down to the river. You'd lay there at night and hear the stallions snort with your kids and hubby, and there was not much between you and six to eight brumbies who would come down for a drink. You'd slowly unzip the tent and the kids would look out and they'd love it. That was our first interaction with Barmah brumbies, and we kept that warm and fuzzy feeling for about ten years. And then things changed.'

What changed was that the Barmah State Park became the Barmah National Park in 2010. The Victorian premier at the time was John Brumby, but the Labor man's surname would prove no good omen for supporters of Barmah brumbies. Before long, the brumbies would be relabelled as 'feral horses' and, in a classic case of bureaucratic language, as 'a threatening process'.

'When the Barmah State Park was relabelled as a national park, that changed everything,' Neubauer says. 'We no longer could be sure that the brumbies were going to stay there for future generations.' But by 2018 it was starting to look like present generations wouldn't see the brumbies either. As mentioned, drought was decimating the herd. 'They were emaciated walking zombies out in the park,' Neubauer recalls. 'So we established the Barmah Brumby Hay Angels to save them.' Donations poured in. After fundraising, the Hay Angels spent more than $10,000 on feed. They purchased lucerne hay at $15 to $20 a bale, the good stuff with no seeds so that no introduced seeds would be brought into the national park. Another group called the Barmah Brumby Preservation Group did similar work. But no one did more than Kaye and Gerry Moor.

The Moors are a retired couple who live in the small town of Barmah at the edge of the forest. Gerry was a racehorse trainer in his day. 'Between them, they've probably got 120 years of being out in Barmah,' Neubauer says. 'They know the mobs intimately. Kaye even has a little logbook and goes out in the car and notes down the details of each horse.'

Kaye Moor's logbook would have had a fair few red lines through it. The drought had gotten so bad that many horses had already died before the Hay Angels started feeding the 'emaciated zombies' like Scruffy and her family. Parks Victoria euthanised a number of them, and for once nobody argued when they pointed a gun at a horse and pulled the trigger. Indeed, locals appreciated their efforts.

When a horse enters the final stages of starving to death, it sits down and pretty much shuts up shop. At that point, most of them won't eat even if you feed them. Kaye and Gerry Moor attended countless horses in this state, sitting with them until they passed, or until a Parks ranger came along to administer a humane bullet. 'It's hard to comfort a wild animal,' Neubauer says. 'You don't want to stress them out. Parks knew where they were mostly thanks to Kaye and Gerry, who were out there every single day for months and months and months. It was incredibly heroic work.' From a humanitarian perspective, Neubauer wasn't much short of heroic herself. She fed the ones that had half a chance of survival, even in the face of hefty fines, because feeding any wild animal, native or introduced, is of course strictly forbidden in a national park. But she was desperate for enough of the mob to survive to preserve a genetically viable population. And survive they did.

The rains came. The drought broke. Grass grew in the forest. The survivors recovered. The Hay Angels and others had saved the herd. Some landholders with properties adjoining the Barmah Forest played their part too by letting the brumbies graze there. Neubauer had driven up to the forest as often as possible during the drought, always making a point of putting out feed for Scruffy and her family. The Hay Angels' efforts paid off. Scruffy developed into a beautiful young mare. 'She probably didn't get to the size she should have, but you'd expect that from her stunted start in life,' Neubauer says. 'But she certainly made up for it in her attitude. She holds her own in the herd and many of the bachelor brumbies are now very interested in her. Her father is so protective of her that he chased one bachelor stallion away. He didn't want anyone coming around his girls! But a time will come when a bachelor stallion will challenge, and then it'll be all over, red rover. But for now, Scruffy's family is quite unique. Mum, Dad and her little sisters, Hope and Chance, they're all so tight together.'

* * *

There's a certain type of bureaucratic language employed in official land management documents that is cold, detached and dispassionate, as perhaps it should be in order to reduce often hotly contested land management issues to the basics. At its worst, such language is almost comical. The term 'threatening process' (in reference to brumbies) mentioned a couple of pages back is a good example of that. But mostly, the language is bland to the point of being soporific. Examples of such language abound in the Barmah Strategic Action Plan.

'The ecological health of the area is essential to Traditional Owners' cultural and spiritual connections to the land and it supports valuable recreation and tourism activity,' it states on the summary page. Which is perfectly reasonable, even if – as noted – it's a little dispassionate. But if you want an example of what the traditional owners really think, look no further than the Joint Management Plan For Barmah National Park produced by the Yorta Yorta Traditional Owner Land Management Board. This is a land management document with attitude, especially in the preamble. It begins:

> From the earliest days of the British invasion on to this Country – in what become known as Australia, Victoria and New South Wales – the Yorta Yorta people were left out in the distribution of their lands and waters. Without the consent of the Yorta Yorta Nation, the British explorers, squatters, and convicts trespassed on to our territory and claimed it as their own.
>
> The Yenbenon have fought for their rights, and even waged a frontier war up against the colonisers, much of which happened around the Moira Lakes, which is now called the Barmah Lakes. Yorta Yorta people became the victims of massacres, violence, rape and exploitation. All without recognition of our rights, our loss of liberty, without justice or reparations.

Massacres, violence, rape and exploitation. British trespassers. This is confronting stuff. And the strong, evocative language continues in the third paragraph, which speaks of 'days of great distress', becoming 'beggars', ancestors who had to rely on 'the mercy and charity of the white man'. It talks of 'black women and their children' who were used 'to quell the lust of the white man and used and bartered as slaves'. It tells how early colonial land owners would have achieved little without 'Aboriginal labourers who were paid in rations and misery'. And it says the Yorta Yorta Nation 'speaks this truth not to find guilt or for pity', but to forge their determination 'to fight for our rightful place for our Country'.

For the record, 'Yenbenon' translates as 'our people'. Otherwise, the meaning of the preamble in the Joint Management Plan For Barmah National Park is unmistakably clear: it's the Yorta Yorta's forest and it's high time it was treated with respect. 'Just because you came here 200 years ago, it does not mean that it diminishes or takes over the rights of people who have been here for over hundreds of thousands of years,' Yorta Yorta woman Monica Morgan told *The Age* in April 2021. 'In fact, it is an insult to the memory of those ancestors who fought to live, to die, to breathe and to be on country.' The Joint Management Plan was a collaboration between the Yorta Yorta and numerous land management bodies. It was released in 2020, and not before time. It had taken ten years to come to fruition since the (John) Brumby Labor government entered into a Traditional Owner Land Management Agreement with the Yorta Yorta Nation Aboriginal Corporation. Uluru-Kata Tjuta National Park and Kakadu National Park are examples of two iconic Australian parks that operate under similar arrangements. Around the same time the Joint Management Plan was released, Parks released its Barmah Strategic Action Plan. Plans, plans, plans, and none of them good news for brumby lovers. But, for one reason or another, the Yorta Yorta took more heat than

Parks over the intention – stated in both plans – to reduce brumbies by 100 a year, then eventually eradicate them. Billboards were erected in the area with images of brumbies and Monica Morgan, saying, 'This is the face that signed their death warrant'. The Barmah brumby wars had turned very, very ugly.

* * *

It's tempting to look at a river red gum forest, scraggly and a little rough to the eye, and go, oh, surely this place can handle a few horses. But only someone unfamiliar with Moira grass could say that. Moira grass is an aquatic grass that for years thrived in the open wetlands of the Barmah Forest, bursting into life when floodwaters arrived. Like sphagnum moss in the High Country, it's a keystone species that holds the whole ecosystem together. It provides a nesting place and foraging habitat for waterbirds. It houses the frogs, insects and yabbies on which birds and other species depend for food. It filters the water as it makes its way to the river after floods. But the change in the Murray River flow due to dams and irrigation altered the seasonal inundation of the forest. Typically, the forest used to flood in the heavy rains of winter, and with the High Country snowmelt of spring that eventually flowed downstream. When that cycle was broken, the Moira grass started disappearing. Barmah was listed as a Ramsar wetland in 1982 but since then the extent of Moira grass has more than halved. By one estimate, it could be gone by as soon as 2026. Barmah is running out of time.

To save the Moira grass and preserve the forest wetland ecosystem, you can't just go and plant Moira grass the way you'd seed a lawn, as the seeds lie dormant waiting for floodwaters, and anyway, the area that it should be covering is too vast. For a healthy carpet of Moira grass you need water, and lots of it. Keith Ward is a senior wetland ecologist working for the Goulburn Broken Catchment Management Authority (the Goulburn and Broken are both significant tributaries of the Murray). For going on 30 years now, he has been taking extensive fauna and flora surveys in the Barmah Forest and fighting for environmental flows to be released down the Murray, and with some success. But there's one thing undoing all his good work. Grazing animals.

Cattle from nearby properties used to be allowed in the forest, but they were kicked out for good in 2008, a couple of years before the national park was gazetted. Ward copped more than his share of intimidation from the Barmah Forest Cattleman's Association while all that was going on. These days he's an enemy of the horse lovers. Ward says the horses are doing all sorts of damage – pugging the ground, dispersing weeds like Paterson's curse that can take over whole patches of forest. The Barmah brumbies even create little receptacles with their hoof imprints that fill up with water and encourage species like giant rush to grow where there should be Moira grass. So an invasive species (the horse) is turning a native species (the giant rush) into a pest species in the context of the forest. It's a complicated, messy ecological disaster unfolding before our eyes.

'Flora and fauna on the floodplains are driven by hydrology, and changed flooding regimes are the number one threat to the Barmah Forest,' Ward says. 'We've always held this and it gets lost in the pro-horse groups. But there has been a lot of money and time and effort invested by the government, and horses are undermining the outcomes of that investment.'

Speaking to Ward and his Goulburn Broken Catchment Management Authority colleague Tim Barlow, the concept of Alec Costin's Kosciuszko 'ice cream plants' comes to mind. It begs the question: what flavour is Moira grass?

KEITH: 'It's sweet.'

TIM: 'It's blue ribbon vanilla, it's a staple, it goes with anything.'

KEITH: 'But the vanilla's always left to last and horses eat the Moira grass first.'

TIM: 'Not if it Street's Blue Ribbon.'

YOUR HUMBLE NARRATOR: 'Maybe Moira grass is more of an exotic vanilla like vanilla bean?'

KEITH: 'Yep. Yep, that's it.'

So that was a moment of levity in what was otherwise a pretty sober discussion. The Barmah battle is just as bitter in tone as the High Country showdown, and Keith Ward gives the impression of a bloke who's lost patience with the bullshit and just wants to get on with his important work.

'On the Parks Vic website, there's a fact sheet about horses, and part of it is an excellent summary of the horses in Barmah,' he says. 'Essentially, there is no conservation value. They're a mongrel breed, they're not native, and they're in a wetland of international significance. There's absolutely no need for these horses. They're as feral as deer, black rats or house mice.'

* * *

In early June 2021, Barmah Brumby Preservation Group (BBPG) president Julie Pridmore was the subject of a story in Victorian rural newspaper *The Weekly Times* which had the headline 'Brumby cull fight heats up'. In the face of an imminent Parks Victoria cull of the first 100 brumbies, she said the group had raised $90,000 towards a 120 hectare 'haven' for the horses on a property adjoining the Barmah National Park. She said the goal was to move the horses out of the park, with some sold to the public or passed on to other groups, while maintaining a viable breeding mob on the property 'to keep our culture and history alive'. In the large image accompanying the story Pridmore stared straight at the camera, lips pursed in steely resolve. BBPG vice president Murray Willaton was considerably less restrained in his Facebook posts around the same time.

'Well the revolt has come! We have had enough,' he said. The post stated that the Barmah Brumby Preservation Group and its supporters had tried their best to work with the Victorian Labor Government, Parks Victoria and the Yorta Yorta Corporation. It claimed that the BBPG had provided them 'an easy way out by building a sanctuary for the Barmah Brumbies' and said it was a 'disgrace' that Parks Victoria would rather shoot the Barmah brumbies than trap and rehome them in their sanctuary. The post said it was a 'sneaky and underhanded way to treat people from Australia and around the world who have donated money and their time to save these heritage horses'.

The post added that the Barmah Brumby Preservation Group would take a stand and was organising an event. It called 'all passionate and brave horsemen and horsewomen' to duty. The revolt was on. Except then it wasn't. Melbourne had yet another COVID outbreak and regional Victoria was locked down for another week, so the event was called off. Parks Victoria then beat the BBPG to the punch. Allegedly, they actually started shooting horses. For better or for worse, for richer or poorer, it appears that a land management body in Australia had finally undertaken the only method of brumby management that is quick, cheap and highly effective. Parks Victoria were unable to confirm or deny this – they had signalled in the early months of 2021 that no information would be released about the culls in advance. But Julie Pridmore posted a message on Facebook on 7 June. In it, she did not hold back with her language or tone.

'It is with disgust and sadness that I inform you that PV have been in the Barmah National Park SHOOTING Brumbies secretly and deceitfully at night,' she wrote. Pridmore went on to speak of 'low life poor excuses for human beings'. She said the alleged cull showed an 'absolute disregard for you the public and all the hard work we have put in'. She said the count was unknown as Parks Victoria would not disclose it, but said Parks had 'taken full advantage of the Covid lockdown and just shit on all of us'. She then urged her followers and supporters to take to the bush in four wheel-drives and to keep their eyes open. 'It's a sad time and a regretful thing to have to inform you of, but you all have the right to know of this disgusting act,' she concluded.

You would not, repeat not, want to wear a Parks Victoria uniform into the Barmah pub anytime soon. Between the Yorta Yorta, Parks Victoria and brumby-loving locals, this part of Australia is at war with itself.

* * *

So in this game, as in any game, you can fight with your fists, your tongue, or your brain. Victorian animal rights lawyer Marilyn Nuske has chosen the latter method. Nuske is a horse lover. She grew up on a property in Victoria and went through pony club, had her own horse, the whole deal. She even married a horsey type. Her ex-husband was a French studmaster, and if that's not a phrase that belongs on a T-shirt, nothing is.

Nuske has been interested in brumby protection in the High Country for ten years or so, but the trigger for her to ramp up her involvement was an impending cull in late 2018 at the Lone Pine Barracks Army Base just outside Singleton, in the NSW Hunter Valley. There was a local herd of more than 200 brumbies, and for various reasons Defence didn't want it on its land. It had tried rehoming with limited success, and ground shooting from the perimeter of the base without much luck either. Its solution was an aerial cull, which was permissible because the base was on Commonwealth land, therefore the Bob Debus moratorium didn't apply.

Nuske started writing to Defence Industry Minister Christopher Pyne's office. She threatened an injunction. Jill Pickering and the Australian Brumby Alliance had set out a plan to remove the horses. They'd arranged to install trapping yards and lined up people who knew how to gentle a brumby for rehoming, everything. One of Minister Pyne's staff told Nuske they'd get back to her before 9 pm on 19 December 2018. Never happened. The shooting started. 'I'll never forget it,' Nuske says. 'I was on the phone to some people there and I could hear people saying, "Oh my God they've herded the brumbies, oh my God, they're shooting them!" I couldn't believe what was taking place. And it was my birthday.'

After Singleton, Nuske launched a change.org petition calling for legislation to protect Victorian brumbies. The petition has thus far garnered a whopping 178,000 signatures. At a rally in 2021 she invited Victorian Environment Minister Lily D'Ambrosio to meet on the steps of parliament and receive it. The minister didn't show, but Opposition Leader Michael O'Brien wasn't going to look a culture wars gift horse in the mouth, so he turned up and had it handed to him.

As Nuske got to know people in the pro-brumby movement like Renée Neubauer, with whom she has become quite friendly, she realised that brumby protection in Victoria wasn't just a High Country issue – Barmah had to be included too. She also realised that there were flaws in John Barilaro's NSW legislation, which she doesn't see as robust enough. So she sat down and drafted Victorian legislation herself. This process has taken her the best part of 18 months. In that time she has cosied up to sympathetic politicians, mostly on the conservative side of the fence. One of them is Wendy Lovell, an MP in the northern Victoria region which includes the Barmah Forest area. Another is Shadow Environment Minister Bridget Vallence.

'It's obvious the bill would get great support in the upper house,' she says. 'There's a big question mark in the lower house, unless we can win over more MPs.'

Nuske says her proposed legislation is all about horse management, all about appointing a panel, about considering the environment. 'It's not about shooting brumbies. There are ways of keeping brumbies out of sensitive areas and it's not necessarily shooting them.' She takes a big-picture view, arguing that humans introduced species like horses into our Australian bushland, and that now it's up to us to deal with them humanely. 'If they are causing damage, and I'm talking about all species, we can't go back to pre-colonial times,' she says. 'If we're going to do that, then we're going to have to rip down the ski lodges and Snowy 2.0 and the whole shebang.

'A lot of brumby group people are country people and they really have strong feelings. They have a very close bond with horses because they ride them. The brumby people don't all get along well, but the last rally in Melbourne brought together a lot of different brumby groups. There is now a united front, and I honestly believe part of that has been kicked up because of my legislation.'

It's coming. It's absolutely coming. In our great Australian democracy, no party rules at state or federal level for much longer than a decade. And maybe the November 2022 Victorian state election goes to Dan Andrews, the way other states have remained with the incumbent during the COVID period. Or maybe Victorians, having been burdened by more lockdowns than any other state, blame him for the mess and turf Labor out. Either way, it's coming eventually. One day the Libs will win, and the bill drafted by Marilyn Nuske, or something like it, will make its way into Parliament House on Spring Street, Melbourne, and it will be debated and, quite probably, pass into law. And Victorian brumbies will be protected as the Kosciuszko brumbies are protected. Just how many, and what the management controls will be, is all up for grabs. But it's coming. And whether Scruffy the brumby survives the Barmah guns or not, many other brumbies will be given a gift a lot more sustaining in the long term than a few bales of lucerne hay.

CHAPTER TEN

IRREGULAR AND RASH

Banjo understood. The great mythmaker was a truthteller too. A denizen of the city but a native of the bush, Banjo grasped the Great Divide in Australian society as well as anyone. The partition is comically captured in his 1893 poem 'The Geebung Polo Club', which tells the tale of a polo match between a mythical bush team and a posh city line-up. The contest is so brutal that every last player dies, and the ghosts of the fallen players haunt visitors to their row of gravestones on Victoria's Campaspe River, much like the ghost of the swagman can be heard by anyone passing the fateful billabong in Banjo's 'Waltzing Matilda'.

Now, you could argue that 'The Geebung Polo Club' is no more than a whimsical, tongue-in-stirrup commentary on the rough-n-toughness of bush life in general and especially bush horsemanship, which today can still be seen in small town rodeos and, as many believe, in brumby running. But it seems likely that Banjo was up to a little more than that. Perhaps he was saying that the bush will never win against the city, that the average people of the land will never triumph over those with money and power and status, and the best they can hope for is death by their own design, perhaps taking a few city folk down with them. Maybe the same message lies in 'Waltzing Matilda', with the uniformed trooper symbolising authority and the establishment, and the jolly swagman standing for freedom and defiance. There was, after all, a shearers' strike at the time of the anthemic poem's writing, and the object stolen by the swagman was a jumbuck, or male sheep. Rebellion and freedom, no matter what the cost: the theme runs deep in both poems, and is of course embodied in the stripling's daring ride in 'The Man from Snowy River'.

'Paterson I admire as one of the greatest of all Australians. Around campfires and all the rest of it, "The Man from Snowy River" has loomed incredibly large in my life.'

The words come from Phil Maguire, brumby advocate, High Country cattleman and famously prickly character. But on this wet April day with an early-season cold front coating the nearby High Country in its first autumn snows, Maguire presents a softer, warmer face. It started at the gate, where Maguire sat waiting in the cab of his ute. When people of the bush want to present a welcoming face to visitors, this is a small kindness they'll offer, in case you happen to miss their property and drain half a tank of petrol before you find the right driveway. The gesture was certainly appreciated on an afternoon of driving rain.

His house is neat. His paddocks are green and the fences appear well-enough maintained. There are dogs and cows, and everything appears in order in this prosperous and well-watered lowland valley in western Gippsland, just south-west of the snowfields of the Baw Baw Plateau. This is not his High Country property in the Bundarra Valley, near Omeo. This is where he resides with his wife, Louise – a highly accomplished equestrian who is away competing – and their three children, Cara, Anthony and James, whose ages range from about 20 to 15 in that order. Maguire serves tea and a generous plate of delicious jam biscuits, not too jammy, not too biscuity. Carrot sticks with dip too. Baklava is given in return, which he stashes away in the cupboard. Will the baklava later be hurled into a bin or will it perhaps be savoured for the excellent baklava it is? Who can say? We're playing tea parties here and everything's out of whack. Mr Angry Shouty on Facebook is being Mr Nicey Nicey with his three perfectly well-mannered children. What happens next here? What was the reason for this visit again? What can the purpose possibly be now that he's not displaying his bombastic, confrontational Facebook persona? Cochran was in character. That interview, if you could call it that, pretty much conducted itself. This is different.

The brumbies, obviously. Talk about the brumbies. Because in recent times, Maguire has been a leading voice in Victoria on the issue, louder than Australian Brumby Alliance president Jill Pickering, louder perhaps than anyone. As mentioned in Chapter Five, he has often been extremely outspoken on social media in the process, while presenting the face of the charming, if eccentric, bushman in public, or at least holding said face for as long as possible before someone or something made him think of Dan Andrews or greenies – at which point, look out! Incoming!

The thing is, Maguire reckons he's done with brumbies. He's made whispers about this before. Done with the brumbies, onto something else. But it seems like maybe he means it this time. For one thing, he trod a financial tightrope with his legal battles in 2020. Even though he raised serious money through his Rural Resistance website and Facebook group for the action against Parks Victoria's planned brumby cull in 2020, which got nowhere in the Victorian Supreme Court, an astronomical financial burden would have fallen largely on his shoulders if he'd made it to the High Court of Australia and lost. You'll recall that in 2020, with his blood running hot, he boldly stated that he'd sell his property to finance a High Court battle if he had to. He seems to have cooled off since then.

'This last year was hell. I hated it, the impact it had on us,' his son Anthony says.

'I risked these kids' future,' Maguire adds. 'As a matter of principle, 600 horses are alive now that wouldn't have been. But there was the potential for us to lose everything.'

There is word now in the mountains of a defamation suit or two against Maguire. Maguire himself mentions something about pending action from a leading brumby figure, the details of which are nobody's business. That's the thing about the bloke. The way he played his cards, he was always going to make both enemies and friends. In adopting the role of defender of the rights of brumbies to live in the High Country, free from the threat of Parks Victoria bullets, Maguire positioned himself as agitator not conciliator. His personal brand is firebrand. And that explains why Maguire says he cops it from all sides, both inside and beyond the pro-brumby movement.

There is a civil war within the brumby wars in Victoria and beyond. There's a war between rehomers and brumby runners over whether trapping or roping is crueller. There's a war between those who believe no horses whatsoever should be removed from the High Country, and the pro-brumby advocates who concede the need for some degree of management. There's a war between the hardline no-management folk and the runners and rehomers who help facilitate horse removal. And there's a war between Phil Maguire and pretty much everyone. Maguire is no ally of Jill Pickering or of the animal rights lawyer Marilyn Nuske. For one reason or another, he also has enemies in and around the Bundarra Valley, where his property is located. One of them was the revered brumby runner, and all-round High Country legend, the late Ken Connley, with whom Maguire co-owned the property before they fell out. Maguire is also continually at loggerheads with the brumby rehomers, many of whom he resents.

'There are people who have been making money out of brumbies,' he says, without naming names. 'What's happened is that the old horse dealers of ill repute have rebranded themselves as brumby rescuers. There are basically three steps. First, they establish themselves as brumby lovers. Then they take to social media and say they've got some brumbies on their property and need a whole winter's worth of hay, which might be $1000. Then they expand and say, "There are ten of us and we're going to buy a property and we need to raise some money." And then the money disappears.'

Evidence of such elaborate scams has not been uncovered. It is known that some brumby rescuers are lazy or deliberately cut corners. They'll take horses that Parks have trapped, then sell them on horsey websites as 'project horses' – the equine equivalent of a real estate 'fixer upper' or 'renovator's dream' – without doing any of the gentling work that a wild horse needs before becoming someone's pet or farm horse. But then there are the credible brumby rehomers. The ones who do tireless, important work. Erica Jessup up at Guy Fawkes is one. And by far the most prominent and successful rehomer in Victoria is Colleen O'Brien. Maguire doesn't get along with O'Brien either. He and his wife have disagreed with her on Facebook more than once. That doesn't bother her. Indeed, O'Brien's off-the-cuff, one-line synopsis of Maguire is intriguing to say the least.

* * *

It all started in 2001 with an ad in Victorian rural newspaper *The Weekly Times*. Colleen O'Brien was a city kid who grew up reading Elyne Mitchell's *Silver Brumby* books, and who eventually became a horse trainer and riding instructor after completing a degree in equine management. As an adult, she never thought much about High Country brumbies. To her, they were characters in Mitchell's works of children's fiction. Then she saw the small ad in *The Weekly Times* advertising Snowy brumbies for $120 a head. She was intrigued, so she called the number. It was a good six-hour trip from her property at Glenlogie in central Victoria to Bairnsdale in

Gippsland, and the seller told her it was a long drive without a horse float just to take a look. 'You're not going to buy any brumbies, are you?' O'Brien's husband, Dave, asked as they hitched up the float and drove off to Bairnsdale. She didn't know. She honestly had no idea.

'We pulled up, got out of the car, and the knackery truck pulled up right behind us,' O'Brien recalls. 'I looked at these brumbies and some of them were really cute. And one of the things that struck me was their size. One thing I knew through my riding instruction background was that we don't have a lot of middle-sized horses. You've got a lot of ponies up to about 12 hands, then lots of horses from about 15 hands upwards. Too many kids go from little ponies onto retired racehorses. We call them "heartbreakers". But these horses were the sort of solid, middle-sized ponies that I needed. I thought, *I could home a lot of these.* So I chose two and asked what was happening to the others. The chap said, "Oh, they're going to the other truck." So I loaded two onto my float and then another two ran on and he said, "I'll get 'em off", and I said, "No, leave them, leave them."' So it was that Colleen O'Brien headed home with her first four High Country brumbies. From day one, it's a decision she has never regretted.

'I was immediately blown away by the things brumbies have that domestic horses don't,' O'Brien recalls of those early days. 'Alpine brumbies are quiet by nature because you can't waste calories being an idiot in the High Country. But they're also very sociable because a brumby on its own is in danger, so they have very strong bonds with family, and also with their human families. They're dog-like in domesticity, and horse people think I'm nuts when I say that, but they just want to be around their person. My brumbies would view me as their family, and my mares are always on the nearest fence line when I'm outside. They are also very sound physically, again because they can't afford not to be when living in the wild. So you had these quiet, sound, sociable horses of a mid size. And I just thought they are such an asset.'

O'Brien started taking four or five or six brumbies each year from the same seller, who was running them out of the mountains. After having her second child in 2006, O'Brien was doing it tough with postnatal depression. Yet the brumbies were still on her mind. She felt she needed to do more. Saving a few wasn't enough. She wanted to lobby for them, and to educate the public about how great they are. 'My husband was a business manager, and he said, "Plan it. Work out how you're going to manage it, do all of that." I said to him, "You know that round yard we were going to build – could you build it this weekend?"'

With upgraded facilities in place at her 150-acre property, O'Brien started taking larger groups of brumbies. She formed a body called the Victorian Brumby Association, and in 2008 approached Parks Victoria and came to an agreement to take every single brumby trapped on the Bogong High Plains – the foals, the mares, the older stallions, all of them. She met with the aptly named Steve Horsley from the NSW National Parks and Wildlife Service and negotiated to take 40 horses a year from those trapped in northern Kosciuszko. She negotiated with NSW forestry authorities to start taking horses from the Bago State Forest, a heavily timbered plateau on the western flank of Kosciuszko National Park which is high enough for snow gums and small snow grass plains, and which was solidly populated with brumbies until the January 2020 fires.

Cut forward to today. O'Brien says she has successfully rehomed around 700 brumbies over the years. Almost all of them were rehomable, which is a real feather in her cap because, unlike some of the brumby runners, she takes all horses, not just the young ones or the ones that are easy to train and sell. Of those that couldn't be rehomed, most are in her paddocks. She manages to rehome about 50 brumbies a year these days, at an average price of around $800 per horse. Some people resent the fact she gets horses for free from Parks and onsells them. But when you factor in transport costs, vet bills, feeding costs, gentling work, and the opportunity cost of 150 acres that might otherwise be put to productive use, it all adds up and then some.

'Sure, it would be nice to cover costs but we never have and likely never will,' O'Brien says. 'There are always people who think there's money in brumbies. Being able to sell 50 brumbies a year for $800 when you've got a $60,000 hay bill, let's just say I'm lucky my husband has a good job.'

O'Brien is a deep thinker on the brumby issue and the environment more broadly. She's a fan of a relatively new movement called 'compassionate conservation', which is defined by the Centre for Compassionate Conservation at the University of Technology Sydney as 'an interdisciplinary field which promotes the treatment of all wildlife with respect, justice, and compassion'. In other words, don't kill something just because it's not originally from around here.

'Whether species are common or rare, whether native or not, all wildlife have intrinsic value. Compassionate conservation creates space for open dialogue, with the goal of helping to shape conservation thinking relevant to the Anthropocene,' the centre's website explains.

The key word there is 'Anthropocene', an unofficial unit of geologic time which is used in issues like climate change to describe the recent period in the earth's history when human activities began significantly impacting ecosystems. It's actually a central concept in all of this. Is anywhere on the planet anything like it was before humans became the dominant species? To bring all this back to the brumby debate, is it therefore fair and just, in a world so radically altered in so many ways, to pick on the mountain horses and shoot or remove them all in the name of a thing called 'conservation'? Conservation of what, exactly?

But there is a strong counter-argument, which can also be expressed as a question: Is it right to allow invasive species to prosper while standing by and watching precious landscapes decimated and native animals condemned to extinction?

You have to be very, very careful wading through these ethically murky waters. In a sense, 'compassionate conservation' is a deliberately sneaky phrase. It's a bit like fossil fuel industry–funded climate science denial groups using the word 'climate' in their title. Because the essence of 'conservation' is preserving the stuff that's already there, and that has been there for ages, not the stuff that arrived unannounced yesterday at dinnertime with a six-pack under its arm, and that might get drunk and break the good plates.

This is not to denigrate the majority of adherents to the idea of compassionate conservation, least of all Colleen O'Brien. Wanting to avoid shooting the absolute shit out of animals like brumbies is a perfectly humane principle, and that's essentially where her interest in the field lies. 'We're really good at killing stuff,' O'Brien says. 'We killed 600 koalas in the Otways because of overcrowding.' This is true. Wildlife officials killed over 600 starving koalas in 2013 and 2014, in the overpopulated koala stronghold near Victoria's Great Ocean Road, in a cull which was conducted covertly to avoid a public backlash but which inevitably leaked to the media. Nobody likes to see mass culls of any animal, native or introduced. But with regard to brumbies, is there a management solution that fits with the 'respect, justice, and compassion' of the compassionate conservation movement?

O'Brien believes there is: fertility control. She knows she's on a treadmill with rehoming. There are only so many people capable of taking horses, and even if there were more there are not enough dedicated rehomers like her. Unlike many brumby advocates, she accepts that the High Country will be damaged if the mobs keep breeding up each spring without significant management measures. So why not stop them breeding? O'Brien points to America, where wild horse management is as fraught as it is here. One control measure showing signs of success is fertility control with dart guns, where mares are darted each year until they're around seven years old.

O'Brien concedes that the practice is labour intensive and hard to administer in rough terrain. She admits that mares tend to live longer when they're not giving birth each year, which somewhat negates the effects on population control. But she still believes it would work, and has approached Parks authorities in both New South Wales and Victoria to suggest trials. No dice. This frustrates her. O'Brien says Parks Victoria spent around $180,000 on trapping 51 brumbies between 2012 and 2015, which equates to about $3500 per horse, and reckons fertility control could do the same job over a similar period for a fraction of the cost.

O'Brien doesn't always see eye to eye with Parks but has a reasonable working relationship with them. Indeed, that's one of the reasons some people in the pro-brumby movement don't like or trust her. But she couldn't even get Parks Victoria to meet with leading US fertility control experts who the Victorian Brumby Association and Australian Brumby Alliance brought out to Australia in 2017 – though, to be fair, some Kosciuszko National Park staff met with them. Although Parks have contracts with groups to shoot animals such as deer on public lands, they refuse to permit community groups to use dart guns on the same lands to carry out fertility control on brumbies. Fertility control on brumbies sounds great on paper, but in reality it would be incredibly difficult to coordinate on a meaningful scale in the Australian Alps.

Colleen O'Brien has had her successes and failures, her frustrations and triumphs. But give her this: she is a doer. Though based in Victoria, she has even served on the community advisory panel to the *Kosciuszko Wild Horse Heritage Act* in New South Wales, helping shape the new plan of management, although she quit recently because she lost faith in the panel's ability to deal with the issues.

The fact that she's a doer, not a spruiker, starts to give you a pretty good insight into why O'Brien doesn't get along with Maguire. 'Some of us are just good at making statements that get the issue on the front of the papers,' she says of Maguire, and leaves it there.

So if women like Colleen O'Brien and Jill Pickering are doing all the hard yakka for no financial gain (and in Pickering's case huge financial loss), maintaining arm's-length civil relations with land management authorities while Maguire blusters away and alienates himself from people and achieves no-one's-quite-sure-what apart from delaying that cull of Eastern Alps brumbies in 2020, it has to be asked: Is Phil Maguire really such an important figure in the scheme of the brumby wars? The answer lies in a Banjo poem. Because of course the answer lies in a Banjo poem.

* * *

Who are you?

When you're sitting in a bloke's house, and that bloke has a history of being a belligerent presence on social media and beyond, and that bloke wants you to see him as a family man, a sensitive man, a man of passion, not hatefulness, then it behoves the situation to ask that man a simple question.

Who are you?

'Primarily I'm a husband and father. Philosophically and religiously I'm a Catholic. I'm pro-life. I believe everyone conceived in this world has a right to life. I'm on the side of humanity, that's where I stand. I am also very strong on just treatment, on justice. When I look at the stars at night, I wonder, "What is justice? Is it something we came up with as human beings?"'

That's a tough one.

'Therefore I believe I should be just in all my dealings.'

In fairness, Maguire deserves points for self-awareness. 'Maybe my brakes aren't too good,' he says.

You get a different portrait of Phil Maguire through his website and Facebook group Rural Resistance, which recently disappeared into a private social media netherworld. His power base, such as it is, lies there, and his supporters look to him for more than just brumby advocacy. In Maguire they see a champion of old-school bush values. You'll recall the quote from Maguire in Chapter One of this book:

'The brumbies have become emblematic of a cultural heritage that is besieged by leftists and fake environmentalists ... If the brumbies go ... Another huge slice of Australia's identity will be lost. We must win this war for the sake of our country.'

That's what his war is really all about. Identity politics, but not of the left-wing variety. He seeks to preserve the rapidly disappearing identity of the bushman and all that goes with it. Like Peter Cochran over the border, Maguire has his own reasons for wanting brumbies running around – namely, that their presence keeps the door ajar, no matter how slightly, for the return of cattle grazing to the High Country. Remember, Maguire lost his prized access to the Bogong High Plains from his Bundarra Valley property back in about 2005. It's a wound that hasn't healed. But there's more than self-interest at play. Maguire loves the brumbies. He loves the horses themselves, he loves their links to the Walers and the war trade – tenuous though that link may be – and, above all, he loves that they represent the bush heritage celebrated by his beloved Banjo.

Maguire says he writes poetry and the odd song or two himself. He says he's had a few unique ideas in his time. One of them was to start a modern-day re-enactment of AB Paterson's 'The Geebung Polo Club'. As in, an actual polo match between a High Country team and a bunch of city toffs. This was more than 30 years ago. The event still takes place to this day on Easter Sunday at Cobungra Station near Omeo. High Country real estate agent John Castran has run it for most of that time. In the 1980s Castran developed Dinner Plain, Australia's only freehold village above the winter snow line (ski resort property within national parks is all leasehold), on the road between Omeo and Mt Hotham.

'I was with Phil in the Dinner Plain Hotel when he came up with the idea of the re-enactment,' Castran recalls. 'This was just after we'd started Dinner Plain and had about 25 or 30 buildings, and people were starting to come up in droves at Easter time but there was nothing for them to do. Phil had been saying, "We've got to get more things for people to do", he was like a termite in everyone's ear. I liked him, he was colourful. He ordered a Cobb & Co–style stagecoach to be made to go between Dinner Plain and Hotham. He was going to be a man riding a stagecoach back and forwards. I thought that would be a bit problematic when the road got icy and I remember Ken Connley said, "What the fuck is he thinking?" And then Phil said it'd be good to have a polo match up here, and I thought it was exactly the sort of thing we needed. But when it came to actually implementing it and doing it, it'd be fair to say that Phil moved on to other things but he definitely did come up with the idea.'

Though based in Melbourne and more often seen in a suit than a pair of boots, Castran is well known and liked in the High Country, and has a bushman's yarn-spinning prowess. And when he talks about the Geebung Polo Club re-enactment, you get the feeling it's exactly the sort of good-natured bush high jinks Maguire envisaged. The polo match really took off when Ken Connley had the idea of using mountain brumbies as polo ponies. It was the leveller that was desperately required, because – just like in the poem – the mountain cattlemen who played for the Geebung team were far superior horsemen, but the city blokes who came up to ride for Cuff and Collar were better polo players.

'Ken Connley said, "Why don't I go catch a whole lot of brumbies and break them in?"' Castran recalls. 'So he got something like 15 or 20 brumbies, and then the brumbies all came up on trucks. The horses were just broken in and had never played polo. I'd hold 15 straws in my hand and the players would pick from longest to shortest. The longest got first pick of the horses, and bingo, we got the handicap worked out.'

The polo match became the centrepiece of the long weekend festivities, but was by no means the only event. 'It was fucking lawless, what we used to do,' Castran recalls with a hearty laugh. 'In the first year, 1988, we had about 200 people. Then it got up to 3500. The polo was always on Easter Sunday and Saturday was the Omeo rodeo. The rodeo was a big, fun event and a lot of refreshment was had by all. So one year we were ready to go on the Sunday morning. The Cuff and Collars had turned up, but where was Connley? We were waiting round for an hour and then the local copper turned up and said, "Why haven't you started yet?" I said, "We've got no fricking horses or captain." And the copper said, "Oh, I've got Connley locked up for drunk and disorderly last night." In those days Hotham had a heli, so I said, "Can we bring him up here, and you can take him back straight afterwards?" So we flew him up, played the game, and the copper had him back into custody the same night. Ken loved it. He was like a rock star coming out of incarceration and onto a polo field.'

Times have changed in the High Country, even since the 1980s and '90s. 'The police knew it was really good for their profile to be interacting at these sort of events,' Castran says. 'One year we had a tug-of-war between a police car and a Cessna 182. People loved it. But somehow word got back to command in Melbourne and we were all dragged up before the police. We said everyone loved it, it was all very innocent and no one was getting hurt. They had an inquiry in St Kilda Road and said, "Next time, perhaps try an egg-and-spoon race."

'So whether you like Phil Maguire or not, he's a maverick and he was a thousand per cent correct. The Geebung Polo Club match was a great idea. It was done in the spirit of bushrangerism, of the folklore of the High Country. The identities that came out of that High Country weren't holier-than-thou and weren't politically correct. They were totally imperfect because it's a tough environment up there.'

That's the spirit that Banjo was writing about. And it's the slow, inevitable passing of that spirit that Maguire seems to lament when he speaks of his admiration for Banjo. In a way, it's a shame that Maguire's brazen persona has spilled over into classic far-right-wing territory. But we live in a world of OH&S and environmentalism and a whole swag of things that constrain the impulses of a High Country free spirit, and that'll inflame a man's passions in all sorts of ways. As for the wild and free brumbies, they symbolise a loss more profound than even the lucrative High Country grazing leases. They symbolise the loss of the whole way of life. Understand that and you understand Maguire himself. Somewhere beyond the bluster, insults and anger, he's in mourning for the High Country hero the modern world won't quite let him be. And if you understand that, you understand the passion of many others in the pro-brumby movement. They pine for a time when they could muck around and wreak havoc and raise hell and no one would tell them what to do. You can't carry on any more like the blokes in the 1965 *Buckrunners* documentary. Not without some parkie lurking behind a snow gum waiting to write you a ticket for who-knows-what. And that tug-of-war between the Cessna and the cop car? Banjo himself would've struggled to find such a perfect metaphor for the struggle of modern High Country life. A vehicle that flies as free as a bird on one side, a vehicle that constrains and enforces rules on the other.

'You have to remember that Banjo himself in many ways was like an action-adventure hero and he wrote a lot of his commentaries and poems and stories reflecting that,' Grantlee Kieza, author of the book *Banjo* says. 'And while he was based in Sydney and was quite a wealthy young bloke who became a pillar of the establishment in middle age, he kept going to bush places and he knew what these people were like. He was writing about characters he had rubbed shoulders with in a part-time capacity, and for a lot of these people, life and death was very tenuous. Banjo was knocking around with so many self-destructive characters. He even played polo against Breaker Morant – how much more self-destructive could you get?'

On a quick survey, 'The Geebung Polo Club' reads like a comic farce. But it may, in fact, be one of the least romantic of Banjo's works. As mentioned at the start of this chapter, the great mythmaker was a truthteller too. And the truth is that the bush was tough, but locals loved it that way. There was freedom in trying to eke a living off the land, no matter what the cost. And Phil Maguire believes in the gospel of the Holy Banjo. He believes that you should fight for the High Country way of life no matter what the cost, even if every polo player dies on the field. He has lived much of his life like the polo players in Banjo's poem, whose style is described as 'irregular and rash' in the first stanza. But being irregular and rash hasn't always worked out for Maguire, because the world is the world and it is, for the most part, regular and ordered. And his family is his family, his responsibilities are his responsibilities and his life, tragically, is not a poem. That's why he seems to be reassessing things now, trying to rebrand himself as a High Country statesman, not a rogue. When you keep that big picture in mind, it seems like Phil Maguire is not such a bad fella after all, deep down, in a place not everyone sees or understands.

CHAPTER ELEVEN

THE BATTLE OF LONG PLAIN

But we all see different things in landscapes. A remote valley that echoes with an old adventure poem is for others a place of contemplation and quiet. A thinly timbered hill enlivened by the flash of manes and tails is for others a landscape invaded, bespoiled.

Australia's early landscape painters could never get the light right. It was always too washed-out and milky. Were they unable to replicate the brilliance and harshness of Australian light because their European palette couldn't cope with it, like a Casio watch trying to run Windows 10? Or did they not want to see it? And what don't the rest of us want to see? Do we all view landscapes through a lens?

* * *

When you drive up from the Tumut side of the plains of northern Kosciuszko on the Snowy Mountains Highway, your first close-up look of the mountains comes from the roadside Black Perry lookout. From there, you get a great view of the Bogong Peaks Wilderness. This little-visited area should not be confused with Victoria's Bogong High Plains, or Victoria's highest peak Mt Bogong, from whose summit, incidentally, you can clearly make out the Bogong Peaks Wilderness some 200 kilometres north-east as the mountain raven flies.

The lookout is popular. Fire ran right through it in 2020, severely charring the whole area, but everyone still stops there. Families, motorbike groups, grey nomads, people with horse floats on their way up to the bridle trails of Long Plain – everyone.

There's a sign at the lookout that says:

'Wilderness'
From this point you can see around 10,000 hectares of Bogong Peaks Wilderness. Wilderness areas in Kosciuszko National Park represent some of the least disturbed parts of the Australian Alps bioregion. They are places in which natural processes can continue with minimal human interference, places of refuge for rare and threatened plant and animal species, and repositories of genetic material. They also provide for natural settings in which people can undertake self-reliant recreational activities and find solitude, inspiration and a sense of renewal.

Natural settings in which people can undertake self-reliant recreational activities and find solitude, inspiration and a sense of renewal. But what does that mean? What is a self-reliant activity? It seems to be code for walking, and perhaps also cross-country skiing. It seems to be saying there are some places you can't bring an esky, and you're staring at one of them. And such places are needed. Indeed, the Bogong Peaks Wilderness is one of just three strongholds of the northern corroboree frog. It deserves to be left alone by all but those who tread lightest.

But is wilderness the only place in which we can find 'solitude, inspiration and a sense of renewal'? Must those experiences be the sole preserve of those with fitness, agility, expensive outdoor gear and advanced backcountry navigational skills? If national parks truly belong to the people, do not people deserve to experience solitude, inspiration and renewal without venturing far from the roadside? And what is solitude, inspiration and renewal anyway? On Long Plain, perhaps more than anywhere else in Kosciuszko, that's up for debate. Long Plain is the largest of the vast northern Kosciuszko snow grass plains and the most visited by horse riders. It has a network of bridle trails as well as designated campsites for people with horses and floats. It also has numerous mobs of brumbies. Long Plain is loved by thousands. For them, it is the finest and most easily accessible area where they can indulge in passive or active horse-related recreation. And, of course, Long Plain is a place where people lament the loss of a once pristine subalpine treasure.

* * *

The famous track that wound back to Gundagai was long ago replaced by the Hume Highway. Then they turned the highway into a four-lane dual carriageway that bypassed the town of Gundagai. The town's iconic statue of the Dog on the Tuckerbox, 'five miles from Gundagai', now sits at a rest area off the highway, just near the KFC and the 24-hour Shell service station. The manager of that service station is Karen Ferguson, and Karen Ferguson works hard, and nothing comes easy, and when she wants to get away from it all, she drives the hour and a half through Tumut and up to Long Plain. And when she gets to Long Plain, she sits down on her favourite rock, gets out her camera, and exhales.

Ferguson grew up on a farm near Adelong, just west of Tumut, but she says she wasn't really a 'horsey person' as a child because the rule in her household was: boys out on the farm, girls in the kitchen. Her grandparents had a house on the south coast of New South Wales, which meant the family often drove over the mountains. It was on those trips that she first saw brumbies out the window. 'I was in awe of them,' she recalls. 'In my twenties, I started visiting the mountains every couple of months. Then life would happen and I wouldn't go for a year or more. But I went up there as often as I could. Then after the 2020 fires, everything changed. Dad got hit by the Dunns Road fire pretty bad. He managed to save the house, but he lost everything else – machinery, fencing, animals. It was the first time in a very long time I'd seen my dad cry, and he's not an emotional person so it was a pretty big thing. Anyway, once I knew my family was safe, my next concern was for my other family, so as soon as I could get up there, I went for a drive. It was very emotional. I spent a full day up there and I saw dead brumbies and wildlife. Luckily, I found some mobs that I had sat with previously that had survived the fires, and I made a commitment to myself that I would go every single month.'

She upheld her commitment. And then she started going weekly, taking more photos than ever before. She started a small, private Facebook group called The Memory Keeper's Pocket where she could post and share the photos. Its description reads: 'Photos of my journey with the Snowy Mountains brumbies … A peaceful place for people who share a common interest. No politics, no judgement and no negativity.'

Ferguson says Long Plain is her happy place. Her peaceful place. A place where she can forget work. The sketchy phone reception helps with that. She's got a favourite spot or two out on the Plain. A rock here. A glade of black sallees there. Couple of protein bars, small slab of chocolate, bottle of water and she's good to go for hours. She knows a lot of the horses by sight, and some of them now know her. She says she can't really pinpoint a favourite because 'they're all amazing for different reasons', but there's one that she loves more than most. She calls him 'Bestie', a grey with a pink strip down his nose. 'I met him on my first visit after the fires and it was a memorable experience,' she says. 'I was sitting in a pile of wet grass taking photos, and there were basically 20-odd horses. I think the mobs were displaced after the fires. Then out of the corner of my eye, I spotted three greys. I tend to sit very still because that makes them comfortable, but they kept coming towards me. One veered off to the side but Bestie came up and put his nose on mine. It was mind-blowing, and after that I seemed to run into him regularly.'

Ferguson never feeds the horses. She knows they're wild animals and feeding them is wrong for all sorts of reasons. She says she understands they need to be managed, but she also believes the brumbies have earned their right to live in the park. 'They're part of our heritage and they have been there a very long time,' she says. 'I understand the alpine areas need to be protected, but in the big scheme, the park is a huge area. I'm not saying they don't do damage, but I've walked a lot of places up there and I don't see the extremes that the other side sees. The brumbies are a drawcard. When I'm up there, do you know how many tourists approach me that want to know where to take photos? There must be a solution that makes everyone happy. Somewhere in this mess, there's got to be a win for everybody.'

* * *

Old Paleface was never too hard to find. He favoured the rolling country in northern Kosciuszko near the Snowy Mountains Highway around Kiandra and Selwyn Snow Resort. When John Barilaro went to see him for a photo op after his legislation passed, there he was. That's Paleface on the cover of this book, by the way, fighting with another stallion. The extraordinary photo was taken by Michelle Brown, a Cooma-based photographer, brumby advocate and rehomer of a beautiful bay brumby yearling that Parks trapped up on Long Plain. 'Paleface knew he was a celebrity,' Brown laughs. It was Brown who told Barilaro's people where he could find Paleface that day. 'He knew who to trust and who not to trust. If he knew you meant no harm, you were accepted.'

But one day in late December 2019, Brown sensed that Paleface was in mortal danger. Fires had raged further afield for months, but Kosciuszko had escaped them up until then. Brown and her husband, Ian, were driving to Victoria just before Christmas when they stopped up near the crest of the range at the car park of Selwyn Snow Resort, whose grassy green slopes were favoured by the local brumby mobs. There was Paleface, grazing with his mob on the ski runs. 'They were always safe there. It was their safe place. The Selwyn staff loved Paleface,' Brown says, tearing up. 'He looked so happy, and we saw his daughter Jinka and her new foal and the stallion that she was with, and then we saw the son of Paleface, which is Bogong. We saw him and the filly that he had.'

Talking to Michelle Brown is like reading a Silver Brumby book. There's an endless procession of horse names dropped casually into the conversation. Where do the names come from? 'We name them and that's how we keep track of where they are and who they are,' she says.

The Browns cut their trip to Victoria short. For one reason or another, they sensed that something was up. On 28 December 2019, the Browns again stopped at Selwyn. The mountain march flies were bad that day. 'Never been eaten alive so badly in my entire life,' Brown recalls. 'They were huge. I don't think I'm a superstitious type of person, but to me it was just not right, because we'd never had that many march flies on us before. It was very still. There was no wind. It was really, really hot and a few brumbies were sheltering from the heat under the shady snow gums.' But there was no sign of Paleface. This was just days before the Dunns Road fire came roaring over the western flank of the mountains, ripping through Selwyn and destroying the infrastructure of the ski resort, chairlifts and all. Michelle Brown would never see Paleface again.

'The king of the mountain is not there anymore. The most iconic brumby stallion and his mob are gone,' she says.

Michelle Brown is more than just a brumby photographer. She's a brumby appreciator, a brumby lover. To her, the brumbies are as Kosciuszko as snow gums. 'They are the living spirit of the mountains,' she says. 'Without the thundering hooves and the presence of an animal that's been there for 180 years, the mountains wouldn't be alive. Kosciuszko National Park is where the brumbies roam. It's their home, it's where they were born. The environment has evolved around them. Everything has evolved around them.'

Brumby photography days start early for the Browns. Ian makes the cheese and tomato sandwiches before dawn and then they're up there, while the grass is still frosty or dewy, with their hiking poles, first-aid kit, snake gaiters, sunscreen, hats, the lot of it. They like the Kiandra area but they often venture further afield to Long Plain, Currango Plain, anywhere in the north of the park. Sometimes the brumbies get quite close. One day, for example – and this was actually on their honeymoon – a bay stallion called Bob, so named because of his bobtail, crept up behind them and looked at them 'as if to say, "Hi guys, you again." We knew Bob already and he was looking at me and I'm looking back and I'm like, "Well, hello to you too."' The Browns swiftly moved towards their car and Bob eventually slipped off into the scrub. All was well. 'It's just a thrill when you get that encounter with a wild horse, you know? Many of the brumbies know us.'

Despite her love of the Kosciuszko brumbies, of their beauty in full flight, of the odd frightening run-in, of their lineage and family trees which she takes such delight in collating, Brown understands the needs for management. 'Yes, I'm a horse lover and yes, I could sit here and blow shit out my arse saying horses don't do damage. But I'm not saying that. I'm not saying they're not to be managed. They have to be managed, but you need to find that balance, and the balance needs to be done properly.'

Michelle Brown's Snowy Brumby Photography Adventures Facebook page has around 70,000 followers. This former Sydney girl has many admirers in the mountains, but there are also those who have a different outlook.

One of them is Alan Lanyon of the Snowy Mountains Brumby Sustainability & Management Group. Lanyon is one of the loudest, most active advocates of Kosciuszko's brumbies and when you meet him in person, well, let's just say he's a little different to what you might have expected.

* * *

So let's imagine that they never built the dual carriageway Hume Highway, and that there was still a track and a shack, winding and old-fashioned respectively, at Gundagai. That shack might look a little like Alan Lanyon's house, which is not to denigrate his pleasant suburban home. It's just to say that it is a modest, unassuming dwelling in a quiet back street of Gundagai near the dilapidated state heritage–listed Prince Alfred Bridge over the Murrumbidgee. When a bloke has been as noisy as Lanyon over many years in an impassioned public debate, you half expect him to live in a grand homestead with a broad verandah or some such. But Lanyon is a working man and proud of it. 'I've been a worker all me life,' he says as we chat over a beer on his back porch, looking out over his well-tended lawn while two of the world's loudest kookaburras disrupt the conversation.

In 2019, they closed the particle board manufacturing plant in Tumut, where Lanyon had worked for years. Before that, he used to do public phone maintenance for Telstra, or Telecom Australia as it was back then. Lanyon is now 66 and semi-retired. He lives with his wife, Cheryl, and has four kids and 'a tribe of grandkids'. Originally from 'out the other side of West Wyalong', Lanyon's first trip to the mountains was in the 1970s when his mate took him fishing there. Lanyon was the one who got hooked. He just loved it up there.

'In those immediately post–snow lease days, the management was very different,' he says. 'There weren't all the impediments to travel throughout the mountains. Bob Carr's wilderness bullshit legislation hadn't come into being, and the country still showed all the hallmarks of pastoral grazing. Rabbits and blackberry were non-existent, sweet briar was non-existent, there were some pigs but they're a transient sort of animal. There were wild dogs in the park but they had been controlled, as they had been for 150 years. The place had all the hallmarks of having been looked after.'

Lanyon soon took to horse riding in northern Kosciuszko on Long Plain and further afield. He used to love 'poking through the bush, minding your own business'. He loved finding old fence lines dating back to the 1800s, old rusting machinery, things that reminded him of tough men eking out a living in tough country. 'My story is not a "Man from Snowy River" story,' he says. 'There's nothing fanciful there. I just get on my horse and I have an affinity for the bush and our cultural history within the bush.'

The fear of many recreational horse riders like Lanyon is that if too many brumbies are removed, a zero-tolerance policy for horses in Kosciuszko could come into play and Parks will come for riders next. Horse riding is not permitted in the designated wilderness areas of Kosciuszko but it is allowed in around 50 per cent of the park. There are no indications whatsoever that Parks has plans to change those rules, brumbies or no brumbies. But you can understand how some would put two and two together.

Lanyon is a combative character. But give him credit. He has put in the hard yards to save the brumbies. In the early 2000s, when he heard strong whispers that Bob Debus's moratorium on aerial shooting was potentially in danger of being overturned, he drove around the Riverina region of New South Wales in his white Ford Falcon, garnering signatures for a petition. It was what he does best – putting himself out there among what he calls the 'true blues' and rallying them to the cause. When Lanyon dived into the pro-brumby fight in the early 2000s, it's fair to say that he was naive about politics and its tricks. He soon clashed with

Peter Cochran and has engaged in a lot of to-and-fro with him over the years. It's probably best to leave their relationship there because the lawyers of the world are wealthy enough. It's probably best to keep a lid on much of what Lanyon says, well intentioned though it may be. Suffice it to say that Lanyon has not gone away. He doesn't get the headlines or the slots on Sydney talkback radio, but he continues to fight for the brumbies and to rail against the science, which he has called 'unmitigated bullshit'. It was his Snowy Mountains Brumby Sustainability & Management Group (SMBSMG) that took the NSW government to court over the trapping and removal of several hundred horses which had strayed into three sensitive new areas in northern Kosciuszko after the 2020 fires, as mentioned in Chapter Seven. He lost, but his supporters dug deep and raised over $50,000 for legal costs. The man has pulling power. The true blues love their true blue leader.

What Lanyon has been up to lately is puzzling to say the least. A recent video on his SMBSMG Facebook page showed brumbies running out of their temporary trap yard on what looks like one of Kosciuszko's northern plains. Who opened the gate is unclear, but the video was accompanied by the following post:

G'day true blues, at a time when fair dinkum brumby supporters have gone past desperation point with unadulterated political bull...t and agendas and the anti-brumby zealots and their bed mates, we are pretty happy to bring you this short clip. Most true blues would be aware of some pics that circulated last Friday of a deathpen of trapped brumbies with their offspring outside the pens whinnying for their mothers. The article mentioned that NPWS turned up, don't know what the yellowshirts got up to but this is the end result of some pro-brumby activity – just hoping the split mob picked up their foals and didn't stop running … as they should be, running free … might be calling for volunteers for some more pro-brumby activity REAL soon.

Back in Lanyon's backyard, as the cockatoos take over from the kookaburras in the battle of the raucous birds, Lanyon hits a familiar refrain. 'We're fighting, or the greater proportion of pro-brumby activists are fighting, to retain our cultural heritage.' The exact manner in which they're fighting right now is unclear. And, for various reasons, not much more can be said.

* * *

Di Thompson doesn't much care for the two things that most nature lovers love most about Kosciuszko: the snow and the wildflowers. She's got no love for the brumbies either, and that's putting it mildly. To understand all that, you've got to understand the background of one of the most fascinating and gutsy characters in the brumby debate.

As mentioned earlier, Thompson grew up in Western Australia, the daughter of a drover. When she talks about her dad, there's this intense mixture of love and sorrow and a hundred other emotions, most of them sweet. 'My father was an itinerant worker who died in his early 60s under an assumed name because he hated the government,' Thompson explains at the dining room of her suburban Canberra home. 'And I'll tell you why he hated the government. He was raised in a family that was very poor in East Perth and his mother had diabetes and was going blind, so he and his two brothers were taken away from the family as neglected children.'

Thompson's father was reared in orphanages and drifted up north as a young man. He worked as the barman at Fitzroy Crossing in the Kimberley. He worked as a gravedigger, a shearer, and a wheat lumper, hauling 'hundredweight' bags, which were in fact 112 pounds, about 50 kilos. And he worked the famed De Grey Stock Route. 'It was a very tough life,' Thompson deadpans with the sort of understatement only someone who grew up in hardship could have. But when talking about her upbringing there's one aspect that she's naturally expansive about. 'I knew that Dad thought the sun, moon and stars shone out of me,' she says. 'There was nothing I could do wrong – isn't that a beautiful thing? It doesn't matter how poor we were. I was Dad's shadow all of my childhood, I went everywhere with Dad. I sat under a table for a week when I had to go to school and missed the first year because I didn't want to leave Dad.'

After floating around the north of Western Australia throughout Thompson's very early childhood, her parents ended up share farming in Western Australia's wheatbelt. But they were no further from the breadline than they had been up north. 'Our last house had dirt floors. We'd sew these wheat bags together, whitewash them and hang them for our walls,' Thompson recalls. 'But I didn't know it was rough. I had a wonderful childhood. I used to sit watching mallee fowl for hours. I'd sit on Dad's knee and steer the old truck, a 1928 model Chev which you had to crank. And the wildflowers of the wheatbelt ... acres and acres of wildflowers, as far as you could see.'

Eventually, Thompson's mum moved to Perth when she was about seven, taking little Di with her, while her dad continued to work away from home. They lived by Scarborough Beach, which working people could afford to do back in the '50s, and Di would spend her time wandering the bush and the sand dunes. Her dad would write to her frequently and in the springtime he'd send pressed flowers in the letters. Sweet-smelling boronia and a delicate little flower called the green birdflower. To this day, those flowers are a hundred times more beautiful to Thompson than anything she's seen in Kosciuszko's remarkable spring and summer blooms. So that explains that. As for her aversion to snow? Well, it's cold, and she's never been a skier so it's not much use to her. Flowers and snow aside, Kosciuszko was paradise on earth for Thompson. The reason? Water. Thompson left school when she was 15, as most girls did back then. She left the west and ended up in Canberra via New Zealand, married to Gary and working as a typist. They first went to Kosciuszko in 1967, the year the park was gazetted, and she couldn't believe the place, especially the northern plains like Long Plain. 'It's a big brown land, and where do I come from? But this big brown land had water, and beautiful clear water! I couldn't believe it. We lived in a five-inch rainfall zone in the WA wheatbelt. Dad used to have to go get water with 44-gallon drums and roll them up onto the truck.'

After having three children, Thompson went to uni and studied maths and stats, which she found an affinity for despite having not studied it at school. She got her first job with consulting actuaries, and her area of expertise later became the interaction between the social security system and the tax system. 'It's a really good dinner party stopper,' she laughs. At one point, she worked with Nill Kyrgios, mother of tennis player Nick, who was a computer programmer. And when the working week was done, Thompson and her husband would take their young family to Kosciuszko. Little could Thompson have imagined that her passion for the High Country would plonk her in the middle of a fight more ferocious than even the most volcanic Nick Kyrgios on-court outburst.

'When I got back to work in the early 1980s, I joined bushwalking clubs and that was the opening of the book for me. You'd go out with these gifted, knowledgeable and kind people that know a lot about the plants and animals and they didn't shove it down my throat, and they were lovely with my children. We did a lot of car camping with these people and you couldn't help but learn.' Thompson has some amazing photos she's taken at the headwaters of the Murrumbidgee River on Long Plain. 'Look at that recovery,' she says as she shows off a 1985 photo. 'This is ten years after they took cattle grazing out. Amazing, isn't it?' It is indeed. The grass is springy, the riverbanks are spongy, the water clear. 'Now look at this one. Same spot. I've been taking photos of this spot for years now. The comparison is just terrible, isn't it?' Again, it is. It's the stormwater-drain look all over again, just like on Currango Plain. 'The loss, the loss,' Thompson says, shaking her head.

When you grow up in the Western Australian bush with hessian sacks for walls, you become the sort of person who's a doer, not a talker. Thompson started getting involved in environmental advocacy with the ACT and NSW National Parks Associations, the Nature Conservation Council of NSW and other bodies. She was involved in orange hawkweed control. She was active in the Kosciuszko Huts Association helping to rebuild after fires. She did tough, physical work in rabbit control, marking out warrens. She sawed down wilding pines that had sprouted in the bush from commercial pine plantations. She has worked with the environmental management of ski resorts, on water flow issues in the Murrumbidgee, on bushwalking tracks on the south coast of New South Wales and much more. For services to the environment, she was awarded an Order of Australia Medal.

For what she endured as a member of various committees and panels in her environmental advocacy on the brumby issue, Di Thompson deserves a medal cast in pure gold, or at the very least a lifetime supply of chocolate from a really classy chocolate manufacturer. She was on the committee for the first Kosciuszko Wild Horse Management Plan in 2002, alongside Leisa Caldwell, and sat on numerous panels and committees thereafter. Horse people gave her hell. As mentioned in Chapter One, she was frequently verbally and even physically intimidated.

'I will never go back on another committee to deal with the horse thing,' she says. 'It's dangerous. I'm an Australian and I should have the right to go without fear. It makes me feel disturbed now to think of the threats.'

Thompson reckons horse people took a particular dislike to her because she wasn't your typical city shiny bum. 'They fear me because I know too much about them, and because I have heritage that probably outranks theirs. But I don't go round saying, "It's my heritage and my right." I never demanded to go somewhere in Western Australia because my dad had worked there or ridden his horse there.'

The Murrumbidgee River is Australia's second-longest river. It rises on Peppercorn Hill at the northern end of Long Plain. Like the Murray, the Murrumbidgee's headwaters are a mess because of horses. The state of country distresses Thompson. The feral horses have denuded her beloved Long Plain, her subalpine paradise, a landscape resembling the West Australian wheatbelt dreamscape of her childhood but with the impossible addition of water and long, waving tussocks of native grass. And it makes her sad. And it makes her angry. And this feisty expert in the interaction between the social security system and the tax system reckons the brumby lovers should get the damn things out of the park and if they really care about them so much, pay for them themselves and stop making the rest of Australia foot the ecological and financial bill for their upkeep.

CHAPTER TWELVE

'WE LOVE OUR HORSES BUT WE LOVE OUR COUNTRY MORE'

In 1995, a new rugby union team formed in Canberra as one of three Australian sides in the inaugural Super 12 rugby union competition involving provincial teams from Australia, New Zealand and South Africa. The new team had a large stadium which it would share with the Canberra Raiders rugby league team, an impressive list of players recruited from scratch, and a high-profile coach in Rod Macqueen, but it had no name. So Macqueen got to work trying to find one. And because the Canberra-based outfit was conceived as being the local team for the whole of south-east New South Wales as well as Canberra, Macqueen looked beyond the capital for inspiration.

'It occurred to me that we could pick up some of the traditions and heritage from the famous Snowy Mountains area,' Macqueen told author Michael McKernan in his book *The Brumbies: The Super 12 years*. 'With this in mind it wasn't long before we were thinking of stockmen and horses and flicking through the poetry books. After many long hours of discussion with family and friends, the name came from an unexpected source. I received a call that night from my secretary Helen. Her son had put forward a name that struck an appropriate chord – the Brumbies.'

Like all the best leaders, Macqueen knew that ideas really take hold when people feel it was *their* idea. So he scrawled down a list of 72 names and photocopied it for the board of the new club. For no apparent reason, the list had an asterisk next to the word 'Brumbies'. That asterisk did its job. When asked to circle five names they liked, it was the only one chosen by all. Thus was born the ACT Brumbies, or Brumbies Rugby as they are now officially known. The irony is that there are no brumbies in the ACT today, even though the highest parts of Namadgi National Park are barely 15 kilometres from Long Plain as the mountain raven flies. Why not a single horse? Because the ACT Parks and Conservation Service has a zero-tolerance policy towards feral horses. Why the hardline stance? In a word: water.

Canberra was founded as Australia's capital city in 1913. After federation in 1901, the constitution stated that the new capital had to be in New South Wales, at least 100 miles (about 160 kilometres) from Sydney. Charles Scrivener was the man charged with surveying potential sites. He knew that an inland city needed water. Eventually the Yass–Canberra area was settled upon. 'I like to think of him travelling over Mt Ainslie or Black Mountain and looking out towards the Brindabellas and wondering what was up there,' says ACT

Parks and Conservation Service regional manager Brett McNamara. What was up there, or at least what was at the foot of the Brindabellas – the high range visible beyond Canberra's western outskirts – was the Cotter River, a beautiful, clear montane river fed by alpine bogs and wetland.

'The importance of that vision well over 100 years ago was that we would be masters of our own destiny,' McNamara says. 'The shape of the ACT is predicated on where the rivers start and where they end.' From day one, nothing would threaten that vision. The Cotter River Ordinance came into being in 1914. Fishing in the river would attract a ten-pound fine or a month in prison. Picnicking or camping by the river was 20 pounds or three months in prison. Before the survey work was completed and the ordinance passed, there had been a smattering of residents eking out a living in the upper Cotter valley. One of them was Jack Maxwell, who contemporaries described as a 'wiry bushman' and a 'bit of a loner' – although the loner later married Ivy Franklin, cousin of the author Miles Franklin whose childhood home Brindabella Station was just over the range. In 1927, the year that Parliament House opened in Canberra, Maxwell was given the job of ranger for the upper Cotter valley. Maxwell was by all accounts extremely proud to hold such an esteemed position. He would always wear a coat and tie when riding into and out of the Cotter catchment. One of his jobs was controlling the feral horse population by brumby running. So it was that a proud bushie was also a proud parkie. A cattleman was also a land manager working for public authorities. A horseman was also a man who knew where horses didn't belong. We did not always have the culture wars in this country. There was a time when even High Country folk understood that land management rules had a purpose, and that obeying or enforcing them did not water down your heritage, freedoms or rights.

Today, ACT Parks has an approach to horse removal which is significantly higher-tech and more efficient. When horses stray across the border into Namadgi National Park from northern Kosciuszko, they will first be spotted by cameras cleverly hidden in trees along the ACT–NSW border, which are in place to detect both horses and deer. Then, depending on a range of factors, the horses might be shot in accordance with ACT law. 'I am proud of the legacy we are privileged to inherit, proud of the vision Scrivener had, and proud I can uphold his vision and keep it going,' Brett McNamara says.

A Canberra native, McNamara is a relentlessly upbeat sort of character despite losing his house, and nearly his life, in the catastrophic 2003 fires which swept into the suburbs of the capital, killing four people and destroying 470 homes. Namadgi National Park was scarred for many years afterwards. It copped it again in 2020 thanks to a Defence chopper whose landing light ignited a blaze that burnt 80 per cent of the park after its crew inexplicably failed to alert authorities for a full 45 minutes after the initial fateful sparks. McNamara takes a long-lens view to land management. 'I have an appreciation of time and how old these mountains are,' he says. 'As humans, we think that 80 years is a lifetime. We don't understand that it's a drop in the ocean on nature's timescales, and that the things we do today, we won't see the ramifications of till tomorrow. A horse grazing up there – what difference is it going to make? The difference is over time, and those are the consequences many people can't understand.

'Look at the sphagnum bogs up high in Namadgi. One of the reasons Canberra still had water flowing into our catchments in 2020 was the critical role of sphagnum, which holds and retains and slowly releases water like a sponge in your kitchen. That's the water that flows into our catchment. These bogs can almost be drained by the rolling and compaction of a 250-kilogram horse. It is not an impact that you will see tomorrow. You'll see a horse mark here and there, but the problem is the cumulative impact over time. And that's why it's so important to appreciate the concept of time. As humans, we fail to appreciate where we stand in the timescale of nature. I've only come to appreciate that in just 30 years. And that's why we've been taking these feral animals out. It's a protection attitude we had 100 years ago, and this idea that we're militants and want to lock everyone out, well, that just goes against the grain.'

While no brumbies roam the mountains of the ACT, there is a very, very famous and popular horse in Canberra, or part of that horse anyway. 'Did you know that Phar Lap's heart is the most requested object at the National Museum of Australia?' horse culture expert Dr Isa Menzies asks. Menzies was working as a curator at the museum in 2011 and vividly recalls the fuss over the famously ginormous ticker of Australia's most celebrated racehorse.

'What fascinated me the most is that parents would bring their small children, and the kids would see this heart in a jar and they'd be grossed out, and rightly so because it's a pretty gross object,' Menzies recalls. 'But the parents would be like, "No, no, this is a very special heart of a very special horse", and the kids, duly awed, would walk away. There was no interrogation of why the heart was important, why the horse was important, but you were basically watching that cultural knowledge being transferred from one generation to the next.'

Menzies became interested in people's deep fascination with horsey objects. She initially thought she might do a PhD focusing on horse parts in museums. Then she broadened the topic. In 2019, she submitted her PhD thesis, entitled 'Horses for Discourses: A critical examination of the horse in Australian culture'. The first few lines of the abstract tell you most of what you need to know:

> The cultural significance of the horse functions as one of the cornerstone narratives in the production and performance of Australian national identity. From Phar Lap's preserved remains to the Opening Ceremony of the Sydney 2000 Olympic Games; from 'Banjo' Paterson's poem 'The Man from Snowy River' to the 2018 Wild Horse Heritage Bill (NSW), the notion that the horse is meaningful to Australians continues to be perpetuated. Nonetheless, the exact nature of this significance remains nebulous and imprecise, and the topic has drawn little critical attention from Australian Studies or Cultural Studies scholars.

The Australian love affair with horses. The only country in the world with a public holiday for a horse race. Why had no one tackled the meaning of the horse in Australian culture in such depth before? Menzies was well placed to do so. 'I was not one of the kids who went to pony club. I was the girl who mucked out the stables of the rich kids who went to pony club,' she says. She later became a trail ride leader in Sydney's Centennial Park. So she knew horses and she knew the people who loved horses. Menzies started her PhD in 2013 and wrote it while passions were high during the process of the 2016 Kosciuszko National Park Draft Wild Horse Management Plan, and at the time when the 2018 Barilaro legislation went through. It's a rich, well-researched, fascinating work. One of the ideas discussed at length is the emotional connection between people and horses. 'I think that's where brumbies get all their support,' she says. 'What the horse really has going for it is the mythology that has been repeated over and over again, so people don't question it. They just accept it and when you say, "horse", most people have some sympathy for that animal.'

Things get really interesting when Menzies moves beyond our emotional connection with horses and into the cultural side of things. If you ask her how Australian horse culture is different from that in other countries, you get yourself one hell of a provocative answer.

'We're a settler colonial nation. There was no treaty with the first people and the horse played a fundamental role in their dispossession, and in the military advantage that it gave the colonists.'

Are you suggesting the horse was weaponised in Australia's colonial history?

'Yes, it has been weaponised through history, and it was put into play in the Australian context particularly effectively,

I guess. The idolisation of the horse is an imposition of an Anglo-European culture.'

Portraying horses as symbols of conquest might sound pretty radical, but Menzies' thinking is much broader than that, especially on the brumby issue. She knows that the brumby debate is not just about kicking the can of colonialism into the 21st century. It's about something we all crave: belonging.

'The impassioned "brumby debate" is symptomatic of the role of the brumby – and the horse more broadly – in mediating what Australian Studies scholars have identified as an anxiety of belonging among Australians. Here, the brumby becomes the epitome of equine instrumentality, serving as a pawn in the machinations of Australian identity politics,' she writes in her thesis.

That phrase 'anxiety of belonging' is a doozy. Menzies is right. The brumby advocates have an anxiety of belonging. But she has another radical idea: they're not alone. Everybody in this debate had an anxiety of belonging. Menzies touches upon it briefly in her thesis, and in conversation with her, she makes it clear it's still very much part of her thinking.

'On the one hand, we're saying, "If horses belong, then we belong." And the opposite side says, "If we are caretakers of the land, then we deserve to be here. If we can maintain the land in a pristine condition, then it's okay for us to be here." So I think there are parallel narratives of belonging, and I don't think one side is completely right and the other side is completely wrong. And I think both sides need to be heard if there's going to be any resolution.'

Both sides need to be heard. That's hardly an insight of groundbreaking academic rigour, but it's some pretty good common sense. But how to bring everyone together? Rob Gibbs tried that and he's still reeling five years later. Where to find something even vaguely resembling a solution?

To answer that, we must venture a long, long way from the High Country. Heave away, haul away – we're bound for South Australia.

* * *

When Gillian Fennell arrives at the boundary to her property, she's still got another 45 minutes until she pulls up at her house. The drive would take an hour for most people, but when you run a million-acre cattle station in outback South Australia, just south of the Northern Territory border, you learn to handle a bumpy dirt track better than most.

Fennell, a mother of three, says her land is surprisingly productive. 'Lots of stuff grows – native herbage and mulga trees. There's a very diverse and rich range of vegetation. Mulga is very palatable for cattle providing you feed them the right supplements to help them digest it. We run about 5000 head of cattle in good years, but we haven't had significant rainfall for five years, so we're down to 3500.'

What happens to those cattle will either put you off your dinner or give you a craving for Macca's. Because they're nice and lean, most of Fennell's herd get turned into mince and sent frozen to America, where the majority of cattle are fed in a feedlot and end up good and plump. Mix the fatty American beef with lean Aussie beef and you've got yourself the perfect burger patty. Yum, yum.

In this vast, largely unfenced country, brumbies are regarded as feral pests, and Fennell doesn't have the slightest hesitation in blasting them to horsey heaven. Outback brumbies are treated with no more reverence than feral camels, donkeys, whatever. They've got to go. This she does not enjoy. Nobody who works the land enjoys killing animals, especially when they love horses.

'I have been horse-mad ever since I can remember but it took me until I was about ten for my parents to afford to get me a horse,' Fennell says. 'Even growing up in a small country town where all my friends had one, we couldn't afford one. But I loved horses, I thought horses were the best thing. I rode on and off through boarding school, went to pony club, which can be a very competitive, bitchy world. I was a terrible rider. We didn't have a lot of money and we always had stock horses from cattle stations that had no idea what they were doing. I spent a lot of time falling off and being very, very jealous of girls whose parents bought them expensive horses from interstate.'

It'd be interesting to know how many of those bitchy girls got as far in life as Fennell. She is a significant figure in one of Australia's oldest industries and sits on the board of the Cattle Council of Australia. She's also still a horse lover, and not every horse that strays onto her property is shot. Some they break in and keep. There are also a few horses living on her property in retirement that people have given her. A couple of ex-racehorses and so on. They live in the 64,000-acre paddock, the one Fennell calls 'the little paddock'.

But overall, horses are not much use to her because motorbikes or planes are used for cattle mustering, and because the way she sees it, brumbies are problematic. 'A lot of people will say that I don't love horses because I'm quite happy to have the brumbies shot and go to the doggers, but that's not true because the life they're going to live is not fit to live. They might suffer an injury that can't be fixed. They will get teeth and hoof problems that will debilitate them. Or they might starve to death. And people will say, "Why don't you treat them?" But they're wild animals and you can't contain them and give them the care that a domestic animal would have.'

Despite their inherent problems, brumbies are sometimes captured and broken in on Fennell's property. For one thing, she feels it's important to maintain and develop the old horsemanship skills. It's also expensive to buy a broken-in stock horse, so why not get one for nothing if you can? But even when you find a good one, you can get problems. Big problems. One likely-looking colt captured on the property ended up being named Broken Head because it repeatedly ran into a railway iron post in its yard. 'He smashed his head open because he didn't want to be captured,' Fennell recalls. 'There were other brumbies in the yard with him, and two of them stood there and watched while he destroyed himself. He was a bay colt, a really nice-looking horse, which is one of the reasons we picked him up. A more perfect example of the Australian Waler you couldn't find. But they don't know what captivity is. They just have an overwhelming fear of becoming enclosed by something. The kindest thing for Broken Head in the end was to euthanise him.'

And according to Fennell, the kindest thing to do to the High Country brumbies would be to euthanise most of them too.

'I can't fathom it. In the outback where I live, we literally have millions and millions of acres. If you kept the population under control out here, a number of them could live here forever and do no damage. But the High Country of Australia, there's not much of it and nowhere else in Australia looks like that. To me, it makes no sense to sacrifice something so unique and precious for horses when we already have too many horses in Australia. We love our horses but we love our country more.'

Fennell laughs a good hearty chortle when you ask her about the prospect of fertility control. 'They're wild animals. How do you propose to do that? In order to sterilise, you're going to first have to capture them, which will cause them undue stress and angst. You'd be better off rounding up 20 of the best shooters from the Australian Army and shooting the lot. Sterilising is probably the most stupid control measure ever considered.'

But Fennell knows a place where the brumbies run free and untethered but are also cared for. She approvingly calls it an 'actively managed wild horse population' and she thinks it's a lot more responsible than having unmanaged populations in any landscape, which she says inevitably results in poor environmental outcomes and poor animal welfare outcomes. Where is this magical place? It's in the far south of her state, a good thousand kilometres from her door, and though its name invokes death, for the brumbies it is life, and a good life at that.

* * *

South Australia has three large peninsulas. There's the Fleurieu, south of Adelaide. There's the Yorke, which protrudes southwards from the coastline north-west of Adelaide like a small version of Italy. And there's the Eyre, a broad triangle of land further west again. At the bottom of the Eyre Peninsula sits the large town of Port Lincoln and its smaller neighbour Coffin Bay. West of Coffin Bay, on a small, almost horse head–shaped promontory, lies a wild and windswept area of huge windblown sand dunes and scrub. This is the Coffin Bay Peninsula, and in this area wild horses roamed for well over a century.

Technically, they were ponies. Timor ponies, to be precise; a strong, quiet-natured breed which were transported to the area in 1839 by a certain Captain Hawson to create a herd for breeding. Stallions from the breed were brought in over the years to add height and other genetic characteristics to the mob, and they were soon prized as polo ponies, army remounts and working horses. At times over the years, such as during the Great Depression and World War II, the herd was in high demand. At other times, the horses were largely unmanaged. But always, they were prized by locals.

The land passed through the hands of various private owners down the years before being ceded to the South Australia government in 1972 for use as a national park. The future of the Coffin Bay ponies was uncertain, so concerned locals formed the Coffin Bay Pony Society. They wanted the ponies left alone. They felt they'd earned the right to be considered part of the landscape, national park or no national park. After the park was established in 1982, the society negotiated with the National Parks and Wildlife Service South Australia to control and manage a small herd within the new park. An agreement was struck: one stallion plus 20 mares and their progeny could remain. Trapping would occur yearly and excess stock would be removed and sold, with the proceeds going to Parks. It seemed like a fair deal all round. But times were changing and the loophole whereby the ponies could remain started looking more like a noose. The 1999 Parks SA Draft Management Plan proposed a wilderness zone on the Coffin Bay Peninsula. The writing was on the wall: the ponies had to go.

No way were Coffin Bay locals going to let their beloved ponies be destroyed. So they raised money to buy a parcel of land where the Coffin Bay ponies could live. In 2003, in conjunction with the state government, they bought 1000 acres just outside of town. It was good land abutted by huge sand dunes, half open, half scrubby, that was not too different from the original run. They called the property Brumbies Run, a nod to Banjo Paterson's poem 'Brumby's Run', and the group administering the land rebranded itself to the Coffin Bay Brumby Preservation Society. And if you talk to people on both sides of the brumby debate today, many will tell you that a brumby sanctuary like Brumbies Run is far from the worst model for compromise in this battle.

The Coffin Bay Brumby Preservation Society's president is local builder and father of three Jody Scharfe. He grew up camping and four-wheel driving out on the Coffin Bay

Peninsula, and he grew up loving the ponies. 'When you watched the horses run down there, they looked so majestic,' he says. Scharfe reckons the horses had been in the area for a long time without doing much damage. That is, of course, disputed. What's beyond debate is that locals valued the horses. And while some locals lost interest in the ponies when they were transferred to a designated property, thereby becoming at best semi-wild, most still highly value the small mob safely ensconced in Brumbies Run. They're even a tourist attraction.

'All sorts of different groups come to see them and everyone falls in love with them,' Scharfe says. 'The property has basic facilities like toilets, showers and running water, and some groups even camp out with the horses.' The property has basic facilities for horses too, including a large hay shed in case feed dries up in the typically dry local summers. But for the most part the horses fend for themselves, running almost wild and almost free, which is a lot better than not being there at all. 'They're left alone. They're still the same horses,' Scharfe says.

Scharfe dedicates a lot of time and energy to the cause. He's always holding sausage sizzles at Bunnings and other fundraisers to pay for hay and the rest of it. Donations also help. The sale of the progeny provides another trickle of income. Scharfe has taken the precaution of legally enshrining his right to have the first dibs on rehoming the horses, should Brumbies Run ever go belly-up. The operation costs around $45,000 each year to maintain. But for now it's still financially sustainable. And it begs the question: could we do it in the High Country?

There are parts of the High Country with snow gums and black sallee trees and wildflowers and snow grass meadows that lie outside of the national parks but that look and smell like the parts of the High Country preserved inside parks. The Bago State Forest on the western flank of Kosciuszko is one such place. It burned like hell in January 2020 but it'll recover. And there's another area on the eastern edge of Kosciuszko near the upper Gungarlin River. Surely a landholder there could be coaxed into selling up for the right price? There are places in Victoria that would work too, such as the area between Omeo and Dinner Plain on the southern side of the Great Alpine Road, or sections of the Eastern Alps. Could fences be built around plots of a few thousand acres? Could enough volunteers be found to ensure feed in droughts and vet care if necessary? Could basic facilities like toilets and brumby-viewing platforms be built? Could enough money be raised to set the plan in motion? If every Facebook slacktivist who's ever thumbsed-up a brumby post chipped in a few dollars, surely it could be achievable. Could fees then be charged for visitors, just as motorists face a daily slug of $30 or more to drive into the ski resorts in ski season? Surely that would be fair. Of course, there would be no point having sanctuaries if brumbies were still running free and wild across the mountains in numbers greatly exceeding 10,000, as they do now. The overall herd size would have to be drastically reduced first. Maybe not to hundreds, but to the low thousands, and everybody agrees that could only be done quickly by culling. You would also have to trap and remove some of the mobs that people value most, such as the Bogong High Plains brumbies. You'd have to do a lot to make sanctuaries happen on a scale that would please those who value their place in the High Country. But is it really such a crazy idea? You reach a point in any deadlocked debate where you've got to bring in fresh thinking. Could it work? Would it work?

'Absolutely it would work,' Scharfe says. 'Give some land back to the animals that are part of our history. We need to build flexibility into land management, and a conservation park or sanctuary is a good solution. Australia is vast. Let's try and manage some sort of area that's fenced off. Surely we could work together to compromise for an animal that has been unique to people's lives. They keep old churches, we restore vintage cars … when an animal has had such an impact on people's lives, surely some sort of management can be put in place without removing them or completely shooting them right out, especially when there are so many other problems like cats, deer, weed issues and so on.'

* * *

It's the colour you notice first. Pineapple yellow and avocado-flesh green. Then the texture of the sphagnum moss, matted and seemingly metres thick. And the tiny stream tendrils that flow through the sphagnum pillows. The water in those little creeklets is as clear as glass. The sphagnum bogs of the Ginini Flats Wetland Complex, high in the ACT on the Brindabella Range, are like no sphagnum bogs in the entire High Country. This place is a miracle.

A kilometre up the hill on the dusty Mt Franklin Road, you wouldn't know this place is here. The road follows the dry ridge line of the Brindabellas – the northernmost range in the Australian Alps – crossing no creeks or soaks for a good 30 kilometres. But this range attracts its share of storms, and in a series of tiny frost hollows just east of the watershed of the border, water collects in a small elevated alpine bog. We're talking a couple of dozen football fields here. That's it. That's the size of the Ginini Flats Wetland Complex, the pristine Ramsar-listed subalpine swamp that ensures a steady flow of water into Canberra's dams, via the Cotter River, in all seasons. But the wetland is valuable in its own right. For one thing, corroboree frogs live here. It's one of just three regions where the critically endangered northern corroboree frog lives. And Dr Ben Scheele from the Australian National University is up here to count them. That is, if he can find any. That is far from guaranteed.

Corroboree frog counting is a weird day out. You clomp around the swamp, stepping on tussocks or heathy bushes to avoid damaging the sphagnum, calling out, 'Hello, frog!' Yes, you actually say, 'Hello, frog!' And no matter how many times you say it, and even though there's no one else around, you feel like the guy who yells at pigeons at train stations. So this goes on for a while and, unsurprisingly, no frogs say, 'Hello human' in return. None croak back either, which is not ideal. There is the wind and patter of light rain on your raincoat and the trickling creeks, but otherwise the swamp is silent. We take a break on a smooth lump of granite on the side of the swamp, cut a few slices of salami and cheese, and pull off the leeches as mist drapes across the wetland.

'The situation with the frog is there's a disease called chytrid fungus which has totally smashed frogs,' Scheele explains. 'It came out of east Asia in the late 1970s, and by the 1980s, this one pathogen had spread right across eastern Australia. Another key threat for the corroboree frog is climate change. Males construct a nest five to ten centimetres below the surface and call their little hearts out to attract females. They only lay 25 eggs – many frogs lay thousands – and the eggs sit in jelly capsules until autumn and winter rains flood the vegetation and the tadpoles hatch. The tadpoles spend winter in pools feeding and growing, even in shallow water beneath snow and ice, then in spring metamorphose into little frogs. So you need spongy vegetation for their nests, but it's undoubtedly getting hotter and drier with climate change, and some of their habitat has turned to dry grassland. And then you have the horses, which make incisions in the landscape, and that drains the bogs and makes them drier and decreases their resilience to climate change. So the overarching threat is chytrid, and there's a range of people working on captive breeding programs to overcome chytrid. But what's the point if you don't have the habitat to re-establish corroboree frogs in? The threat of feral animals like horses and deer destroying habitat is the one problem we can manage relatively easily and cheaply.'

Scheele's a likeable young bloke. House in the suburbs, wife, couple of small kids. No airs or graces about him. He grew up spending time on cattle country in the Monaro, just north of Cooma. Some of his relatives are pro-brumby and he says he gets on with them fine. He gets it. He knows people love horses. He knows they don't hate corroboree frogs either.

Who could dislike a tiny, black-and-yellow speckled frog? It'd be like squashing Christmas beetles.

'I think people genuinely don't appreciate that there is really serious damage to these bog ecosystems from these horses, and to a lesser extent deer and pigs because they are culled,' Scheele says. 'And I'm not advocating for aerial culling of horses. I just think there is a genuine lack of appreciation of habitat damage. I actually think there's a genuine misunderstanding about how science works. People say scientists need to get out of the office more. They say, "Corroboree frogs are everywhere". And it's amazing how many people will send a photo of a little brown frog in their backyard. People see what they want to see. They think what they want to think.'

The mist is slowly rising. The sun feels like it might even pay its respects. As for the frogs, they're no-shows. 'It is kind of depressing working on a species going extinct,' Scheele says. 'This is such an amazing beast. But, you know, corroboree frogs aren't the reason to manage horses in the High Country. There are more important reasons in terms of why do we have a national park if it's overgrazed in parts more than a lot of private farmland? Most of Australia has grazing upon it. Why can't we have some areas that are specifically set aside for the designation of fauna and flora? Why can't we have those? It's about the whole ecosystem for me.'

Walking back to the car, the high Brindabellas are putting on a show. There are the gorgeous cushions of sphagnum and the creeks with water so clear, you feel like you could lift a pebble from the stream bed without wetting your finger. The snow gum bark glows orange with sun-smudged dampness, and the tips of the snow grass tussocks glisten with a thousand illuminated droplets like coral about to spawn. This place is perfection. This place is every bit as magical as the Great Barrier Reef, and no less fragile. It's so important that Parks ACT is protecting it. These mountains have enough problems. And it seems like there are new issues every year. Just recently, it was widely reported that tiny beetles are killing off snow gums across the alps by boring into them and effectively ringbarking them. Alec Costin's daughter, the ecologist and backcountry adventure guide Acacia Rose, had been talking about this for months before the articles started appearing, because she'd been watching the horror story unfold with her own eyes, and all too rapidly. 'We've had two major bushfire events in 2003 and 2020 and now the forest ecosystems are crashing in front of our eyes,' she says.

So the snow gums are in trouble and there are too many deer and too many pigs and the increasingly frequent and intense bushfires fairly blaze, to borrow Banjo's phrase, and the architects of Snowy 2.0 are digging holes like open-cut mines in the Pilbara, and the ski resorts get busier every year despite declining snow cover and the visitors get more dopey and less environmentally aware, and backcountry adventurers are behaving like hippies at a music festival in waterproof clothing out on the Main Range and beyond, and there are 101 problems besides all those. And then you've got the vast herds of horses trampling the place to dirt like a rodeo ring. But the problem of too many horses is something we can fix.

Horses have essentially been invited to wreak havoc for far too long on a landscape that was never designed for hooves and that took half a century to recover from the trampling by cattle. And why? Because of stories. And feelings. And while stories and feelings are what make us human, that doesn't mean you run public policy in accordance with them, otherwise you'd never build a set of traffic lights, because who the hell feels like stopping at intersections?

'This is the hardest, most controversial land management issue you could work on in Australia,' Invasive Species Council CEO Andrew Cox says. 'It's got everything, and I think it's important we move beyond where we're stuck now because this is about the sort of Australia we want. Do we want an Australia full of farmyard animals and exotic plants – a menagerie from everywhere in the world of the most successful invaders – or do we want the plants and animals that make Australia what it is?

'It's a choice we have to make, and this issue is symbolic of that choice. It'd be a different matter if everyone thought it would be a good idea to have horses in the park, but the really offensive thing is most people want native animals in the park.'

It's true that most people believe horses should be managed. A 2020 poll conducted by the Australia Institute of voters in the Eden-Monaro federal electorate showed that just 13 per cent of all voters wanted the horses totally left alone. John Barilaro himself, as reported in Chapter Seven, believes the total of 14,000 in Kosciuszko, or whatever it is now, should come down to three or four thousand. But a small number of people continue to deny that the horses are a problem. And those people influence the horse-loving masses on Facebook who couldn't distinguish the alpine celery shrub from a bunch of celery at Woolworths. And those people hold all Australians to ransom, because our great national parks belong to all of us.

Meanwhile, NSW Environment Minister Matt Kean still hasn't released the long overdue Kosciuszko draft plan. Perhaps he's trying to grow an Afro first. If the plan comes out before this book hits the shelves, that'll be mildly annoying, but it likely won't matter too much because whatever the plan contains, two things are certain. One: it will fuel a conflagration of passion, which will likely include horseback protests in the streets and the rest of it. And two: it won't stop the wars.

'No battle is ever won. In the history of conservation, we fight battles, people declare victory, a bit of time elapses, knowledge is lost, then the battle is fought again. So you have to be eternally vigilant.' These pragmatic, somewhat bleak words come via John McRae, a manager at Tidbinbilla Nature Reserve, in the shadow of the Brindabellas. And he's just getting started.

'If your job is to protect these landscapes for future generations, you have to fight, you have to be vigilant, because the enemy doesn't go away. They just stand down, they regroup, and they come back with a different leader, a different legislation. I've dedicated my life to nature conservation and I see these battles fought again and again. No protection is permanent, no vigilance is too strong, and no battle is ever won. We can have a victory in the brumby wars, we can have a moment, we can do the culling, the control processes that the science tells us needs to be done to protect the High Country and the alpine regions, but we can't be sure that in 20 years, someone will read *The Silver Brumby* or "The Man from Snowy River". And that person might form a brumby group, and there will be a push to protect them again. This battle will never be won.'

He's almost certainly right. This battle will never be won by either side. But that doesn't mean we can't change the tone of the battle.

'I think a lot of this is about human egos, and I think also there's an awful lot of belly-gazing going on,' *Silver Brumby* author Elyne Mitchell's daughter and biographer Honor Auchinleck says.

She's also right. A lot of this is about egos. And there are egos and stubborn characters on both sides. On the conservation side, there are scientists who arrogantly discount all claims of horse heritage as rubbish. There are Parks staff who locals find incredibly frustrating and unwieldy to deal with. And there are one or two political animals working behind the scenes in the conservation movement whose egos could fill Lake Jindabyne in a dry year. But by far the biggest egos are in the pro-brumby movement. That is the indisputable truth, and they undermine the hard work of the decent brumby advocates, many of whom it was a pleasure to meet in the writing of this book. But the treatment dished out to Rob Gibbs and others should never be forgotten. It was intimidation, cowardice and textbook bullying. It was the sort of behaviour that would guarantee instant sacking in any workplace and instant glassing in virtually any pub. If a single scientist or environmentalist carried on that way, they'd be branded 'militant greenies' and talkback radio and the internet would explode with rage.

The brumby advocates need to recognise a good deal when they see it. Never forget that the Draft Wild Horse

Management Plan for Kosciuszko National Park of 2016 co-authored by Rob Gibbs offered to preserve small pockets of brumbies in the national park. Never downplay the monumental significance of this. It was like offering a wing of an art gallery to mud wrestlers. Yet brumby supporters snapped the olive branch over Gibbs's head and jabbed him in the ribs with the jagged edges. Go back to Chapter One for a refresher of the gross invective and abuse. Click on a pro-brumby Facebook group – maybe you'll get one of the nice ones. And maybe you won't. There are a lot of angry people out there. People who have conflated a pro-brumby stance with quasi-nationalistic hatefulness. People who would be the first to say, 'We grew here, you flew here' as an expression of Australian belonging, but who apply the reverse logic to animals. This debate should never be a game of 'I'm more Australian than you'. To love the snow gums of Kosciuszko, the red gums of Barmah, the gorges of Guy Fawkes is as Australian as it gets.

And if you're really into flying the flag of national identity, ask yourself this: What's more Australian than getting along with your fellow Aussie? While this country's frontier wars are a dark stain on our past, there is nonetheless much to admire in our postcolonial society. Unlike America, this country has never had a civil war. Unlike England, we never had the social apartheid of the aristocracy. Unlike France, we never needed a revolution. The Australian way is to band together and work things out. So it should be with the brumby debate.

'We shouldn't have the walls up. We shouldn't be, "I'm right, you're wrong". We should talk about this,' says Jody

Scharfe from the Coffin Bay Brumby Preservation Society. 'Because there is no matter of life or death with the brumby issue. In real wars, you have to make split-second decisions. But we've still got time to get this right.'

We do indeed have time. But the ecological clock is ticking and we need a solution sooner rather than later. We need to compromise. And compromise is difficult, so we need to be just a little bit heroic, even if we're not. We need land managers and anti-brumby folk to say, 'Okay, brumbies are important to many people so you can have some. Not many, but a few, and as few as possible in our great montane and riverine national parks.' And we need the pro-brumby people to stop peddling ecological gobbledygook about horses being good for the Australian environment. We live in the age of misinformation and this is a classic piece of it. The Australian bush was doing fine before brumbies came along. Indeed, it goes without saying that it was doing much, much better. Brumbies are not magical unicorns with fairy-light footsteps and farts that smell like eucalyptus oil. Like deer, goats and pigs, they are descendants of imported ungulates that our most sensitive landscapes are exquisitely ill-equipped to deal with. So it's not ideal, but okay, fine, let's keep small pockets of brumbies here and there that don't overwhelm the native flora and fauna, just as the ecologist and author Elyne Mitchell envisaged in her stories. Let them be a flash through the trees. A glint. A glimmer. A flicker. A vague hint, not a vast herd.

Of course, that's more or less the package that Rob Gibbs and his colleagues tried to sell in 2016. And here we are …

ACKNOWLEDGEMENTS

Thank you firstly to each of the 60 interviewees who agreed to share their passion, opinion and/or expertise in the pages of this book. While this is a book about the debate over wild bush horses, it is first and foremost a story about Australians. About you. I know it was tough for many of you to speak openly on this issue, so thanks for being part of this story. Indeed, thanks for *being* the story. Thank you to my wife Kate and my kids Stella and Leo for holding our little family together while Dad was out in his writer's shed. Thanks to Mum, Dad and Soy for always being there. Thanks, as ever, to Rockdale Library, Sun's Noodle and Ibrahim Pastry for providing shelter and nourishment during daylight hours. Thanks to Toby Stenberg for being a good bloke and because I forgot to thank you in the last book. Thanks to Ricky French for your contacts, ideas, and many years of comprehensive reporting on this issue which was an invaluable research tool. Thanks to Mark Hardy, Tom Smithers, Ben Domensino and the gang at Weatherzone for believing in my love of weather and storytelling, and for providing an excellent escape from the brumby wars for at least a couple of days each week! Huge thanks to all the believers at Hachette Australia, especially Sophie Hamley for being a brilliant psychologist, editor, publisher and much more. Special thanks also to Karen Ward for holding this thing together with admirable calm as the deadline got tight and things became super fiddly. Thanks as ever to the ski.com.au crew for being the most supportive, knowledgeable and entertaining bunch of idiots in the online universe. I really shouldn't, but I can't help saying a massive thanks to the person who asked not to be thanked. Onya mate! Lastly, I'd like to thank the young barber in Bankstown, who provided a much-needed laugh when, in describing the difference between fiction and non-fiction, he said, "One's bullshit bro, and the other's not!" Researching and writing this book, it became less and less clear which was which. Our stories are one of the key things that make us human. But the truth keeps us alive.

hachette
AUSTRALIA

If you would like to find out more about Hachette Australia, our authors, upcoming events and new releases you can visit our website or our social media channels:

hachette.com.au

HachetteAustralia

HachetteAus